Performing with Understanding

Performing with Understanding

The Challenge of the
National Standards for Music Education

Edited by BENNETT REIMER

Based on a Northwestern University
Music Education Leadership Seminar

 The National Association for Music Education

Contents

Teaching for Performing with Understanding in Band and Orchestra Settings

Teaching for Performing with Understanding in Choral Settings

The Standards and Performance in the Context of Culture

The Ideas in Action

Preface
The Northwestern University
Music Education Leadership Seminars

The music education profession, like all others, must engage itself in continual efforts to improve its effectiveness and viability. Such efforts need to be made at a variety of levels, reflecting the complexity of this field. One of these levels, often neglected, requires the profession to nurture the expertise of its most influential members.

The Northwestern University Music Education Leadership Seminars (NUMELS) are conceived as a means of elevating all aspects of the music education profession by providing intensive learning experiences for its top-level leaders, thinkers, and activists. A relatively small number of music educators exercise a high degree of influence on the profession's fortunes. These are the professionals who are the most visible, productive, active, well-regarded people in their respective areas of music education expertise. A great deal of the success of music education, in refining its understandings and reforming its practices, depends on their wisdom.

The continuing education of these national and international leaders occurs by their own, self-directed efforts to keep abreast of the issues most relevant to their work. Seldom if ever is an opportunity available to them to expand their expertise by coming together with people as advanced as they, specifically to serve their needs for continued growth, by learning from each other and from experts in related fields they have invited. The luxury, intensity, and excitement of being a student rather than a teacher is rare indeed for people at that high level of attainment, but is no less needed if their intellectual horizons and professional efficacy are to continue to expand.

In alternating summers, starting in 1996, a small number of people (around a dozen) who are among the leading music educators in the particular aspect of music education on which that summer's Seminar focused, have been invited to be participants. They spend five days at Northwestern University, in informal discussions led, in turn, by each participant, in interactions with guest instructors who have been identified as being able to add useful dimensions to their expertise, in strategy sessions on needed professional initiatives in which they see themselves playing key roles, and in various other activities they mutually devise.

The 1996 NUMELS focused on the topic "Performance in the Context of the National Standards for Music Education." The 1998 Seminar was on "Issues of Multiculturalism in Music Education." The topic of the 2000 meeting is "Teaching Composition in the Schools: A New Horizon for Music Education." Future topics, and the participants appropriate for each, will be chosen to reflect emerging issues and needs of the profession.

The Seminars are not product-oriented in the sense of creating a final report or policy recommendation or consensus document. Their purpose is to deepen and expand the leadership capacities of each attendee, in whatever way each chooses to apply the learnings they have gained. The present book, however, reflects the desire of the NUMELS Director, Bennett Reimer, and the participants in the first meeting, to jointly plan and write a book capturing the insights of the attendees, as a way of spreading their leadership beyond their own, individual involvements. Similar books, written by attendees at successive NUMELS, are anticipated.

The Seminars could not have occurred without the generous and enthusiastic support of the Dean of the School of Music, Bernard Dobroski, who has supplied not only the financial wherewithal required, but whose hospitality at the opening dinner (as well as superb cooking skills) and throughout the meetings has helped make each Seminar personally as well as professionally memorable. For this book the editorial expertise of Margaret A. Senko, Director of Publications for MENC, generously and graciously supplied, was a key factor in bringing it to fruition. The Editor is grateful to her, and to each of the chapter authors for their patience and forbearance in all the arduous, exacting work required to transform the intangibility of ideas into the actuality of a book.

Music Content Standards for Grades K–12

1. Singing, alone and with others, a varied repertoire of music.

2. Performing on instruments, alone and with others, a varied repertoire of music.

3. Improvising melodies, variations, and accompaniments.

4. Composing and arranging music within specified guidelines.

5. Reading and notating music.

6. Listening to, analyzing, and describing music.

7. Evaluating music and music performance.

8. Understanding relationships between music, the other arts, and disciplines outside the arts.

9. Understanding music in relation to history and culture.

From Consortium of National Arts Education Associations, *National Standards for Arts Education* (Reston, VA: Music Educators National Conference, 1994).

Introduction

1

The Power of the National Standards for Music Education

Paul R. Lehman

One of the things I learned early in my term as president of MENC is that it is very difficult to draw valid generalizations about anything pertaining to music education. The nation is so large and music education involves so many people in so many settings that any generalization is bound to be based on a relatively small sampling of cases. But having offered that disclaimer, I won't allow it to deter me from drawing several generalizations.

I believe that the response to the National Standards for Music Education from the nation's music educators—including teachers of performance—has, in general, been very positive. When we published the first draft of the Standards and invited comments, the most common response was, in effect, "It's about time. We've needed something like this, and now we finally have it."

But it's difficult to explain such a complex undertaking so that the details

are immediately clear to everyone. I recall especially the response of a high school choir director who said that she agreed that all of these outcomes were important and that her students should learn these skills but, she said, she simply didn't have time within her schedule to teach "all of this." She went on to explain that when she came to her current job six years ago, she inherited a choir of thirty members. She then developed a large concert choir, an advanced choir, a madrigal group, and a show choir. Her students presented a musical every year. She had an active program of small ensembles. She spent her lunch hours giving private lessons and section rehearsals. She was busy from 8:00 a.m. to 5:00 p.m. every day and most evenings, and she couldn't possibly do anything more.

She was right, no doubt, that she needed more time. Many music teachers do. But her response reflected a basic misunderstanding that I suspect is shared by many readers of the Standards. She thought that the Standards represented a set of learnings that were to be superimposed on her present curriculum. She assumed that they were another layer of skills to be taught in addition to everything she was presently teaching. In fact, the Standards are intended to provide a basic framework for all music teaching that is applicable in every setting, regardless of how much or how little time the teacher has.

Although most teachers seemed to welcome the Standards, I know that there are teachers who see them as largely irrelevant to what they do. I'm thinking, for example, of the band director who believes, "My mission is to develop the best band possible in this school. That involves teaching the kids to play with a good tone, in tune, and in rhythm. It involves giving them the technique to play the notes and the musicianship to interpret the music effectively. Never mind the historical and cultural context or relationships with the other arts. Never mind analysis. Those things are nice, but they're not central to my goals."

I suspect that this group is composed of two subgroups. One subgroup is amenable to persuasion in the face of convincing arguments. The other subgroup is unwilling to broaden its perspective no matter what anyone says. How many people belong in each of these groups and subgroups? No one can say.

Regardless of how teachers have responded to the Standards, the response from the leadership of the various music educators' organizations has been almost unanimously positive. For example, at an annual convention of the American School Band Directors Association, I was given an opportunity to explain why band directors should support the Standards and develop Standards-based programs. I was also invited to present a session on the Standards at an annual Newly Published Music Workshop sponsored by the U.S. Navy Band, and I know that many music education leaders in the standards movement have spoken at similar meetings.

I believe that one of the most impressive demonstrations of support came at the National Music Education Summit sponsored by MENC in September 1994. That meeting brought together some seventy representatives of diverse music organizations to explore how their organizations could work together to implement the Music Standards. These people demonstrated a clear sense of mission and a unanimous view that it was in the best interests of each of their organizations to support the Standards and to seek their implementation in every school district across the nation.

Let's look for a moment at some of the implications of the Standards for the music educator. Some teachers look at the Standards and say, "Everything I do is here. This is all very familiar." They're right, of course. The Standards were designed to reflect the best practices of our profession. Most teachers can teach to the Standards immediately because there's nothing in them that's totally new. But other teachers look at them and find many learnings that they have never taught and perhaps never learned. That can be very intimidating. After all, we can't teach things that we can't do ourselves.

Still, everything called for in the Standards is being taught by good teachers across the nation. What we need are means for those teachers to share their skills and experience with their colleagues who want to learn. We have many avenues to provide those in-service experiences, even though most of the funds for professional development have been shortsightedly eliminated from the *Goals 2000: Educate America Act* by Congress. We have a wide variety of professional meetings organized by all of our professional associations. We have numerous and diverse professional publications. We have large numbers of workshops presented by colleges and universities, especially in summer. We need to find ways to utilize these channels more effectively and to expand them so that professional development opportunities are readily accessible to all music educators.

Exactly what is there in the Standards that causes concern among some teachers? Standards 1 and 2 deal with singing and playing instruments. That's what we do best. That's what we have traditionally emphasized. There's nothing at all that's troublesome here.

Standard 3 concerns improvisation. This has been emphasized almost exclusively in jazz groups and to some extent in elementary and middle-school general music programs. But especially at the earlier levels, we tend to teach improvisation superficially and unsystematically. Our instruction often resembles aural finger painting, in which we accept uncritically whatever the student does and call it creative. We need ways to teach the skills of improvisation more rigorously.

Standard 4 calls for teaching composition. We do this in high school classes labeled Composition and, again, we do it superficially in elementary and middle-school general music programs. But, as in the case of improvisation, we should find ways to bring more rigor and higher expectations to our teaching of composition. We also need to teach both composition and improvisation in more diverse settings.

Standard 5 deals with reading and notation. This is something else that we have traditionally done well. Teachers tend to be comfortable with this standard. Again, there's nothing new here.

Standard 6 concerns listening to, analyzing, and describing music. Many of our colleagues emphasize these skills and teach them very effectively. Others devote less effort to these matters.

Standard 7 deals with evaluation. Our attention to this topic is very uneven. It is probably fair to say that in most instances evaluation is treated in an incidental manner and is not emphasized in a systematic and rigorous way.

Standard 8 stresses relationships between music and other disciplines. Although some music teachers do this well, as a profession, we need considerable help with this topic.

Standard 9 deals with the historical and cultural context of music. Again, some teachers do this well, but many of us need help.

Throughout the Standards there is an explicit call for teaching a broader repertoire. There is an emphasis not only on Western art music but also on Western music from outside the art music tradition, including jazz, pop, and folk music, and there is an emphasis on music from the various cultures and ethnic groups throughout the world. It's unrealistic to expect that teachers can quickly expand their repertoires to include knowledge of a broad sampling of all of these types of music, but it is possible for teachers to learn some representative exemplary works from the various genres and to expand their personal repertoires gradually on a continuing basis.

The Music Standards specify that "every course in music, including performance courses, should provide instruction in creating, performing, listening to, and analyzing music, in addition to focusing on its specific subject matter."[1] This is an idea from the Comprehensive Musicianship Project of twenty-five years ago, to which the faculty of Northwestern University contributed significantly. It's still a good

idea, though it will require a broader perspective than some of us have taken in the past.

Teachers have asked, "Should every student electing a music course at the high school level be expected to meet all of the standards for grades 9–12?" The answer is "not necessarily." At the high school level the standards are designed for students who have completed relevant course work. A student electing orchestra, for example, should be expected to do especially well with respect to standards 2 and 5. The level of expectation with respect to the other standards will depend on the emphasis placed by the director on the skills called for in those standards. One would expect that a student who elects any course in music would do better on all of the standards than a student who elects no music, but every student will do better on some standards than on others, depending on the subject matter emphasized in the course(s) elected.

The critical issues in this discussion are these: Why are standards important to music teachers? Why should music teachers support the Standards? Why should they implement Standards-based programs? Here are some of the major reasons, in my view:

1. *Standards will benefit students.* They'll benefit students because they can help to ensure that every young American has access to a comprehensive, balanced, and sequential program of music instruction in school. If we can sell the Standards to the public and

muster the resources to implement them, every future citizen will have a better life because of music and the other arts. Music programs exist to bring joy, beauty, and satisfaction into the lives of people: to enhance the quality of life.

2. *Standards can focus our efforts.* Standards make it possible to bring every aspect of education into alignment. Now that we have achieved a national consensus on standards specifying what every student should know and be able to do, we can use those standards as a basis for developing curriculum, reforming teacher education, assessing learning, and improving every other aspect of education. Standards provide a basis for rationalizing the entire educational process and making it consistent in a way that has never before been possible.

3. *Standards clarify our expectations.* That's important because, if we can't state clearly what it is we want our students to learn, then we can't expect to be taken seriously by school administrators or by parents. And if students don't know what it is that we want them to learn, they may never learn it, and we can't blame them. Someone once said that if students understand what teachers want them to learn, that's half the battle. Schools have standards already; the problem is that too many schools don't say what they are. The standards are set by default and by individual teachers. So no one is held accountable. Whatever the student does, we find some excuse to accept it. As a result,

these de facto standards are so low that we would be embarrassed to state them publicly.

4. *Standards bring equity to our expectations.* Every year one-fifth of the nation's students move to new schools. Their new teachers have no idea what they can do, especially in music, because curricula are so different among districts and states. Teachers can't assume anything. Further, some schools currently have high expectations for students and some have low expectations. Is that fair? It's morally inexcusable and it's socially devastating to expect less of some students just because they come from a certain area of town or a certain socioeconomic background. Basic fairness demands greater equity in our expectations, and standards make that possible. If we expect students to learn, they will, and if we don't, they won't.

5. *Standards move music beyond entertainment.* The Standards give us credibility in claiming that our programs, like those in the other basic disciplines, are based on teaching specific skills and knowledge. They strengthen our argument that music is not simply an activity. It is not merely something to be engaged in as a respite from the serious business of education. It is not primarily entertainment. There is indeed an important body of skills and knowledge to be taught and learned.

6. *Standards give us a basis for claiming needed resources.* If we want students to know and be able to do specific things, then we will need specific mini-

mal levels of time, materials, equipment, and support. With standards we can argue for the resources we need to do our jobs. MENC's Opportunity-to-Learn (OTL) Standards specify what music educators need with respect to curriculum and scheduling, staffing, materials, equipment, and facilities to implement the Standards.[2] The development of OTL standards was originally an important part of the *Goals 2000: Educate America Act,* but, unfortunately, OTL standards became a political casualty and have disappeared for the moment. That doesn't matter much to teachers of math and English because they usually have the time and other resources they need. But OTL standards remain important to music teachers because too often what we have is far short of what we need.

7. *Standards give us a basis for insisting on qualified teachers.* Having standards enables us to bypass the argument about whether music should be taught by classroom teachers or specialists. If the outcomes we seek are vague, imprecise, and undemanding, then it doesn't matter. Anyone can teach music. We don't need music specialists. But if we want to teach specific skills and knowledge as outlined in challenging standards, then we need teachers who possess those skills and that knowledge. If a teacher can teach students to read music and to sing in tune, in rhythm, and with a good tone quality, then it doesn't matter whether the teacher is labeled a music specialist or a classroom teacher.

Most teachers who can do those things will be music specialists, but what counts is the result. However, if a school district expects classroom teachers to teach to the Music Standards, then it has to ensure that the classroom teachers it hires possess the necessary skills and can achieve the necessary results.

8. *Standards give us a basis for assessing music learning.* The standards movement has changed the educational landscape utterly and completely. I believe that the standards movement has set the stage for an assessment movement, and I believe that assessment may become the defining issue in music education for the next decade. Developing standards and defining clear objectives that flow naturally from standards make assessment possible where it was often not possible before. But standards do more than make assessment possible. They make it necessary. Standards have brought assessment to the center of the stage and have made it a high-priority, high-visibility issue. Standards and assessment inescapably go hand in hand. We cannot have standards without assessment.

9. *Standards give music a place at the curricular table.* If we want to play in the game of education reform, we have to play by the rules. Today, increasingly, the rules require standards. Where would we be in the struggle for time in the curriculum if every discipline except music had standards? At the very least, our standards should earn for music a place at the table in the major forums

where education reform is discussed. The Standards further strengthen our position because they represent a broad national consensus. They were developed not by music educators alone but through a massive consensus-building process involving representatives of every group with an interest in the arts or in education. These are not MENC's standards; they are America's standards. They give us a banner around which to rally our supporters and a basis for claiming a fair share of the school curriculum.

10. *Standards provide a vision.* Perhaps the most compelling reason for adopting standards is that a school is more likely to be effective if it has a clear vision of what it seeks to achieve than if it doesn't. I believe this is a commonsense notion that will be accepted by most Americans once it is explained to them.

In implementing the Standards through performance, the task that lies ahead is threefold. We should seek to persuade our colleagues to (1) broaden their teaching emphases to include aspects of performing, creating, and analyzing music in every music class, (2) broaden the repertoire they teach to include Western art music, Western music from outside the art music tradition, and representative music from the various cultures and ethnic groups of the world, and (3) implement Standards-based programs.

Some of our colleagues will probably pay little attention to the Standards, but I think there is considerable risk involved in that attitude. We cannot expect to exist in isolation from what is happening elsewhere in education. We must understand the process that is taking place around us and participate in it effectively if music education is to survive and flourish in the twenty-first century. If we offer high-quality, Standards-based programs and if we develop good assessment procedures, our programs will almost certainly be less vulnerable to cutbacks or elimination than if we don't.

I have tremendous confidence in the nation's music teachers. I believe that as a group they are well-qualified, committed to their students, and dedicated to their art. I believe that they are willing to change if and when a strong case for change is presented. The opportunity available in the coming years is historic in its dimensions. Standards will not solve all of the problems facing music education, but they can be a powerful weapon in our arsenal as we seek the support we need to preserve and enhance our programs for the sake of the young people of America.

Notes

1. Consortium of National Arts Education Associations, *National Standards for Arts Education: What Every Young American Should Know and Be Able to Do in the Arts* (Reston, VA: Music Educators National Conference, 1994), 42.

2. Music Educators National Conference, *Opportunity-to Learn Standards for Music Instruction, Grades PreK–12* (Reston, VA: MENC, 1994).

2

What Is "Performing with Understanding?"

Bennett Reimer

Background

Throughout its history in the United States the music education profession has devoted much if not most of its energies to teaching young people to sing and play instruments. To this day, singing and playing are dominant involvements with music in most general music classes and are the only music electives offered in most secondary schools. All music education majors in colleges and universities are required to study performance seriously, and most of them intend to become teachers of performance in elective school music programs. The relative few preparing to be general music teachers in elementary schools spend a good deal of their training learning how to teach singing and playing appropriate instruments, and those preparing to be general music teachers in middle or junior high schools also must be proficient in teaching the performance electives, most commonly choral ensembles.

Given the historical and continuing emphasis on performance as the principal way to involve students with music, the achievements of American music education in this endeavor have been impressive indeed. The community of music educators devoted to performance is active, vital, and well organized. The level of performance of the typical school music groups—bands, orchestras, and choruses—is often remarkably high, especially in that most members of those groups have no intention of pursuing performance study in any serious way after graduation from high school. The number of students in schools electing to become involved with performance, estimated to average somewhere between 9 percent and 15 percent, compares favorably with other school elective offerings and certainly outstrips elective choices and opportunities in the other arts. So in many ways the music education profession deserves to be—and is—justifiably proud of the excellence of its performance endeavors.

The Concerns

But beneath that merited pride has been a long-standing undercurrent of concern about the quality and depth of the musical learnings accruing from school performance activities. The concern is usually not about the level of technical ability students are able to achieve. Music educators are deeply savvy about what is reasonable in that regard and are expert in helping their students develop acceptable if not admirable technical control. The concern has more to do with what students are or are not learning beyond the level of proficient sound production—learnings that cause their singing and playing to be musically authentic, genuinely expressive, fully artistic, and thereby deeply satisfying for themselves and their audiences.

Why should such a concern exist? Two reasons for it have often been expressed, both by performance specialists and others.

First, the performance experience of many students tends to be limited to the correct production of notated sounds as instructed to do so by a teacher who makes every substantive decision about how those sounds should be made. Such students, it is often argued, are not being given the opportunity to develop the individuality and responsibility required to be an artist—in this case, a performing musician. Rote instruction, while producing results quickly, leaves students dependent on the teacher, when what is desired is the development of musical independence on the part of students.

The teacher, under pressure to produce public performances with inadequate time to do much more than whip an ensemble into shape, and working with literature at the edges of the students' capabilities so as to make the best impression possible, does not have the luxury to spend time on matters not directly and specifically connected to getting the right sounds made in the right way, "right" meaning as the notation requires and as the teacher interprets.

Students in such very common situations, it has been argued, can become very proficient at being able to do what they are told, but are left with minimal ability to make musical decisions when left to their own devices. They have not been helped to become performers in the genuine sense; that is, people whose excellent craftsmanship is based on their finely developed musical sensitivities, their imaginative ability to make music come alive in personally expressive ways, and their wide and deep perspective on how to accommodate their creative decisions to the demands of particular pieces in particular historical, cultural, and individual musical styles. Performance experiences in schools, it has long been argued, should foster this kind of genuine musicianship to the highest possible level for each student. The concern is that this goal becomes usurped by the pressures of a demanding public performance regimen.

The second concern about the quality of much school music performance experience is an outgrowth of the first.

This concern has to do with the future consequences of instruction that has been narrowly conceived and limited in focus. What happens to the students who have undergone such experiences once they graduate from high school?

Solid research on that question is scarce.[1] But a good deal of evidence based on the experience of many professional musicians and music educators allows for several pertinent observations.

For the very small percentage of students who go on to become music majors in colleges and universities, and who therefore are almost always required to continue performance study either as their major or as an important component of their programs, it has been widely expressed that their technique tends to be quite good to remarkably good. Of course, different collegiate institutions have different expectations for what acceptable performance expertise consists of, but even the elite among college, university, and conservatory music programs are generally able to find students fulfilling their high expectations (with, of course, some exceptions for the less common instruments). The problem with students entering music programs, it is widely observed, is not the level of their technical achievement but the shallowness of their musical understandings and the narrowness of their musical perspectives. There seems to be a disjunction between musicianship in the limited sense of technical facility and the broader sense of solidly grounded artistry.

The task for collegiate level education is to bring the two into better balance and to foster the continuing growth of both as being interdependent; that is, to develop mature performing artists.

The cream of the crop of school performers choose to continue in music, and what is left is the vast majority, whose lives will no doubt have been enriched in various ways by their performance experiences but whose continuing involvements with music are likely to change radically from what they were in school, given the exigencies that life will present to them. Some few, who have gained deep satisfactions from having been performers, will be reluctant to just give it all up, and will seek continuing involvements as amateurs in a variety of settings depending on what opportunities they find in their communities. Most will seldom if ever pursue performance in any substantial way again. What will they have gained from their brief experience as performers that will inform and enhance their musical experiences throughout their lives, albeit that those experiences are unlikely to come from performance? What will be the residue of musical understanding they have gained from performing, and will it be sufficient for, and relevant to, an enhanced ability to incorporate music into their lives as a precious source of pleasure?

The Larger Picture

The concerns about the depth, quality, and real-world applicability of performance learnings are part of a much larger movement occurring throughout the education enterprise at this point in history. In every subject matter field in education, an intensive self-analysis has taken place to determine whether traditional approaches have been too narrowly conceived to foster what is quickly becoming recognized by education scholars and leaders as the primary goal of education—the development of understanding. The mechanism for that analysis has been the creation of national standards for describing what all students should know and be able to do in each subject area. The effort to produce these standards—to identify the most important knowledge and skills for each field—has had an enormously positive effect on each field's sense of its central values and its central knowledge base. Every field, including music, has had to look itself squarely in the eye and ask itself what really matters about it and what really matters to learn about it.

In doing so, it has become crystal clear that much material previously considered essential was not optimally connected to achieving the ultimate goal of effective education—the deepening of every student's understanding. Each field, including music but much more broadly than music, has begun to face the challenge of reassessing its previously more limited aspirations and redesigning its curriculum to reflect a concentration on those learnings most relevant to understanding as it is manifested in that field.[2]

The National Standards for Music Education should be read as the attempt, in music education, to precisely define the knowledge and skills required to achieve musical understanding. What leaps out most dramatically from the nine content standards is their identification, as essential learnings, of far more than has traditionally been included. Further, the Standards require that all nine must be represented in all programs within the total music curriculum, including the performance program.

Why these nine? Why should all of them have to be incorporated as essential learnings in Content Standard 1, having to do with singing, and 2, having to do with playing? The answers to those questions require an explanation of what understanding consists of, and, as outgrowths, what musical understanding consists of and what performing with understanding consists of. The following discussions in this chapter will attempt an overview of what a reasonably complete explanation would entail, since a full explanation would require its own book, or, given the complexity of the issue, series of books. The subsequent chapters of this book are devoted to discussions of and recommendations for achieving the understandings required for artistic performance.

Generalities about Understanding

Dictionary definitions of understanding are of little help in providing guidelines for cultivating it, offering primarily synonyms, such as "perceiving the meaning or grasping the idea of something, comprehending, being familiar with, apprehending, grasping the significance," and so forth. What is needed is an explanation of just what it is that such terms actually entail—what mechanism of thinking/doing underlies and operationalizes the achievement of "perceiving the meaning," "grasping the idea," "comprehending," and so forth. Until we are able to identify that mechanism, we are not able to be optimally effective in providing educational experiences useful for fostering understanding.

Several recent considerations of this issue have attempted to clarify what this mechanism consists of. Unfortunately, I would suggest, they do not produce the desired result—a clear, elegant, yet powerful identification of the foundational operation of thinking and doing, which underlies what we generally call understanding, comprehending, apprehending, grasping the meaning, and so on. Most discussions remain at too high a level of generality to supply the specificity needed to focus efforts of educators on cultivating understanding. As Howard Gardner puts it in his book dealing with education for understanding, *The Unschooled Mind: How Children Think and How Schools Should Teach,* "generalizations about understanding are elusive, and those that can be made are necessarily expressed at a high level of abstraction."[3] Precisely so.

How do we get to a level of detail that can guide educational efforts efficiently?

I do not believe Gardner provides what we need, despite the many excellent insights he offers. In the book mentioned above one searches in vain for a concise definition of understanding that pinpoints its particular nature or character. In a chapter called "What Are the Qualities of Understanding?," written for another book, Gardner, along with Veronica B. Mansilla, offers the following reflection:

The quality of students' understanding rests on their ability to master and use bodies of knowledge that are valued by their culture. More specifically, it rests on their ability to make productive use of the concepts, theories, narratives, and procedures available in such disparate domains as biology, history, and the arts. Students should be able to understand the humanly constructed nature of this knowledge and to draw on it to solve problems, create products, make decisions, and in the end transform the world around them. Put differently, students should use knowledge to engage in a repertoire of performances valued by the societies in which they live.[4]

Few would disagree with this hope, including me. But it remains at a very "high level of abstraction." What is required for students to be able to "master and use" valued knowledge? How do they develop their ability to "make productive use" of learnings in various fields? What do we learn of the nature of understanding by the assertion that "Students should be able to understand . . . ?" What we are searching for is an explanation of what, precisely, that *means,* not only what one uses it for when one has it.

Here is another too-abstract explanation of understanding from the same collection, this one from Vito Perrone. "Teaching for understanding—the view that what students learn needs to be internalized, able to be used in many different circumstances in and out of classrooms, serving as a base for ongoing and extended learning, always alive with possibilities—has long been endorsed as a primary educational goal in the schools."[5]

This calls attention to several useful ideas about understanding. It is something "internalized." It is able to be "used in many different circumstances." It is "a base for ongoing and extended learning." But what, precisely, is it that needs to be internalized so that it can serve these functions? Again, we are left with no guidance beyond generalities.

The chapter by David Perkins, titled "What Is Understanding?," takes us closer to what we are searching for. Perkins identifies three desired goals of education—knowledge, skill, and understanding. Knowledge, he suggests, is "information on tap." Skills are "routine performances on tap." Understanding, however, is more subtle, not being reducible to either or both those two:

So what is understanding? One answer lies at the heart of this book and this project; it is simple but rich with implications. In a phrase, understanding is the ability to think and act flexibly with what one knows. To put it another way, an understanding of a topic is a "flexible performance capability" with emphasis on the flexibility. In keeping with this, learning for understanding is like learning a flexible performance—more like learning to improvise jazz or hold a good conversation or rock climb than learning the multiplication table or the dates of the presidents or that $F=MA$. Learning facts can be a crucial backdrop to learning for understanding, but learning facts is not learning for understanding.[6]

So now we may regard understanding as an ability to do a specific thing—"to think and act flexibly." Unfortunately, we are again given no explanation about the particulars that would allow thinking and acting to be flexible. We cannot yet identify just what it is that allows knowledge and skill to be "thought with" in a variety of situations; that is, flexibly.

Perkins explains that understanding in the thinking dimension requires a "conceptual model"—a structure in the mind that represents a particular situation, idea, system, and so forth. He labels this "mental model" idea of understanding the "representational view." In this view the model one holds in one's mind is the basis for the actions one takes. The action is not the under-standing—it is a signal that the appropriate representation is possessed.

In contrast is the "performance model" of understanding, which argues that the only way we can recognize understanding is through its manifestation in flexible performances—doing things that demonstrate that a person can "operate on or with the model."[7]

Now, there seems to be little difference between the conceptual model and the performance model. Both allow for and depend on mental representations and actions that operate on or with them.[8] The difference turns out to be one of degree. The conceptual model tends to emphasize the structures of knowing, on which actions depend, as being the key factor while the performance model emphasizes the actions one takes as being the key factor, the underlying structures being secondary. As Perkins concludes, "the performance view of understanding yields a brand of constructivism [engaging students in their own efforts to build understanding] that might be called *performance constructivism* because of its emphasis on building learners' repertoire of understanding performances more than on cultivating the construction of representations."[9]

Where does all this leave us? The distinction between thinking and acting is extremely helpful, as is the recognition of their relative interdependence. It would seem that the emphasis teachers put on either mental models or perfor-mance models might depend on subject matter. For example, philosophers and psychologists are specialists in articulating the mental models underlying our knowledge, skills, and understandings. Making such models explicit is what they do. The education of philosophers and psychologists (among many others), therefore, would seem to require that students in these subjects be assisted in developing knowledge about the models' underlying actions and in developing skills to explain them conceptually.

On the other hand, musical performers are specialists in making explicit, *through their actions,* the musical thinking underlying the sounds they create. The education of musical performers would seem to require a focus on their actions—their skills of creation of musical sounds—as these are founded upon their musical knowledge and internalized musical models whether explicit or implicit.

The implications of this idea for teachers of performance are clear and profound. Performance teachers must be able to help their students internalize musical models—inner representations of appropriate musical expression—which form the basis for independent artistic decisions carried out in acts of performance. The "mental/musical models" are, for performers, means, not ends. For music theorists, music psychologists, music philosophers, and others, the building of such models is an end, which can then be used by others as means. For performers, the end is realized in their artistic actions. When those actions are based only on their teachers' internalized models rather than on their own, the performers remain dependent on others for artistic decision making. When they are helped to gain and appropriate within themselves the musical models they need to call upon, they are enabled to become independent musicians/artists.

Teachers of performance, then, must (a) have internalized valid models relevant to performance in general and to their special area of performance in particular; and (b) be able to make the details of those models explicit, that is, communicable to students in a variety of ways including explaining them, helping students discover them, providing exemplars in actual performance, whether their own or others', providing musical challenges that encourage the application in action of the model aspects being explored, and so forth. Good teaching of performance, this suggests, develops students' mental/musical models as a means to the end of independent, musically grounded, artistic creating.

As useful as the insights of people like Perrone, Gardner, and Perkins can be, they still leave us without a description of what understanding actually consists of, their discussions remaining at too high a level of generality to supply the insights we need in order to do our jobs as teachers optimally. I will attempt a remedy in the next section.

Before doing so, two ideas of great importance, held in common by the

three scholars I have been discussing and by many others, need to be brought to attention. They have wide-ranging implications for the topic of this book.

First, understanding exists in degree. There is no single point at which one can say, "Now I have achieved understanding." No matter the level of one's understandings, further understandings are always possible. The responsibility of education, then, is to continually build upon, expand, and deepen students' understandings, recognizing that no hypothetical end point will ever be achieved in potential growth of understanding.

Second, understandings exist in kind—they are specific to the contexts to which they are applicable. There is no such thing as a "general understanding" separate from the specifics of the kinds of understandings called for by particular situations.

The term usually used in the scholarly literature for this contextual embeddedness of understanding is "domain specific." Often the domains in which specific understandings are called into play are considered to be the subjects studied in schools—languages, math, science, arts, history, geography, government, and so forth. Each of these, it is claimed, requires its characteristic ways of understanding. The most influential recent conceptualization of the domains in which understandings are achieved is Howard Gardner's notion of "frames of mind," in which seven categories of mindful functioning (called "intelligences" but applicable to understandings as well) are identified: the linguistic, musical, logical-mathematical, spatial, bodily-kinesthetic, interpersonal, and intrapersonal.[10] (Gardner has more recently considered adding the "naturalist" domain and, possibly, the "spiritual" or "existential.")

Whether domain specific understandings are conceived to reside in school subjects, in "frames of mind," or in other conceptualizations,[11] it is important to recognize that when we teach musical performance we must focus on developing the specific understandings relevant to that role. We can offer a general definition of understanding applicable to all specific role contexts (I prefer a focus on roles rather than domains), but in actual practice the understandings needing to be developed take their particularity and purpose from the role context in question. What then, is the answer to the question of what understanding specifically consists of? And what does performing with understanding consist of, given that it is a particular way, or role, in which understanding is achieved? Further, how can we best help our students achieve deeper understandings in their role as performers?

The Specifics of Understanding and Performing with Understanding

I want to propose that the specific, underlying operation of thought and action required for understanding is the forming of relevant connections.

Three concepts are embedded in this proposal: (a) connections, (b) forming, and (c) relevancy.

(a) Connections are interrelations—the ways things have something to do with other things. These ways range broadly over every possible relation that one thing can have with another, from identicality, to similarity, to affinity, association, proximity, pertinence, contrast, dissimilarity, incommensurability, opposition, variation, resemblance, imitation, and on and on with all the myriad operations of the mind in which some level of and sort of connectedness is identified.

The mind's ability to connect disparate things (objects, ideas, experiences, feelings, and so forth) is the basis for human understanding. Without this ability the world we experience would be chaotic—a "booming, buzzing confusion." Meaning, significance, wisdom, knowing, accomplishing—all human endeavors, intentions, and undergoings—are founded on and dependent on our ability to recognize relationships. Recognizing relationships is understanding.

Necessarily, then, as previously explained, understanding exists in degree. Recognizing that one leaf looks like another leaf is a necessary step in understanding leaves. A subsequent step, adding to and broadening that understanding, is the recognition that some leaves differ from others. Identifying, by the connection of dissimilarity, that differences in leaves can be in color, size, shape, texture, thickness, and so forth is a still further step toward understanding leaves. The understanding of leaves can continue to grow through successive levels of complexity, breadth, depth, and inclusiveness, leading to, perhaps, a worldview of the nature of life itself. At every step toward more comprehensive making of interconnections, we may say that understanding has grown.

(b) Forming is the function of the mind actively bringing connections into being. That function requires, consists of, and could not exist without imagination. Here the dictionary is precise: "Imagination is the faculty of forming mental images or concepts of what is not actually present to the senses." Connections among things are not present in factual sensory inputs—they are *constructed* from the sense data we receive. This construction ability is so deeply embedded as a primary function of human minds that it seems to be "given" with the sensory data we receive. It is not. We *attribute* the connections among things, as minds process those things to make experience out of them—to turn them into meanings. The level of our forming—our ability in particular instances to transform data into connected phenomena so that meaning occurs—is the level of our understanding.

Understanding, then, is an accomplishment, something we create at every moment in our conscious lives. Our minds are, inherently, connection-making devices, or, to put it into the context of this discussion, understanding

generators. The levels of connections we are able to process about similarities and differences among, say, leaves, from the most limited to the most comprehensive, are levels of imaginative construction. We form the connections—we imaginatively create them—as our experience with leaves, our learning about leaves, our application of those learnings in wider, more inclusive interrelationships, leads us to deeper understandings about leaves and their role in life on earth. Humans are active agents in forming connections—in making understanding. Teachers are active agents in assisting this process.

(c) The connections, or interrelations, we form, or imaginatively construct, must be relevant to the task at hand in order to qualify as understanding. In a second-grade classroom studying nature, the children are engaged in the role of learners, in this case about leaves. If the teacher were to show several different leaves from different trees and ask the students what they noticed about them that was particularly interesting, answers demonstrating that connections were being made ("They're all green," "They don't look the same— some are bigger than others," "They look like they come from different trees") are, in fact, demonstrating the level of understanding achieved. If one child's answer was "They all seem to be from deciduous trees, probably from a Northern climate, and from trees still in the growth stage of the season," the teacher would have reason to be impressed at that child's unusual level of understanding—of being able to form wider, more completely imagined interconnections than one would expect in that context. Similarly, if another child answered, "My Dad gets really mad when my Mom asks him to rake the leaves," the teacher might register that that child's response was not entirely relevant to the task of learning about leaves as part of nature—that that child didn't understand what relevant connections were being sought in this context.

A useful way to conceive the contexts in which connections are made—contexts that unify and give coherence to the many ways interrelationships among sensory inputs can be constructed—is to focus on the roles we play in our lives. Connections, to be meaningful, must serve some purpose. Our purposes depend on the roles we are pursuing. The teacher in the above scenario was pursuing the development of particular kinds of interconnected recognitions — understandings. He was also, as a teacher, sensitive to clues—connections—signifying additional issues needing attention among his students in relating this lesson with several others. The many connections this teacher was responsible for making in the classroom setting, for his students and for himself as their teacher, constituted his professional role, a role calling on particular, focused, intentional understandings to be exercised.

The students had a different role. They were in school to learn—to build the depth and breadth of their understandings, in this case about one aspect of nature. School is a place that makes sense, that means something, because it delineates to students one of the roles they are expected to play in their lives, a role focused on developing their understandings in a variety of contexts.

Now let us switch the above scenario to that of a music educator who is teaching students to perform. Several things remain the same as in the previous scenario. The teacher in both cases is going to play a particular role, calling on a coherent set of understandings related to the role of the teacher. In this case the role of the teacher is that of imparting and developing performance learnings. While still a teacher, the specificity of this particular role influences everything the teacher will do in her professional task of enhancing her students' understandings, specifically in their role as performers.

The performer role requires understandings to be developed—relevant connections to be formed—in a variety of interrelated focuses. One focus for performance understanding, for example, is on the physical actions required to produce the sounds that will serve musical purposes. Breath, vocal cords, throat, mouth, fingers, arms, tongue, lips, diaphragm, hands, wrists, legs, feet, all are involved in various ways depending on the performance medium. Performers must develop complex, subtle successions of interrelated connections (understandings) regarding such matters, not only as mental constructs but as internalized action patterns. Teachers helping this process to occur—teaching for understanding about the physical making of musical sounds—use a variety of devices such as words, gestures, diagrams, modeling, and touching, as means to the end of getting students to so deeply internalize the actions being sought as to render them automatic. Until the actions occur as habituated, they have not been "learned" as performers must learn them. So understanding in this context requires the sets of connections about sound producing to become tacit, in the sense of understood with no verbal expression of that understanding as the understanding is being demonstrated. The teacher's ability to make the relevant connections explicit, using a variety of means to bring them to awareness, is part of her arsenal as a professional. The end in view, however, is "awareness in action."

Another focus for performance learnings—for understandings to be developed as required to become a competent performer—is on notation (when, as is dominantly the case in American music education, the music to be performed exists in notated form). I will not attempt here a delineation of all the virtually endless connections that must be formed in order to deeply and widely understand the workings of musical notations, whether standard staff notation or various others. Readers will be able to do that for themselves.

Still another set of understandings are those that must be developed in order for each piece to be performed, in its particulars of pitch, rhythm, dynamics, tempi, articulations, harmony, texture, and form, and on and on with all the specifics comprising "a piece of music." When does one "fully understand" all the musical interconnections existing in even a simple piece, let alone a very complex one? That is, when has a performer become aware of, and transformed into automatic bodily behavior patterns, all the possible musically meaningful (interconnected) events in a piece being performed? Well, remember, understanding is always a matter of degree.

The three dimensions of performance understanding mentioned above—physical actions, notations, and pieces—are, of course, separable from one another only theoretically. In the actuality of the performance experience, all function interdependently. Think, then, of the staggering complexity of the multifaceted understandings required for a performer to (a) be able to physically produce the sounds required for music, (b) be able to translate notated symbols into musically sonic gestures, (c) be able to do both those things as relevant to the particularities of musical meanings contained within the piece being performed, and (d) be able to so coordinate all those facets of understanding that they are unified in the singular act of performing. This challenge, I suggest, is among the most daunting with which humans can be presented.

The Standards and Musical Understanding

Until the advent of the National Standards for Music Education it was (and, of course, continues to be) often assumed that if students were able to learn, to an acceptable degree relevant to their age and experience, the three dimensions of performance understandings delineated above—physically producing the needed sounds, being able to interpret notation, and making the pieces they were performing sound "musical" (that is, appropriately expressive)—they were learning all that was necessary to be competent performers. And, as I have pointed out, that in itself has been a formidable task.

The challenge of the Standards is the requirement that many other important dimensions of understanding be added to those traditionally assumed to be sufficient. This challenge signals a sea change in professional expectations of the performance role. It represents the growing awareness that students limited to those three aspects of performance understandings are limited in two important ways—in their musicianship as performers, and in their understandings of music outside the performance context. The Standards are conceived and designed to broaden and deepen musical understandings so as to include all major dimensions of music as a human endeavor. Both for those who will continue to perform after high school, whether as professionals in some aspect of music or as amateurs, and for

those who will no longer perform, the inclusion of those dimensions of musical learning will, it is now believed, enable all students involved in performance to more fully achieve musical meanings and satisfactions than under the previous, more limited expectation system.

The Standards represent the "grand plan" of all the dimensions of understandings achievable in music. Each of the nine content standards constitutes its own vast panoply of possible understandings—of potential relevant interconnections of meanings and actions. But none of the nine stands alone. Each requires and depends upon understandings in all the others to complete it and allow it to serve as a part of a larger whole. Each can serve both as a primary focus to which all the others contribute and as a complement to the others.

The success of music education in the future, I suggest, will depend in large measure on the profession's utilization of the Standards to guide the development of a meaningful general education program in music and of meaningful specializations in each of the nine.[12] The purpose of this book is to clarify how the Standards can serve as the basis for the development of performing with understanding, understanding as newly conceived, in breadth and specificity, by the Standards. My definition of understanding as the forming of relevant connections now comes fully into play.

Standards 1 (singing) and 2 (playing) are those focusing on performance. The connections required to do those things successfully, I have suggested, go beyond the three aspects traditionally associated with performance. Each of these two standards requires that understandings about the other eight—the forming of relevant connections within each of the eight—be incorporated within them. How does that actually play out?

Within Standard 1 is the requirement that, in addition to gaining the craftsmanship necessary for effective production of sung sounds, being able to translate notation into sung sounds, and musically appropriate singing of the piece being performed, understandings about solo and ensemble singing be developed ("alone and with others"). Further, the "varied repertoire of music" clause requires that requisite understandings of the inner workings of pieces in a wide variety of musical expectation systems (styles) be attained. So even before branching out to the other eight the breadth of understandings related to singing has been expanded.

How would Standard 2, having to do with understandings related to performing on instruments, be relevant to singing? Several aspects of singing are similar if not identical to playing. Both require that vibrations be produced to cause sounds. Both require exquisite physical control over the mechanisms of sound production, sound projection, and sound manipulation. Both are used for the same purpose—to form successions of sounds conceived as musically

meaningful in particular cultural/historical/aesthetic contexts. Both require enormous physical/mental/affective energy in order to produce the desired musical results. Both require actions within and according to the parameters of a particular "piece"—a set of composed sound-ideas being brought to sonic reality. And on and on with all the shared aspects of performance whether singing or playing. Understanding that these aspects apply equally to singing and to playing enhances the understanding—the aggregate of connections—of students involved with each.

But there are differences between the two, and these are equally as relevant to understanding as are the similarities. Unlike sound production on instruments, the vibration mechanism for producing sung sounds is an organ of the body rather than a mechanical device manipulated by the body. The experience of sound producing and manipulating is therefore subtly (or perhaps substantially) different. Instruments are able to produce sounds different from those produced by the voice, and vice versa. Voices are typically combined with other voices according to criteria quite different from those for combining instruments. Vocal music practically always entails words, while instrumental music does not, a significant and far-reaching distinction affecting how voices and instruments get used to make music. And on and on with all the differences between singing and playing. Understanding these differences enhances the understandings of those involved with each mode of performing.

How can teachers go about adding understandings from Standard 2 to Standard 1? Surely the Standards do not require all singers to become players in addition to becoming singers. But supplementing the learnings focused on the development of the skills and understanding required for singing, by referring to, discussing, demonstrating, and even trying to produce the similar and different ways playing relates to singing, broadens the connections singers are able to make. Awareness of how singing and playing are in many ways alike and in many ways not alike adds a significant dimension to the understandings being developed in Standard 1.

Each of the rest of the standards presents rich opportunities for connections to be made with singing, as illustrated by the example of how Standard 2 can do so. As the profession comes to grips with the wealth of learning opportunities—opportunities to develop understandings—in each of the standards, and as the interrelations among them become more obvious, several realizations are likely to occur.

First, we will begin to recognize with more specificity and more clarity how limited our perspective has tended to be on musical learning in general—and, since the dominant musical learnings we have pursued have been those connected to performing, how limited our

conception has been of what is required to be a broadly educated performer. The vague sense we have had that performance learnings have tended to be restricted in scope and depth, as mentioned at the beginning of this chapter, will take on specificity as we use the Standards to delineate the particular understandings that need to be fostered in the ways performance requires; that is, as awarenesses transformed into the actions of performing.

Second, we will learn how to examine the dimensions of musical understanding represented by each of the standards, in search of the particular array of connections each affords—the particular sets of interconnected ideas and actions each embodies. As our awareness increases of the particularities of the understandings available in each of the nine dimensions of musical involvement, our ability to envision interconnections among all of them will also grow. We will be able to significantly broaden the number of specializations within music study beyond performing, each of them retaining its individuality of focus but also being enriched by learnings from all the others. And we will also become more clear than we have ever been about the purposes of a general education in music; that is, an education embracing all the dimensions rather than focusing on one particular dimension. As related to the concern of this book, our ability to provide performers with all that educated performers should understand will grow exponentially. That will achieve two things we need very much to achieve—the fostering of more genuinely artistic performing musicians, and the enhancement of their musical enjoyments beyond performing should they choose not to continue as performers.

Third, we will gain more respect for music performance as a human achievement of monumental proportions. As our understanding of the complexities of performance grows, as a result of our deeper awareness about the breadth of interconnections it takes to perform with understanding, the attitude that performing is simply a pleasant but relatively trivial entertainment will yield to the realization that performance, in its embracing of all dimensions of musical understanding, and in its transformation of them into bodily behavior, is a paradigm of the union of knowing and doing. The unification of mind, body, and feeling required for performing with understanding may well be an example of human cognitive potential at its farthest reaches. Teachers of performance are developers of that potential.

The Contribution of This Book

Each of the following chapters makes a particular contribution to our ability as professionals to help students perform with understanding.

Chapter 3, by Dorothy Straub, offers a broad overview of the total music program in the schools and how the Standards apply to the performance aspects of all programs. She then dis-

cusses the role of professional leadership in encouraging change in the direction of performing with understanding, and the rewards to be gained by this emerging vision.

In Chapter 4, Will Schmid provides specific, practical, and extremely thoughtful suggestions for changing choral and instrumental practices from the "get ready for the next public performance" mentality toward the incorporation of the Standards as subject areas infusing all performance learnings. We have had many successes as teachers of performance, he points out, but also some serious failures. It is time we "change the landscape" of our teaching in the direction of the fullness of learnings the Standards stipulate. His pinpointing of learnings essential for educated performance, and the specificity of his recommended activities for achieving it, reflect his years of experience as a successful mentor of students who can perform with both competence and comprehension.

Performance is an integral component of a general education in music. In Chapter 5, Suzanne Shull expresses her devotion to involving all students in the doing of music through performance. With wide-ranging examples she draws a picture of how the Standards can make performance a direct route to musical understanding, achievable through practical, workable, teachable activities general music teachers can supply in abundance. She ends with several pointed, tough questions we all need to answer, and with the plea that performance not be regarded as only for the "talented few." There is no excuse, she argues, for any student to be deprived of the opportunity to experience music as an active, educated, performing musician.

Marvelene Moore's discussion in Chapter 6 focuses on the role of bodily movement in performing. Throughout history and in many cultures movement has been and continues to be inextricably linked with performing. And when movement is added to performance it assists not only in the development of musical understandings but also in the crucial task of internalizing, within the body's knowing/acting system, the understandings that must be displayed in performing. Movement, she points out, can be utilized in many of the standards to add a powerful, positive influence on the development of inward understandings.

Rehearsals are the major setting for developing more refined understandings among participants, argues Patricia Hoy in Chapter 7. In her wide-ranging and penetrating analysis of the rehearsal as a means for concentrated teaching, she covers a variety of musical elements needing to be explored and important teaching strategies needing to be employed. For each of the musical elements she provides detailed suggestions for incorporating the Standards to broaden student learnings.

Robert Gillespie, in his focus on the school orchestra in Chapter 8, provides a series of model rehearsal strategies incorporating the Standards to build understandings. While the pieces he uses are for string and full orchestras, all ensembles can apply the principles he delineates. His strategies range widely over the nine standards, incorporating them as essential learnings for performers of orchestral (or any other) literature.

A fascinating glimpse into the mind of the exemplary conductor/educator Larry Rachleff is given in Chapter 9. In interview format, Rachleff reflects on what musical understanding consists of for performers and how performance directors can best cultivate it. He also comments on audience education, the role of orchestral music in our culture, how the Standards deepen the understandings of performers, and the point and purpose of music and musical performance—to enable feelingful response. Among many other issues discussed, his vision of music as serving both the heart and the brain is paramount.

In Chapter 10 Mary Goetze describes her devotion to performing choral music beyond that of the Western tradition. Her analysis of the issues involved in doing so, both musical and pedagogical, reveals her deep understandings both as a musician and as a performance director/teacher. Her practical suggestions for broadening the repertoire performed, and thereby broadening the musical understandings of the performers, are based on real-life challenges she addresses with her International Vocal Ensemble, as she explores with them the various modes of musical expression in our multimusical world.

Bruno Nettl brings his wide cultural/musicological perspectives to bear on the issue of the attempt in the United States to implement the new vision of music education embodied in the Standards. He describes what "standards for musicianship" consist of in several cultures outside the West, and discusses the issue of whether music is intended to transmit culture or change culture, illustrating the issue as it operates in Persian music and Blackfoot music. The U.S. standards, he points out, are attempting something "rather unprecedented," in attempting to change the musical culture in the United States in the direction of dramatically greater breadth than has heretofore existed, enabling all young people to be full members of their culture's diverse musical community.

In the last chapter, Editor Bennett Reimer presents and discusses ten guidelines, generated during the seminar, which can serve as an action agenda toward making performance as broadly and deeply enriched with musical understanding as students deserve it to be. Achieving that agenda will also strengthen music education as an essential component of schooling through its enhanced contribution to our musical culture.

Notes

1. For a useful review of research on effects of school performance involvements on subsequent listening experience, see James K. Kjelland and Jody L. Kerchner, eds., "The Effects of Music Performance Participation on the Music Listening Experience," *Bulletin of the Council for Research in Music Education* 136 (1998): 1–55.

2. The growing literature on education for understanding is indicated in the notes section of Martha S. Wiske, ed., *Teaching for Understanding: Linking Research with Practice* (San Francisco: Jossey-Bass Publishers, 1998), 351–73.

3. Howard Gardner, *The Unschooled Mind: How Children Think and How Schools Should Teach* (New York: Basic Books, 1991), 118.

4. Wiske, ed., 162.

5. Ibid., 13.

6. Ibid., 40.

7. Ibid., 47.

8. Perkins claims that one can have an enactive (performance) understanding without an explicit mental model. But a model need not be explicit in order to be functional. We have so internalized many of the mental models we hold as to often not be able to make them explicit except with great difficulty. That does not mean we do not have them. We simply do not have them readily available in verbal-conceptual form.

9. Wiske, ed., 57.

10. Howard Gardner, *Frames of Mind: The Theory of Multiple Intelligences* (New York: Basic Books, 1983).

11. See, for example, Philip H. Phenix, *Realms of Meaning* (New York: McGraw-Hill, 1964), and Elliot Eisner, ed., *Learning and Teaching the Ways of Knowing* (University of Chicago Press, 1985).

12. An argument can be made that viable

music specializations exist in each of the standards except, perhaps, number five, having to do with reading and notating music, which are skills useful or necessary in several of the others but not constituting, by themselves, a field of endeavor as do the others. This argument awaits further elucidation as to its persuasiveness.

Teaching for Performing with Understanding in the K–12 Music Program

3

A Snapshot of a Quality K–12 Music Program

Dorothy A. Straub

Performing with understanding quite accurately describes an essential aspect of an excellent K–12 school music program. Until recently, a quality school music program meant different things to different people. Marching bands, competitions, public visibility, and entertainment were the expectation of some students, parents, and school administrators. Others expected music theory, history, and literature, with an emphasis on aesthetic appreciation. Music teachers themselves held vastly different opinions on what defined good music education in our schools. Should music reading be a priority? Does "pop" music have a place? Should we focus instruction for students who are "musically talented"?

One need only observe the products of our schools—today's adult population—to realize that music in their education varied greatly from state to state and from school to school. Adults are generally able to read and write, and they possess basic skills and knowledge in mathematics, science, and history,

but what are they able to do in music? Lack of a clear answer would indicate discrepancies in their music education.

Enter the National Standards for Arts Education. During the administration of President George Bush, education reform charted a future for education in America. In 1989, the nation's governors called for a national effort to improve the education of America's children. That initiative developed into the *Goals 2000: Educate America Act* during the Clinton administration. *Goals 2000* called for national standards in mathematics, science, English, history, civics and government, foreign languages, geography, economics, and the arts. The arts were defined as dance, music, theatre, and visual arts. National standards in the arts, like standards in the other disciplines, would describe what every child in America should know and be able to do at the end of grades 4, 8, and 12. They would be voluntary world-class standards—something to aim for.

In March 1994, the National Standards for Arts Education were presented to U.S. Education Secretary Richard Riley at a press conference in Washington, D.C. Now we had a model for music education in our schools. The national consensus process brought credibility. The funding process and the appointment of a national advisory committee brought public awareness and support.

The introduction to the K–4 Music Standards states:

> Performing, creating, and responding to music are the fundamental music processes in which humans engage. Students, particularly in grades K–4, learn by doing. Singing, playing instruments, moving to music, and creating music enable them to acquire musical skills and knowledge that can be developed in no other way. Learning to read and notate music gives them a skill with which to explore music independently and with others. Listening to, analyzing, and evaluating music are important building blocks of musical learning. Further, to participate fully in a diverse global society, students must understand their own historical and cultural heritage and that of others within their communities and beyond. Because music is a basic expression of human culture, every student should have access to a balanced, comprehensive, and sequential program of study in music.[1]

The National Standards call for a comprehensive music education for all children. With the Standards as a model, performing with understanding is now a fundamental musical expectation for every child.

A Look at School Music Programs

What is actually happening in music classes in our schools today? Are the National Standards in place or at least recognized as a goal? Let us take a glimpse of music education at the three most common levels of American schools—elementary school, middle school, and high school. The following are my personal observations based on my experience as a music teacher, music administrator, and most important, as a past president of the Music Educators National Conference (now MENC— The National Association for Music Education). In these capacities I have visited music classes in more than thirty-five states and interacted with thousands of music educators.

Elementary school (commonly grades K–5).[2] There are elementary schools in this country where the National Standards are being met or nearly met. In these schools, all of the content standards in the National Standards are addressed sequentially, beginning in kindergarten. A structured sequence of skill development and knowledge building provides for success and enjoyment at each incremental step in each class. Instruction is child-centered and hands-on. Performing, composing, improvising, and listening are supported by discussion and reflection, each enhancing musical understanding.

The emphasis is on nurturing the musicianship of every child.

In elementary schools with excellent music programs, all of the children are singing, in tune and with good tone quality, and they are enjoying singing. They know many songs, from folk songs to art songs, from American patriotic songs to songs from many different lands. They sing beautifully in unison, and they also sing comfortably in two and three parts by the time they reach fourth or fifth grade. A choral experience is a regular part of the curriculum for fourth and fifth graders, and a special chorus provides an opportunity for students who aspire to do more.

Beginning in kindergarten, where developing a sense of pulse and rhythm is an important goal, sequenced movement activities are an integral part of each class.[3] Listening to examples from excellent music literature and from a wide variety of cultures brings the treasures of the world of music to each child, opening the doors to a lifelong richness. Reflecting on this music—its form, style, and expressive content— deepens its personal meaning and value for students.

Performing on instruments is a part of every class. A large collection of pitched and nonpitched instruments is used for rhythmic activities, for accompaniment, for improvisation, for composition, and for learning musical form, timbre, and score reading. Since the instruments are from a variety of cultures, projects with classroom teachers

are a natural outgrowth.

Music reading develops along with reading of language. Early exposure to notation symbols, as well as use of the soprano recorder and pitched percussion instruments, facilitates music reading skills. Technology assists the children in music reading, facilitating individual progress and familiarizing them with the piano and electronic keyboards. New skills continue to be introduced by rote because the aural aspect of music is the strongest and most direct connection to the humanness of the child.

When children have learned a large repertoire of folk songs and are comfortable playing simple patterns and melodies on pitched and nonpitched instruments, improvising melodies or rhythmic variations, creating new patterns, or improvising interludes is achievable by all students and personally rewarding to each. Creating accompaniments to a poem or story captures the imagination of the children. Building on simple creative experiences, children expand on their improvising skills, strengthen their aural acuity, and take ownership of their individual musicianship. Improvisation occurs in a variety of styles, including the jazz idiom and world music.

A string and orchestra program begins in the third or fourth grade and is well subscribed. The band program, which usually begins a year later, is healthy as well, and the specialists who teach orchestra and band work cooperatively with each other and with the general music teacher to ensure consistent curriculum delivery, to avoid conflict or competition, and to keep the best interests of the individual child as the primary focus.

School concerts are an outgrowth of instruction. They do not drive instruction. Demonstrations for parents are common, and whole-grade or whole-school project demonstrations often present the products of integrated learning units in which music plays an important part. Special visits from professional performers are planned and presented so that artistic and personal impact is maximized, enhancing the musical life of the children and bringing excitement to the whole school.

Music teachers are key figures in their schools. Not only do they teach every child in the school, but they often do so for the child's entire elementary career. Music teachers work closely with classroom teachers and administrators, keeping the development of the whole child as the primary focus and keeping the total school curriculum in mind. Ongoing communication with music colleagues in other elementary schools, middle schools, and high schools, as well as with parents and the community, is routine. Of course, there is a written curriculum that is updated regularly, and adequate instructional time is provided. Performing with understanding is an important dimension of the total music curriculum in these schools.

Is this elementary music picture typical of most schools? No, but it is not the rare exception either. The good news seems to be spreading. School principals, school districts, and parents are increasingly aware of what should be happening musically for children. They are also aware of the advantages of an excellent school music program.

Middle school (commonly grades 6–8). A continuation of this comprehensive music education is the logical next step for optimum development of musical growth in every child. With the rich musical background developed in the elementary school, children are well prepared and motivated for more advanced musical experiences. They are able to achieve the National Standards for grades 5–8 by the time they complete middle school. Very few middle schools, however, provide that kind of music program. Is the changing voice the problem? Is it the nature of the adolescent child and the attraction of teenage "pop" music? The successful middle school music teacher will respond "no." These are natural changes in the growing-up process, and excellent music education can continue to flourish with adolescent youngsters.

What would a model middle school program look like? The core of music instruction, music class (or general music) continues for all students in grades 6, 7, and 8, with all the Standards being addressed. Singing experiences are adjusted for adolescents, but these children do continue to sing. Music reading skills become more necessary and used in exciting ways with computers and MIDI keyboards, which provide opportunities for composition and improvisation. Music listening experiences now include appropriate examples of symphony, opera, ballet, the Broadway musical, and jazz, which stimulate the adolescent. In addition, listening experiences include musics of a rich variety of world cultures and a variety of popular music from our own culture. Guitars, keyboards, and perhaps handbells or other instruments encourage students to expand their musical performing skills. Integration with art, dance, and theatre is ongoing, as are interdisciplinary projects with social studies, language arts, science, and math. Music is a viable component of the academic curriculum of the school while maintaining its authenticity as a genuine cognitive domain.

In addition, students may elect to participate in performing ensembles, continuing their instrumental and/or choral experiences. String orchestras and bands are offered for students in each grade, with students grouped according to their achievement level. Small-group instruction is provided for all instrumental students, in like instrument classes, so that students continue to advance their musical skills. A full orchestra experience is also part of the curriculum, allowing string players an opportunity to play with selected woodwind, brass, and percussion players and to perform appropriate arrangements of orchestral masterworks, as well as

lighter selections. A variety of choral experiences are offered, and chorus may be elected by any student. Choral participation is encouraged, particularly for students in band or orchestra. Enrollment in performing group ensembles involves a large percentage of the school (as much as 90 percent), and band, orchestra, and chorus are held in high esteem by the entire school community. Instrumentation in the bands and orchestras is well-balanced.

To meet students' special needs and interests, ensemble opportunities include string quartets; brass, woodwind, and percussion ensembles; vocal or instrumental jazz ensembles; strolling strings or fiddling; and ethnic music ensembles that reflect the population of the school. A healthy number of students participate in area youth orchestras, bands, or choirs. Concerts are an outgrowth of the curriculum, and visits from musical artists enrich the musical life of the school. Music is a vital part of the middle school years.

Now let us take a look at a typical middle school program. When a trend in education caused many junior highs to redefine themselves as middle schools, it affirmed a middle school philosophy that learning should be more student-centered and less compartmentalized by subject. These years would be a time for exploratory experiences. High school, then, would provide an opportunity for students to continue to pursue selected areas of interest that they explored in middle school. Usually, middle schools follow a block schedule designed to encourage teachers to plan cooperatively and integrate instructional experiences. Students are grouped into communities or clusters in an effort to create a positive social and learning environment.

A typical middle school block schedule distinguishes an academic block from a related or unified arts block. The arts block usually occupies two periods each day or a total of ten periods each week. (A period is generally forty to fifty minutes.) Included in the arts block may be not only music, art, dance, and theatre, but physical education, foreign language, computer science, health education, sex education, and substance abuse education. Limited instructional time for music, and its classification separate from academics, weaken its effectiveness.

If a middle school does require music—and some do not—a student may usually select only one course. A student may choose to be in band or orchestra (if there is one), chorus, or general music. What actually happens? Most elect to participate in a performing group. This leaves general music class with the students least interested and least motivated in music and, usually, those with discipline problems; hence, the poor image of middle school general music. Band, orchestra, and chorus classes are usually large, grouped by grade level rather than ability, and meet two or three times each week. The expectation is strictly performance.

Extending the students' skills in music fundamentals is a challenge. Exposure to anything beyond performing music is nearly impossible. When will these children, who are the highly motivated musicians of the school, hear a Stravinsky ballet, a Beethoven symphony, or a Mozart opera? When will they learn about the music and the people of Egypt or Japan or have an opportunity to experiment with musical composition?

In reflecting on a typical middle school and the objective of performing with understanding, we might conclude that the performers are lacking in understanding while the students in general music classes are lacking in performance skills. In reality it is easier to fix the general music classes. Successful general music teachers are utilizing piano keyboards, guitars, computers, and MIDI instruments to turn on even the least motivated students to music. Ironically, the music achievers in band, orchestra, and chorus are denied a comprehensive music education. The middle school music teacher who is committed to a comprehensive music education for all children is often frustrated by his or her inability to provide this kind of a music education for the students, particularly for those students in performing groups, but it is important to note that the music teacher should not be blamed for program inadequacies.

High school (commonly grades 9–12). In an ideal high school music program, performance courses are offered at varying skill levels, providing for sequential development during the high school years. Every school should have a band, orchestra, and chorus. Instrumental lessons are provided for students in band and orchestra. Courses in which performance is not the primary focus attract the general student body and satisfy a fine arts requirement. Vocal and instrumental jazz ensembles, music theory, music history/appreciation or a related arts course, music technology lab, piano class, and guitar class are offered.

Performance does not drive the curriculum, but excellent concerts are the norm. A variety of performing groups are featured on each concert. Wind and percussion players are shared between band and orchestra, and instrumental students are encouraged to sing. Extracurricular auditioned groups stimulate and challenge the most advanced musicians, and students have the opportunity to participate in a variety of small ensembles.

Presently, at the high school level, music courses typically are elective. Performance courses (band, orchestra, chorus) are the most highly subscribed. Some music programs offer music theory, and some offer music history or appreciation, but these courses are often underenrolled and therefore canceled. Music technology lab or music composition, piano class, and guitar class are offered in some schools. Orchestras exist in fewer than half the high schools nationwide, primarily because of the absence of viable string programs in the lower grades.

The emphasis on performance courses varies from an intense focus on performing and competition (marching bands, contests) to a more comprehensive musicianship approach. Teaching performance with understanding is less the norm, but it is slowly growing because of the advent of the National Standards and examples such as the Wisconsin project, which applies long-standing principles from the Comprehensive Musicianship Project. The two major impediments to teaching performance with understanding in the high school are: (1) middle school programs that limit students' music experiences to the technical aspects of performance, and (2) teachers who are not comfortable or prepared to teach using a comprehensive musicianship approach.

The percentage of students currently enrolled in music courses at the high school level is relatively small. *Arts Education in Public Elementary and Secondary Schools* compares music teachers to the total school teaching staff, and music space to the total school space.[4] It reports that, while 94 percent of the secondary schools in the United States offer music courses, the average number of music teachers in each secondary school is only 2.1, and the average number of rooms used for music instruction is 2.6.

If music education preceding high school were more comprehensive in nature, producing a higher level of musical skill and knowledge on the part of entering freshman, there might be greater interest among some students in continuing instruction in keyboard, guitar, or composition, or in music history/appreciation. It should be noted that technology has made music much more accessible to students, not only to develop skills but to utilize and expand their musical creativity. A student with minimal skill can successfully engage in music improvisation and composition. Technology can be the catalyst that brings the disaffected rock musician into the school music program.

An increasing number of states are requiring a fine arts credit for high school graduation. This statewide recognition of the importance of the arts, along with the influence of the National Standards, has caused an awareness that many high school programs tend to be somewhat elitist. High schools need to offer a variety of music electives to meet the individual needs of students not involved in performing groups.

An overemphasis on the technical aspects of performance has been characteristic of many high school music programs. Can that emphasis be shifted to meet the needs and abilities of the individual student performers? Many directors fear that such a shift in emphasis would result in diminishing the quality of the performing group. These directors need only look and listen to performing groups in which performing with understanding underlies instruction. The results are convincing.

Quality is not compromised but enhanced by the musical understanding and personal commitment of the students. Most important, high school directors need to be reminded that a high-quality performance is only one of many valid outcomes of music education.

The Importance of Leadership

If we believe that performing with understanding is our goal for the music education of all children in America, substantive change is needed. The vision of where we should be is miles from the reality of K–12 music in schools today. How can change take place? Where can it begin? Leadership is needed to raise awareness, bring appropriate parties together, build a plan, and effect change.

The role of the K–12 music supervisor/coordinator. Along with the National Standards in music, MENC published another important document, *Opportunity-to-Learn Standards for Music Instruction.*[5] It defines the aspects of a PreK–12 school music program that must be in place in order for the Standards to be achieved, including recommendations for curriculum and scheduling, staffing, materials and equipment, and facilities. The document states: "In order that the instructional program of every student may be adequately coordinated and articulated from level to level, one music educator in every district or school is designated as coordinator or administrator to provide leadership for the music program."[6]

K–12 supervision or coordination of a music program is essential for instructional continuity, for curriculum development, and for monitoring the curriculum that is taught. The role of the music administrator is essential in ensuring a balanced, sequential program for all students in the district. The quality of the instructional program from kindergarten through grade 12 is an overarching concern. Key responsibilities are assessment of the instructional program and student achievement, accountability, and communication with and among all the music teachers, administration, parents, and the community.

As school budgets have tightened, limited financial resources have resulted in the elimination of many subject-area supervisors nationwide. The quality of all disciplines is compromised by this absence of what might be viewed as middle management, but music is uniquely vulnerable to loss of quality without program leadership.

Consider a principal's responsibilities. In an elementary school, language arts, social studies, math, and science are taught by each classroom teacher. Supervision of these teachers is distinctly different from supervision of the one music teacher who teaches music to all the children in the school. Classroom teachers communicate with each other regarding the articulation of the curriculum from grade to grade in the subjects they teach, unlike the music teacher who is responsible for all curriculum articulation in music, as well as

for communication with the instrumental music specialists who teach in the school. Most principals have limited expertise in music curriculum and pedagogy and are therefore unable to provide the curriculum supervision a good program requires. The task is left for the music administrator, who provides ongoing support for the music teachers and provides continuity among schools at the same level and from elementary school to middle school to high school. Music teachers, like other teachers, need constant oversight for a quality program to remain effective and efficient.

Aspects of the K–12 program that call for districtwide coordination include curriculum development and assessment; teacher evaluation; meetings of the K–12 music staff; inventory of school-owned instruments; purchasing, issuing, and maintaining a library of band, orchestra, and chorus music; maintaining a calendar of concert dates and music activities; providing professional opportunities and resources for music teachers; and organizing districtwide festivals.

Without program leadership, there is no guarantee that music teachers will work together. An important role of the music administrator is to maintain a balance in the program and among teachers so that all aspects of the program are strong, not just those taught by teachers with dominant personalities.[7]

The role of higher education. If performing with understanding is a major goal of music education, then performance teachers themselves must be able to perform with understanding and be able to teach it. The National Standards call for rigorous musical and professional skills on the part of teachers. Who will prepare these teachers? The potential for dramatic change rests with the colleges and universities who prepare students for careers in teaching music and who provide ongoing professional opportunities for teachers to continue to learn and grow. Updating of teaching skills and knowledge is now needed on a regular basis. A particular challenge for college faculty is keeping in touch with the changes occurring in the schools.

How can colleges and universities be expected to graduate first-rate professional music educators when the students they receive are products of weak music education programs? Of course, higher education cannot solve the problem alone, but its role is critical, and without assertive action from colleges and universities, there is little hope for improvement in school music programs. Those institutions that have strengthened their entrance requirements and intensified their course of study in order to prepare music educators to teach to the National Standards are to be commended.

The role of professional associations. Professional associations have not only increased their services to music teachers but have also taken initiatives to strengthen music education in the schools. Our national association, MENC, had the commitment, tenacity, and political clout to bring about

National Standards in music, perhaps the single most significant development in the history of music education. Now, MENC and other associations, including American Choral Directors Association (ACDA), American Orff Schulwerk Association (AOSA), American String Teachers Association with National School Orchestra Association (ASTA with NSOA), National Association of Teachers of Singing (NATS), National Association of Pastoral Musicians (NPM), National Band Association (NBA), Organization of American Kodály Educators (OAKE), Suzuki Association of the Americas (SAA), and many others are actively pursuing a wide variety of strategies to help teachers improve their teaching and expand their musical horizons. The magazines, publications, resources, and information services of these professional associations reflect a responsiveness to the needs of music teachers. In addition, workshops and state conferences, division conferences, and national conferences are perhaps the most valuable means for regenerating our professional energy in times of change and challenge. The personal interaction experienced by members at these conferences is a rich benefit in itself.

The role of the individual music teacher. Each of us is challenged to adapt to the new expectations of the National Standards—to teach to a higher level and to assist others in doing so. School music educators who teach in a setting where no district leadership is provided face a particularly difficult challenge.

How can you advocate change in your school and in your school district? What can you do to motivate complacent colleagues to strive for higher standards for their students—to teach performance with understanding as well as all the other musical learnings the Standards include?

You can begin by reading the literature and taking full advantage of professional opportunities. Invite your colleagues to join you in attending a state, regional, or national conference, asking your building administrator to provide financial support. Be sure your building administrator has a copy of the National Standards and the Opportunity-to-Learn Standards for music. Speak directly with appropriate administrators about specific positive changes that need to occur in your school so that your students can achieve the National Standards. Always keep the focus on the benefits to students.

The Rewards

Teaching performing with understanding, an important component in achieving the National Standards in our schools, is a monumental undertaking! Is it worth it? Is the intended change important enough to warrant so much time, effort, and stress? If excellence in music education is important, the answer is yes.

Imagine the rewards! The American public, being educated in music, would be able to perform, understand, appreciate, and personally value good music as a regular part of life. Community

bands, orchestras, and choruses would spring up throughout the country so that adults could continue to enjoy music making. Families and friends would come together to play chamber music in homes. Adults and children would share music together. Symphony orchestras, ballet companies, opera houses, chamber music societies, and musical theatre companies would experience a demand for subscriptions. Everyone in attendance would join in singing at worship services and at community events. Retail sales of recordings, print music, and musical instruments would reach an all-time high. Music would be good for business and good for the economy. Being a professional musician or a music educator would be a highly respected career choice.

Most important, all of us would experience a more meaningful enjoyment of music, enriching the quality of our daily lives by singing, playing, and listening to music we have learned to cherish. Support for music in our lives and in our schools would be enhanced. We would discover a deeper understanding of the music of other cultures and a better understanding of the people themselves, bringing the music of the world into our own world. Results like this, meaningful and life-enhancing, make all of our efforts worthwhile.

Notes

1. Consortium of National Arts Education Associations, *National Standards for Arts Education: What Every Young*

American Should Know and Be Able to Do in the Arts (Reston, VA: Music Educators National Conference, 1994), 26.

2. Research has shown the importance of music study in the elementary school years as it relates to musical potential, and, in fact, to other learning. Thanks to the pedagogies of Koldály, Orff, Dalcroze, Suzuki, and others, and the initiative of teachers in studying and applying these pedagogies, the elementary music classes of today are dramatically different from those in years past. Find an excellent instructional program in music and you have found an excellent school. In *Strong Arts, Strong Schools* (Oxford University Press, 1996), Charles Fowler reported, "The Florida Department of Education, . . . found a direct correlation between active fine and performing arts programs and increased student motivation and a lower dropout rate. The Manchester Craftsmen's Guild in Pittsburgh, an organization that apprentices 'at risk' inner city students in the arts while teaching them math, English, and other subjects, found a correlation between the arts and student academic performance. At the Duke Ellington School of the Arts in Washington, D.C., students graduate at an astonishing 99 percent rate, and 90 percent go on to higher education" (p. 138).

3. A sense of timing is recognized by a growing number of educators to be a key to success in activities such as reading, writing, and speaking. "Research in the area of movement and music confirms that arts education contributes to the overall quality of life and specifically to children's academic and social development. For example, the High/Scope Rhythmic Skills Study (Weikart, Schweinhart, & Lamer, 1987), done with 358 children in Michigan, found that their beat-keeping ability, as measured by the Rhythmic Competency Analysis Test (RCAT), was positively and significantly correlated with California Achievement Test total scores at the end of first and second grade. . . . Kiger (1994) also found that RCAT scores were positively associated with gross motor skills and the reading group level of 128 children in grades 1, 3, and 5 in Ohio and Georgia" (from Phyllis S. Weikart and Elizabeth B. Cariton, *Foundations in Elementary Education: Movement* [High/Scope Press, Ypsilanti: Michigan, 1995], 385). Other research suggests that movement activities also develop attending skills (listening, processing information, following directions), thereby strengthening other learning.

4. U.S. Department of Education, National Center for Education Statistics, *Arts Education in Public Elementary and Secondary Schools* (Washington, DC: U.S. Department of Education, Office of Educational Research and Improvement, October 1995), 13–15.

5. Music Educators National Conference, *Opportunity-to-Learn Standards for Music Instruction, Grades PreK–12* (Reston, VA: MENC, 1994).

6. Ibid., 6.

7. Because of parent involvement and performances, the music program is more visible to the public than most subject areas. A quality music program results in positive public relations for the school district.

4

Challenging the Status Quo in School Performance Classes
New Approaches to Band, Choir, and Orchestra Suggested by the Music Standards

Will Schmid

At a recent workshop on the future of choral music education, participants were asked to imagine a choral rehearsal in the years 1927, 1957, and 1997. What differences would there be between them, if any? Has the everyday job of delivering a music education to students in performance classes changed significantly over time? The overwhelming response of the workshop participants was that the rehearsals would probably look remarkably similar—warm-ups followed by rehearsal of three or four pieces, all with the teacher/director firmly in control.

"Is there anything wrong with this?" many asked. "Haven't these time-honored procedures produced great choirs (and bands and orchestras)?" Others asked, "Why change? If it ain't broke, don't fix it." Yes, clearly the tradition of bands, choirs, and orchestras in America has been one of our greatest successes. And now we have the new National Standards for Music Education, which have been adopted or adapted in most states, raising the bar even higher on what we can expect to accomplish in the future.

The Successes

In order that we not "throw out the baby with the bathwater," it is useful to examine what we are doing well in band, choir, and orchestra classes. First of all, we are striving for excellence in performance, an effort that often produces stunning results. The number of students participating in solo and ensemble festivals at the local, district, and state levels is staggering. The level of difficulty of the literature being performed is high because states have closely monitored the lists of acceptable repertoire and because peer pressure among directors is also high. Students work toward a I (A) rating with the possibility of moving on to the next level. This widespread activity, if handled properly, can continue to be one of the best aspects of performance education. Math, science, and language arts education only occasionally approach this level of excellence and involvement with their science fairs and speech contests.

Another strength of performance education today is that students learn about music as active, firsthand participants in the art. Students who have felt what psychologist Abraham Maslow described as a "peak experience" when performing want to replicate that experience through continued performance activity.[1] Given the right kind of opportunities, this natural motivation can lead to a lifetime of satisfying experiences with the art and with other people. The value to the community of continued performance in church choirs or community orchestras, bands, or choruses is enormous.

Beyond the purely musical value of the band, choir, and orchestra experi-

ence lie the social and human values. During the adolescent years, when peer pressures to fit in are greatest, it is very helpful to have a place in school where, as the theme of the television show *Cheers* puts it, "everybody knows your name." It is also clear that students in performance groups are learning the value of discipline, teamwork, and focus—attributes much prized in today's workplace. Parents find it hard to discount the significance of the high correlation between years of participation in performance ensembles and higher SAT scores, even though a cause-and-effect relationship has not yet been proven.

The Failures

In the midst of stunning successes are also, depending on one's viewpoint, dismal failures. Most obvious of these is the failure of music performance to rise above the level of an extracurricular activity in the minds of the general public. In their capacity as "service" organizations, ensembles have often appeared as the entertainment at a wide variety of events, from athletic halftimes to breaks at Rotary Club meetings. When this turns out to be the dominant exposure of the general public to our field, we have a public relations nightmare. In the worst-case scenario we are slated for cuts along with activities such as athletics. What often comes to mind is the old saying "If it looks like a duck and walks like a duck, then it must be a duck." When we look like an extracurricular activity to the general public, we are our own worst enemy.

Equally problematic is the frequent failure to teach "performing with understanding." When students reach a high level of technical proficiency with their instruments or voices without knowing much about the musical form, history, or cultural background of the pieces they play, music rehearsals can come to resemble a typing class. Parents often ask their children, "What are you working on in orchestra (band, choir) these days?" When the child's answer is "I don't know," parents are left with a bad impression of the music program. This impression may be reinforced by a typical school concert that presents a parade of pieces without a perceptible purpose. When nothing is said about curriculum, the prevailing notion—and all too often the truth—of what goes on is that there is no curriculum or plan of instruction.

The Challenge of the Music Standards

The arrival of national, state, and local music standards since 1994 has presented the field of music education with old challenges in newly codified forms. Although our field has believed in most of the principles contained in these standards for a long time, it has never before made such a convincing or coherent case in such a politically potent form. Indeed, the National Standards for Music Education will serve for some time as a watershed, to be ignored by music teachers only at

the peril of their programs.

One way in which the Standards have been used is as a platform for personal and program renewal. Both individuals and school districts have seized the opportunity to move their curricula to the next stage of growth using the Standards. Some districts have gotten grants for teacher in-service programs, while others have used this reform platform to bring in outside experts and clinicians. Individual teachers have sought funding from district and state sources, citing how the Standards could move their curriculum to a higher level.

The Standards have also been used as a measuring stick to assess whether individuals and school programs are doing their jobs well. Teachers who attend workshops on the Standards often say that they do so wanting to see how their own programs measure up. Part of this response may be the legacy of state and district contests and festival ratings.

During my years as president of the Music Educators National Conference (now MENC—The National Association for Music Education), I was able to get a good sense of the nation's response to the Standards as I conducted conference sessions on this topic. It soon became clear that four of the nine content standards were already being taught to a considerable extent, while the other five needed more attention from educators in order to gain parity with the others. Teachers were very clear where their teaching stood on each standard and were able to comment in detail on what needed work and what did not.

In teachers' own assessments of their teaching, content standards 1(singing), 2 (playing), 5 (reading and notating), and 6 (listening, analyzing, and describing) seemed to be the most frequently addressed. The one exception to this was that instrumental music teachers underutilized singing (Standard 1), while choral music teachers tended to underutilize playing of instruments (Standard 2). In fact there appeared to be a distinct possibility that many teachers mistakenly thought that the Standards applied across districts or schools rather than in each individual music classroom. These teachers seemed to think that if the choral teacher was addressing singing (Standard 1), the instrumental teacher did not have to worry about it.

The five content standards that most teachers felt were least addressed were Standards 3 (improvising), 4 (composing and arranging), 7 (evaluating), 8 (understanding music in relation to other arts and other disciplines), and 9 (understanding music in relation to history and culture). Of these five, the creative standards (3 and 4) were felt to be the most neglected. Performance ensemble teachers of band, choir, and orchestra (with the exception of jazz teachers) often admitted that they had almost no background in improvisation, composition, or arranging. In addition, most performance teachers could not

easily see how Standards 3 and 4 could be taught in the context of band, choir, or orchestra. Of the underutilized five standards, Standard 9 seemed to be the one getting the most attention.

Changing the Choral Landscape

The Standards present a comprehensive picture of music teaching that widens the scope of choral music education. This includes helping students:

- sing with good vocal technique
- have experience in a wide variety of small and large ensembles
- work on solo repertoire
- know how to independently select, analyze and interpret, and develop the performance of music for personal use
- develop personal and group presentation skills
- employ appropriate instrumental accompaniments in a wide variety of historical and cultural styles
- form their own vocal/instrumental groups
- play commonly used accompanying instruments, such as keyboards, guitars, drums, recorders, handbells, chorded zithers (such as Autoharps or ChromAharps), dulcimers, or MIDI synthesizers/sequencers
- sing harmony parts by ear
- improvise appropriate embellishments in a variety of styles
- learn songs and vocal parts from recordings without the aid of notation

- put together "head arrangements" of songs for personal or small-group use
- make up (or write) their own songs, including melodies, lyrics, and chords
- read notation successfully in standard choral or solo vocal music
- notate music from recordings or their own creations
- listen actively and critically to recordings in a variety of styles
- locate records for personal use
- evaluate personal performances and those of others
- use audio, video, and digital recording techniques as tools for recording and improving performances
- connect musical performance to the traditions of dance, theatre, and visual arts
- understand poetry and prose as it applies to lyrics in vocal and choral music
- write lyrics for their own songs
- know that a "good" vocal tone varies from culture to culture around the world
- sing the music of different historical periods with appropriate styles
- approach the music of the world's cultures according to the norms of each culture, rather than filtering all music through Western concepts

The kinds of behaviors listed above are commonly practiced by successful singers—both professionals and amateurs—in the real world outside of schools. For many school choral teachers the list may seem overwhelming. It need not be. Following are some strategies for opening up the way things are done to include some structures the Standards require. In a way, this is a "if we build it, they will come" way of thinking, which implies that new wine does indeed require new bottles.

"We are what we eat" might be paraphrased to "we are what (and how) we sing." So if the Standards suggest nurturing growth in musical independence and decision making by the individual (something great teachers have always done), then more time must be spent on those behaviors. The rehearsal "conductor" who makes *all* of the artistic decisions for students is clearly a social and educational anachronism. A good antidote for this is asking questions rather than giving answers. The use of thoughtful, provocative, mind-expanding questions will lead naturally to Standard 7, which expects students to evaluate their own performances and those of others, and to Standards 8 and 9, which involve students in understanding and discussing connections between music and other subjects, history, and culture.

How time is spent will determine much of what is learned. Traditionally, a full-choir rehearsal has been about singing and not much else. The easiest way to begin to change a choral program is to change how time is allocated. Moving away from the iron grip of five large-ensemble rehearsals per week

	Monday	Tuesday	Wednesday	Thursday	Friday
a.	full choir	chamber groups	full choir	sectionals	full choir
b.	full choir	keyboard lab/ sectionals	full choir sectionals	keyboard lab/ theory	full choir
c.	full choir/ sectionals	full choir/ chamber groups	full choir/ theory	full choir/ sectionals	full choir/ chamber groups

Figure 1. Some examples for using five 50-minute periods per week.

opens up other opportunities. Some examples for using the five 50-minute periods per week in different ways are illustrated in figure 1.

These examples suggest that there are many possible permutations for using time other than the traditional full-choir rehearsal. Ironically, recent pressure in high schools toward block scheduling of a four-period day has forced many choral teachers to reexamine how they allocate their time. With 90-minute periods, for example, they must use their time more creatively. When some time is spent with Standard 6 (listening, analyzing, and describing), for example, the landscape changes dramatically to include a much better sense of the musical whole, as well as opportunities for reflection.

Looking at learning time from a year-long point of view also opens up new learning possibilities. Between the goal-oriented concert units can come short units that loosen the iron grip of the rehearsal. For example, students could spend a week or two working in small groups to prepare a fifteen-minute performance of music of their choice. Some years ago the Wisconsin 4-H State Leadership Conference tried an interesting experiment of this sort—the brainchild of Bob Swan, University of Wisconsin Extension professor. Instead of having their usual All-State 4-H Band and Chorus, they chose to take those same 125 students and put them in groups of 25, each with a facilitator, for a period of two days. Students were asked to bring music, instruments, and ideas from home in order to work toward a fifteen-minute performance at the end of the two days. They began their small-group work by brainstorming themes that could unify their presentations. They then went on to select music and decide what resources were necessary to put their ideas into action. The result of this process-oriented education was the empowerment of individual leadership and creativity. And none of it would have happened if the mold had not been broken.

Another interesting departure from traditional models is the so-called vocal/guitar ensemble. An interesting example from Ohio came into being because of two factors: (1) no one was signing up for choir, and (2) there was a strong interest in guitar instruction. So the teacher constructed a new type of class called a vocal/guitar ensemble [notice the absence of the word "choir"], which combined singing with instruction and playing of guitar. The result of this experiment was the growth of a fine ensemble that boasted sixty members.

Students in this new ensemble learned many of the skills now incorporated into the National Standards, such as the ability to read music, taught through the guitar and reinforced by singing; how to sing, alone and with others (in two, three, or four parts) in a variety of settings; how to accompany their singing and play instrumental sections of the music; and how to improvise, arrange, and compose music to suit the needs and the resources of the class. They also gained an understanding of how melody, harmony, and other musical elements actually work, and they performed, listened to, evaluated, and came to understand a wide spectrum of multicultural styles of music. Instituting the experimental vocal/guitar ensemble also had the desired effect of making students want to sing in regular choirs in succeeding years. In addition, there were many choir directors who were very happy to inherit students who could read music and who understood basic theory.

The choral teacher needs to be first of all a music teacher. Passing all student musical needs through a choral filter produces a thin band of light compared to the full spectrum of colors possible without that filter. Particularly problematic are the many types and styles of music that combine singing with playing instruments. Teachers of band, choir, or orchestra frequently feel that such music does not fit their needs or pattern of instruction. Where do the popular amateur music-making instruments like keyboards, guitars, Autoharps, handbells, recorders, hand drums, synthesizers, drum sets, electric basses, and others fit into the structures that now exist in schools? The answer is that they often do not fit: new structures are needed. Teachers who would like to branch out from their traditional patterns of instruction could begin with what some have called *explorations*. These explorations (with possible help from community resource people) can take the form of a "day off" to try something new, such as African drumming, vocal improvisation/ scat singing, handbells or other types of hocket ensembles, singing harmony by ear, collecting songs that the school or community knows well enough to sing by heart, or doing a circle dance and singing American Indian social songs. It is liberating to find out that a few days off from the usual concert-driven agenda will not wreck the choral program.

Changing the Instrumental Landscape

The Standards also present a comprehensive picture of music teaching that broadens the scope of instrumental music education by challenging students to:

- play with a variety of stylistically appropriate instrumental techniques
- sing as well as play
- play in a wide variety of small and large ensembles
- develop solo repertoire with and without accompaniment
- know how to independently select, analyze and interpret, and develop the performance of music for personal use
- play instrumental accompaniments in a wide variety of historical and cultural styles
- form their own vocal/instrumental groups
- play commonly used accompanying instruments, such as keyboards, guitars, drums, recorders, handbells, chorded zithers, dulcimers, or MIDI synthesizers/sequencers
- play harmony parts by ear
- improvise appropriate embellishments in a variety of styles
- learn pieces and instrumental parts from recordings without the aid of notation
- put together "head arrangements" of pieces for personal or small-group use
- make up (or write) their own music including melodies and chords
- read notation successfully in standard instrumental ensemble or solo instrumental music

- notate music from recordings or their own compositions
- listen actively and critically to recordings in a variety of styles
- locate recordings for personal use
- evaluate personal performances and those of others
- use audio, video, and digital recording techniques as tools for improving performances
- connect musical performance to the traditions of dance, theatre, and visual arts
- know that a "good" instrumental tone varies from style to style and from culture to culture around the world
- play the music of different historical periods with appropriate styles
- approach the music of the world's cultures according to the norms of each culture, rather than filtering all music through Western concepts

When students make the decision to play the flute, saxophone, violin, or trumpet, they are often not aware of all the options available to them in the complete world of playing instruments. Often a presentation made in the fourth or fifth grade encourages them to narrow the choices to an instrument needed in a school band or orchestra program. The result of this screening process may be that the student (1) signs up for the French horn and happily plays it throughout life, (2) signs up for the French horn only to find that it is not played on MTV and subsequently drops it or switches to some other instrument, or (3) does not sign up for any band or orchestral instrument because the styles of music represented in these programs are not in sync with his personal choices.

A recent contact with a high school violin player gives a glimpse of the dilemma in which school instrumental music finds itself today. This seventeen-year-old had played Suzuki violin from the first grade all the way through middle school. Then, between the eighth and ninth grades, as her musical-style choices started expanding, she decided to drop orchestra and play in several alternative bands outside of school. Three years later she was still playing violin/fiddle (with a pickup built into the bridge), the mandolin (also with pickup), and the Fender Mandocaster (an electric solid-body, four-stringed mandolin). The styles she described herself playing were rock, reggae, swing, alternative, acoustic folk/bluegrass/country, salsa, blues, jazz, and several others. She also sang and made up her own songs with lyrics, learned music from records, sequenced background tracks on her MIDI computer/synthesizer, had made a CD, could improvise with ease, and had good group playing (chamber music) skills. Because of the limited spectrum of musical opportunities offered by school instrumental programs today, many students such as this one—students who are very musical—must operate outside the confines of their school's program.

In order for real change to take place in instrumental music education, teachers must see themselves as music teachers first and instrumental (and, hopefully, also general) music teachers second. They should not look at themselves just as band or orchestra directors. Such a change could start by putting the students' needs first—before the needs of "the program." This is where the Standards really apply, because they are not tied to any genre or instrumental ensemble; rather, they are based on the lifelong needs of a student who will also have complex adult needs.

Another illustrative story is that of Thomas Miller, a middle school band director who took my course Intro to World Musics at the University of Wisconsin–Milwaukee. During the unit on African drumming and singing, Tom commented that his middle school band students would really enjoy doing the African drumming. His problem, however, was that he could not see how this would fit into his band program. The solution to this dilemma, described in his master's thesis,[2] was to throw out a little bathwater and make room for another baby in the tub. He dealt with the need to infuse some world music experiences into his band program by instituting "explorations." These took place about one day a month when the band did not rehearse as usual. This was a positive first step toward loosening the grip that instrumentation has on music making.

Effective use of time presents many of the same challenges to instrumental music teachers as those described in detail under the choral section above. The clear enemy of change is the locked-in full rehearsal. Any movement in the direction of chamber music, sectionals, solo work, computer labs, theory, listening, evaluating and critiquing, understanding, or other pursuits would be helpful in breaking this lock. Likewise, taking some time to pursue new options in between concert-oriented units would also help speed up change.

Chamber music, in the most liberal interpretation of the word, can provide a good deal of the change needed within instrumental programs. If we really aspire to the goal of having students become independent musicians who can find their own music, form their own ensembles, interpret music on their own, find venues for playing (and singing), and present music well, then we will value chamber music. We must, however, see chamber music as style neutral. This interpretation allows a five-piece rock band to be considered a chamber group. It also makes room for the myriad hybrid groups so interesting to students today. It allows for the use of instruments (such as guitars, keyboards, synthesizers, electric basses, and world music instruments) that are not normally part of either band or orchestra programs. If chamber music is to flourish, it should be scheduled into the regular day and not just be added on as an after-school elective. State music educator associations can aid the growth of this new chamber music by adding state solo and ensemble categories to their festivals to encourage experimentation and flexibility. The Wisconsin School Music Association has done an exemplary job of pioneering these new categories.

The role of the instrumental music teacher in this new type of program becomes less the conductor and more the facilitator. That is why the title "band director" or "orchestra director" used by teachers themselves is so telling. If teachers respond to the question, "What do you do?" with the answer "I'm a band director," then they are probably saying that they see their role as primarily that of the conductor on the podium. The title "instrumental music teacher" clearly communicates a much broader vision of what the Standards require.

The Creative Challenge of Standards 3 and 4

Learning to improvise and compose should be the right of all instrumental and choral students, not just those who find themselves in the jazz ensemble or vocal jazz group. If the need to teach improvisation and composition were taken seriously, creativity would become more of a regular part of instrumental and choral music programs. The following are some ways in which music teachers could do more creative teaching within the dimensions of performance classes.

Group rhythmic improvisation. Determine the rhythmic feel of the piece that you are going to perform. Establish that feel with feet and hands, and be sure to have a solid bass beat. Have students join in and add their own complementary patterns. *Option:* Add solos in call-and-response fashion after the group feels comfortable with the feel and process of the group rhythms.

Write a rhythm round. A great way to help students understand staggered imitative entries (fugues, motets, masses, madrigals, inventions, rounds, canons, canzonas, oratorio and cantata choruses, overtures, catches, etc.) is to ask them to write a round. The easiest type of round for a novice to write is a rhythm round. This can be done with either standard notation or invented notation. All that students need to do is to write a rhythm and indicate with an asterisk when the next part comes in.

The next step in the growth of sophistication occurs when the student realizes that the rhythms that line up vertically (simultaneously) will sound better if they are complementary and different. You can help them work this out by suggesting that the measures be written vertically on the page so that they can see the result of the combined patterns.

As students improve in writing rhythm rounds, the next step is to introduce pitch. Begin with "no-fault" pitch structures such as the pentatonic scale (*do, re, mi, sol, la*) so that students will be successful. Then have them write rounds that have only one under-

lying chord, gradually progressing to two or more chords at a later time.

Create rhythm ensembles. Choral speaking is an easy next step after writing rhythm rounds. Hand-clapping ensembles or other "found sounds" can be written with rhythm only. Also, students can create rhythmic ostinato backgrounds (beat box, etc.) over which someone creates an improvisation similar to a "rap." The improvisation can be unpitched or pitched.

Group pitch improvisation. Determine the pitch content of the piece that you are going to perform (teacher or students). This may be seen as a scale or a set of pitches. Is there a tonal center (or perhaps several)? Establish the pitch set by using instruments (or voices) as a tonic/dominant (or other) grid. Have students sing/play the scale tones over the drones/grid until they are familiar with the tones in the scale. Model improvisation by echoing short patterns using the pitch material. Then set up a formal structure that uses a fabric of the pitches as a foundation over which various soloists improvise some pitch patterns similar to those that have been modeled. Consider starting with a no-fault set of pitches (such as the pentatonic scale).

Compose an ending for a melody. Students can learn a lot by finishing the second half of a melody. Give them a specified number of measures and tell them what kinds of pitches and rhythms they should use. (You might want to write in the last note.)

Although this kind of exercise has many restrictions, students are not awash in a sea of too many possibilities. This kind of composition exercise can also be done during a rehearsal period while some students are doing other things. Try to play/sing some of the examples for the whole class.

Campy way to practice scales or arpeggios. Challenge students to compose their own rhythms and forms to practice scales/arpeggios. Use nontraditional meters.

Transcriptions and easy arrangements. Many students first discover the joys of composition by transcribing or rearranging something for presentation in a public performance. The very act of either making notes on a page with a pen or a computer printer can in itself be fulfilling. The natural next step is for students to wonder what would happen if the notes were their own. It is important to note that the teacher's role is to put *students* into positions of responsibility.

Harmonize or reharmonize a melody. Use easy-to-play chordal instruments, such as the Autoharp, guitar, Omnichord, or electronic keyboard to work out harmonies that sound good. Always have students create several options. An interesting strategy in the study of any existing piece or arrangement is to look at other versions of the piece and then have students make their own versions. This is a natural lead-in to theme-and-variations form.

Compose a countermelody to a known melody. Once students know a melody well (this can be a piece they are performing), have them try their hand at creating countermelodies. A useful technique for doing this is to record a melody many times on tape or have a sequencer loop it ad infinitum, and then have students practice countermelodies over the top of the tape until they find some that they like and want to keep. This is the process of creating "frozen improvisations."

Improvise on a simple melody. Challenge students to take a simple melody that is well-known and sing/play many variations without stopping. Start by adding ornaments or changing the rhythms, and then change the meter or the mode. This is a skill that can be practiced anywhere by singing or whistling.

The challenge of Standards 6, 7, 8, and 9. Standards 6, 7, 8, and 9 ask performance class teachers to teach "performance with understanding." Always a goal practiced by the best, most comprehensive teachers, performing with understanding suggests the use of some of the following strategies:

- Ask students to set personal goals regarding their own performance and keep track of their progress toward those goals in a log or journal. Evaluating recordings of their solo and small-group performances will stimulate reflective thinking.
- Take time in rehearsals to critique recordings or the work of the total ensemble.

- Set shared ensemble goals and discuss progress made toward those goals.
- Ask students to analyze the structure of the music being performed. Sometimes this can be easily accomplished in subtle ways by giving musical rather than mechanical directions, such as "Start at the second theme" as opposed to "Start at measure number 34."
- Bring in (and ask students to bring in) related music, recordings, art, architecture, and science ideas to help students make connections between the music they are performing and the larger world of other subjects, history, and culture.
- Turn the performance classroom into a treasure hunt for relationships of ideas. Once students catch onto this game, they will start suggesting lots of supplementary material that can enrich the experience for everyone. One example would be having students search the Internet for Web sites on Shaker culture when singing or playing "Simple Gifts."
- Program with cultural, historical, or subject matter connections in mind. By playing or singing a series of related pieces, you demonstrate the importance of a curriculum based on the Standards to both students and stakeholders such as parents and administrators. Have students briefly share what they have learned at each concert.

Conclusion

The golden age of the school performance ensemble could lie just ahead if teachers of vocal and instrumental performance classes continue to modify what they do. The National Standards for Music Education provide a remarkable menu of options that can spur on the changes needed. Areas that need the greatest attention are:

- teaching performance with understanding (comprehensive musicianship)
- more flexible time—breaking the full-ensemble rehearsal mold
- attention to chamber music and individual musical independence
- breaking the domination of band, choir, orchestra instrumentation to allow for other vocal and instrumental options, including nontraditional resources such as electronic instruments, world instruments, or mixed vocal/instrumental hybrids
- embracing a wider spectrum of musical styles
- giving serious attention to the creative standards, 3 and 4

The strong track record of success in band, choir, and orchestra music education is a platform to build on, not a structure to destroy. Great attention must be given to preserving the strengths of what has been accomplished, and change should be evolutionary, with great care given to saving the best of what we now do. Now is the time to use the National Standards for

Music Education to transfuse new ideas into performance education, to create a brighter future for all children and for the field of music education.

Notes

1. Abraham Maslow, *Toward a Psychology of Being,* 3d edition (New York: John Wiley & Sons, 1998).

2. Thomas Miller, "Incorporating Traditional African Music into the Middle School Band Class" (master's thesis, University of Wisconsin–Milwaukee, 1993).

Teaching for Performing with Understanding in General Music Settings

5

What Are We *Doing* in Music?
Toward a Lifelong Involvement with Music

Suzanne M. Shull

A major turning point in arts educa-tion was reached in 1994 when the Consortium of National Arts Education Associations published national stan-dards for teaching the fine arts in schools. Since that time, these standards have been embraced in varying forms by many individuals, institutions, and school systems and have laid the foun-dation for a groundswell of much need-ed change in music education.

In the MENC publication *The School Music Program: A New Vision,* the authors state: "Because music is a basic expression of human culture, every stu-dent should have access to a balanced, comprehensive, and sequential program of study in music."[1] This chapter will address the activities in general music classes that I believe we have neglected in favor of providing students with

knowledge that is assessable using paper and pencil. These are the performance activities that are slowly finding a way back into the classroom, much to the excitement of middle and high school general music students. These activities are giving students the incentive to develop their own musical skills, even though they may not be interested in joining a traditional performing group.

A related issue is that teachers of per-forming groups are challenged to accept the National Standards as a model for planning comprehensive lessons. To help keep the community informed of the work the students are doing, all music teachers need to be innovative, perhaps by holding "informances" and perhaps by extending their programs beyond the traditional school hours to offer music opportunities for adult members of the community.

The Standards also emphasize the idea that *all* students should be involved in performing music. As a music educator, I have long grappled with the dichotomy in schools between the active nature of performance classes and the passive nature of the many general music classes that rarely, if ever, provide performance opportunities. On the one hand, our profession has coped rather well in print and in practice with what music students in performing groups should be able to *do*, and to a lesser extent with what those students should *know*. On the other hand, although we have a philosophy in place for the *knowing* part of a general music experience, the *doing* part is a different story. The Standards strongly suggest that we concern ourselves with what general music students should be able to *do*, and this has been the source of some discomfort for educators who have conducted general music classes that, at best, were watered-down versions of their college music appreciation courses.[2]

In his book *Megatrends: Ten New Directions Transforming Our Lives,* John Naisbitt stated, "We must learn to balance the material wonders of technology with the spiritual demands of human nature."[3] As music educators *and* musicians, we know how human nature is touched by music, and we understand the spiritual experience of being able to sing, play, or create our own music. However, the trend of the last two decades toward the use of personal sound systems has given individuals immediate access to their favorite music, making them feel less of a need for attending live performances, much less for learning how to make their own music. As a result, most U.S. inhabitants of any age have little incentive to study music, and many even refuse to sing, often because of a lack of self-confidence and experience. Yet these same people can become so familiar with a favorite piece of music that they can explain, in lay language, exactly what each artist on a recording is doing and then go on to lament that they wish they could make music like that!

Some of today's schools *are* providing "living music" classes, a name I choose to use because it implies more vitality than "general music." Students in these classes have musical experiences that go beyond listening to music. The opportunities these students are given to sing, play a variety of instruments, and compose—using available technology—enhance their desire to learn more about music, and many begin to see musical involvement as part of a lifelong experience. As an added bonus, when all or most students are served, enthusiasm for the total music program and its impact can be felt by the entire school community, not just the ones involved in elective performing ensembles.

Today it is possible for a music teacher to set up a vital music-making center that contains competitively priced equipment purchased with school and community support. Students who find a music room equipped with guitars, African drums or other sophisticated percussion instruments, computers, keyboards, and MIDI keyboards are much more likely to be interested and accepting of the music curriculum offering. Even if there is an initial lack of funding, many teachers find that an active music-making program can be built with a minimum of equipment. The enthusiasm generated by students can quickly get the attention of outside funding agencies and parent groups.

In all of the arts, it is what students can actually do that is of greatest interest to administrators, parents, and the students themselves. Can you imagine art students who don't draw, dance students who don't dance, or drama students who don't act? Yet secondary music programs frequently provide little or no opportunity for students not involved in performing ensembles to make music. The teachers at this level have chosen a limited curriculum because of deficiencies in their own knowledge or training. Additionally, well-written listening lessons, related arts projects, videos, and reading materials on all aspects of music—all of which are readily available—can provide enough material to keep a general music class busy[4] and quiet[5] for an entire grading period. But these materials should be used as a means of linking information with skills acquired from a hands-on approach.

There is overwhelming evidence that most people learn best through concrete experiences.[6] Math, science, language arts, and social studies teachers who are in touch with current teaching and learning theory have broadened their classroom activities to include hands-on activities in their curricula. It is through "doing" that most students become interested in "knowing." Obviously, watching a basketball game is more exciting to people who have experienced the thrill of "shooting hoops" than to those who have never handled a ball. It should not be any surprise that viewing an art exhibit becomes a significant experience if the viewer has learned about spatial harmony by creating it. In the same way, listening to a work in sonata-allegro form is more meaningful if students have created their own themes (no matter how simple) and placed them into their own compositions in that form.

This issue of the importance of doing, as reflected in the Standards, has inspired me to develop new practices and strategies for the classroom. I think the reader will find those that I will share in this chapter to be useful for most age groups, including adults. While I will deal primarily with what the general music student should be able to do, I will also touch on what the performing music student should know. My ideas are based on knowledge gained from a combination of classroom experience, personal research, graduate study, peer suggestions and observations, in-service classes, and attendance at professional conferences and workshops.

Rather than addressing the complete list of standards, I will tackle those that seem to have created the most anxiety among my fellow music classroom teachers:

- performing music in general music classes at the secondary level
- creating and evaluating music
- reading vocal music
- performing and understanding music of many cultures

Following is a focused discussion of the six standards that involve these areas of concern.

Content Standard 1: Singing, alone and with others, a varied repertoire of music

Content Standard 5: Reading and notating music

Singing is a skill that allows any human to express music. It requires no special equipment. Matching pitch is a muscle-brain connection, and the experience is kinesthetic. All children, unless hampered by physical challenges, can learn to sing on pitch. Toddlers can understand the concept of higher and lower. Young children can grasp the difference between head and chest singing required for attaining a wide range.

However, as important and accessible as skill in singing is, various obstacles interfere with its use in the classroom. From the time when students are about age twelve through high school, classroom singing is a challenge for teachers because of students' diverse attitudes toward singing, their changing voices, and their lack of confidence. All of these factors tend to lead students to off-task behavior. In spite of these obstacles, a teacher who approaches singing with enthusiasm, joy, and genuine concern for musical development in *every* individual can lead learners to discover that singing can bring new meaning into their lives.

The attitude about singing that students bring to middle school often directly relates to the availability and quality of instruction in elementary school. An elementary music teacher who provides positive and caring assistance can promote the kind of comfortable atmosphere that children may need if they lack musical experience outside of the school setting. An important factor is the persistence of the teacher in helping to correct pitch and rhythm. Because all children dislike not being able to perform as well as their peers in group activities, they find it safer to say "I don't want to" rather than "I can't." An indifferent or reluctant attitude usually comes from fear of failure, and this is where the caring, prepared teacher can make a difference.

One successful approach at the secondary level is to approach changing voices and pitch accuracy in singing from a scientific point of view. This removes the stigma of "Am I talented enough to sing?" Discussions about the voice change can be open to the whole class with students allowed to give opinions about which (spoken) voices sound alike and why. Information about the acoustic relationship of octaves is valuable. In a middle school class, most students can sing the A at 220 and 440. Some can sing a high A 880, and a few changed voices can sing A 110. Using the singing voice for experimenting with octave relationships helps reluctant singers relax.

A teacher should express genuine concern for every child to have a positive singing experience and encourage even the most meager attempt. The book *Get America Singing . . . Again!*[7] is a very good resource for teachers who must coax reluctant singers. Teachers can explain that the whole music industry is concerned that few people want to make music. Also, they can point out that the songs in the book have been selected from our national cultural heritage. This often convinces students that they should make an effort, and most will find a song in the book they remember from elementary school, church, camp, or recordings. Additionally, the variety of song styles found in this book gives students a chance to experiment with different vocal styles.

Singing also provides an excellent opportunity for students to perform "their" music in class. Allowing them to sing personal favorites can open the door to greater expression and enthusiasm. Every new pop chart contains at least a few songs that can be sung in a group setting. Whether students are singing Boyz II Men or Schubert, a teacher can work on expression, range, and technical accuracy.

Unquestionably, ear training and sightsinging are skills fundamental to becoming a proficient musician. Some form of ear training and sightsinging should occur in every music class of every type at every grade level. If beginning instrumental students could sightsing simple melodies, imagine how quickly they could relate the pitches in their head to correct fingering. The ability to sing intervals before playing them would allow students to find and correct their own mistakes and shorten the time needed to learn the piece.

An absolutely essential part of the ear training and sightsinging process is the use of pitch syllables. These syllables become the kinesthetic response (mouth to brain) that is the equivalent of fingers on a wind instrument or keyboard.[8] Given sufficient oral and aural practice, singers have little difficulty applying pitches to written musical language. This is also true of rhythmic patterns. Although a lot of high-quality sightsinging materials are available, no such materials are really necessary for this kind of training. Examples may be taken directly from music being performed.

Finally, our performing musicians, choral and instrumental, must work on ear training or sightsinging *every* day. These experiences may take various forms: singing pitch syllables during warm-ups, playing pitch games, singing a phrase before it is played, memorizing scales and arpeggios with pitch syllables, or singing a part while other members of the ensemble play theirs. Exercises need not be lengthy, and they should be a natural part of the daily routine.

Content Standard 2: Performing on instruments, alone and with others, a varied repertoire of music

Opportunities to use instruments in general music classes and vocal ensembles are numerous. However, here I will focus on two instruments that work very well, given the nature of today's classroom.

The acoustic guitar and electric keyboard synthesizer are two of the most accessible and inexpensive instruments available for teaching. With the right materials they can be taught in large- or small-group settings or used in learning centers. They may be used to enhance the study of a particular musical concept or played for the sheer joy of an encounter with favorite music.

Classroom guitar. Music educators have long been aware of the value and appeal of the acoustic guitar as a classroom instrument, and the number of teachers offering guitar courses or teaching guitar in eclectic music classes continues to grow. The acoustic guitar may very well be the most versatile, accessible, and popular of all musical instruments. It is compact and can travel easily in the family car or the school bus, needs no electricity, and can be used to play many styles of music. It can also be played in the solitude of one's room at home, with a garage band, on a camping trip, or in a classroom with thirty-five other players. At all ability levels the guitar can be used as a harmonic or melodic instrument to improvise, compose, accompany, and arrange. Granted, good modeling is always beneficial, but even a teacher with limited skill can be effective, especially since an ever-expanding repertoire of methods and materials is available to aid in the teaching of any style of playing.

What is it about the guitar that makes it such a popular instrument? Obviously its use in popular music is attention-getting, but there seems to be something more that makes it so alluring. The way a guitar is held and the way it produces vibrations make it almost a living object—a personal friend—according to Adrian Legg, English guitarist and recording artist.[9] The social value is also an important aspect in secondary school. Most guitar repertoire can be played in ensembles, and students share songs they've learned from friends, private teachers, or over the Internet. They create melodies and harmonies for original lyrics. Peer teaching can run rampant in a guitar class!

Meanwhile, students are acquiring some of the skills recommended by the Standards. Specifically, students can *sing* while they *play* or they can *accompany* singing. The guitar lends itself naturally to *improvisation,* which, in turn, can lead to *composition* as the next step in the creative process. Also, *listening* to harmonies and recreating them on guitar teaches *arranging* and *playing by ear* while the students gain insight on harmonic structure. Peer performances provide students with opportunities to *evaluate* their own playing and that of their peers, creating forums and positive possibilities for musical growth.

Interestingly, *note reading* is the best equalizer in a multilevel guitar class with students ranging from beginners to garage band players. Beginning students find single-note melodies physically easier to play than chords, and the garage band players have to slow down to think about the challenge of reading music. By suggesting that music reading is a skill that often separates the studio artist from the garage band musician, the teacher can present the idea that being able to read music will enhance one's entire experience with music.

Classroom keyboard. Technological developments in the manufacture of musical instruments have greatly enhanced keyboard teaching in lab situations. While these systems can be expensive, teachers trained to use them correctly praise their creative uses and the speed with which students learn. On the other end of the scale, inexpensive individual electronic synthesizers that can withstand continuous classroom use are also available. On these, students can use preset rhythms and sounds to help develop rhythmic accuracy, add interesting harmonies, and learn about timbre and different styles of music. They can learn to play simple melodies immediately, and, as with teaching singing and guitar, this is an excellent opportunity to have students incorporate their favorite tunes from the pop charts into the repertoire. In situations where instruction time is limited, learning to read notes may be too time-consuming, produce too little music that is satisfying to the learner, and create massive frustration. In these cases, I recommend teaching simple melodies using letter names of the notes and basic chords.[10] These are skills that are fundamental to learning how to play by ear, an activity that a living room musician can enjoy for a lifetime.

Playing by ear appears only at the middle school level of the Standards, although the "outline of sequential learning" in the Standards documents indicates that students at the high school level are expected to demonstrate this skill at a higher level. This is a skill that most amateur musicians acquire without (or in spite of) the aid of formal education on an instrument. Guitar players begin early trying to figure out chord progressions, bass lines, and lead solos performed by their favorite artists. Keyboard players enjoy picking out tunes and finding chords to match. Formal instruction has often ignored this as a desirable skill, requiring students instead to respond as quickly as possible to notes on a page. Yet playing by ear may be one of the most valuable skills a music student can learn. Teaching students to play by ear involves instruction in the fundamental components of the music. It means showing them that melodies are derived from scales and that harmonies can be built on the same scale degrees.

For students who are shy or insecure about their musical ability, the use of headsets with electronic keyboards can provide a safety zone, enabling them to practice privately until they are ready to play with others. It is gratifying for me as a teacher to watch young musicians start out timidly and then blossom with confidence as they share with peers something they've learned. Like guitar, keyboards offer peer teaching opportunities and can be played easily by two people sharing one instrument. The marriage of guitar and keyboard activities further extends the opportunity for students to play together.

Content Standard 3: Improvising melodies, variations, and accompaniments

For every note-bound music teacher, there are countless students who cannot read notes and have no interest in learning. Singing, playing by ear, and improvising are the only ways for these students to participate in music-making events. This alone should be sufficient incentive for music programs and teachers to provide more of these kinds of activities. In addition, they are easy to add to a program. Much like singing, the only requirements for learning to improvise are a good attitude, a willingness to listen and respond, and some fundamental musical information. Of

course, the amount of information and practice time a student receives enhances the level and quality of the improvisation.

What should students know in order to improvise? Vocal and instrumental students should simply have a scale in their ears and/or fingers and a harmonic progression in their memories. They can begin by playing around (or singing, as the case may be) on two or three notes of the scale as they listen to the progression. Limiting the parameters creates a comfort zone for experimentation. As they practice and experiment, students can add notes to their ranges and explore new rhythms, always consciously attending to the underlying beat and style. *Please note: Students must have ample time to experiment in a no-fault environment!* Given the demands of other curriculum requirements, teachers are tempted to move on to other activities too quickly, thus robbing improvising musicians of the time they need to find the level of comfort required for free experimentation.

True improvisation is not simply spontaneous. Student musicians must have some knowledge of the context of the music in which they are involved as well as some ideas for getting started. Modeling by the teacher can help. Also, if students know what is expected, they will better know how to evaluate their own work. Taping performances for instant replay helps students focus on the task and provides a product for evaluation. Here are a few examples of beginning improvisation exercises:

- *Guitar:* One group of students strums an E-minor chord in rhythm while another group plays open E and B strings, working to create interesting melodic patterns that match the rhythm.
- *Keyboard:* While the teacher plays I, IV, and V chords in E-flat minor or G-flat major on an acoustic piano, students experiment with melodies or ostinati on black keys on individual electronic keyboards. Next, students can improvise on white keys while they listen to the teacher play harmonic progressions in the keys of C major and A minor. They should be familiar with the scales and have ample time to explore and discover which notes sound "right" with certain chords.
- *Recorder:* Students should be able to play the first five tones of the G-major scale. They then take turns creating the first measure of a two-measure call and response. The second measure should be a planned pattern played by all participants that moves from dominant to tonic (see figure 5-1).[11]
- *Vocal:* The voice is the quickest and most accessible source of melody and rhythm. Yet, when asked to improvise, most singers become reluctant and dissolve into shyness. Keeping the activity short and simple (e.g., call and response) in the beginning helps build confidence, as does allowing singers to play their responses on pitched percussion instruments before they sing. Note that the recorder example works very well for voices. Making improvisation fun and telling singers that it's difficult to be wrong when improvising puts reluctant singers at ease.[12]
- *Percussion:* Percussion ensembles can provide true no-fault experiences for all students regardless of—or in spite of—ability level. Participants learn that listening to one another is vital. They also learn that someone must keep a very steady rhythm going to provide a foundation on which the improvisation can be built. The students determine which player will be the anchor (e.g., conga drum, bass xylophone). They also can experiment with dynamics, tempo, rhythm, melody, timbre, texture, and style changes. In this way, they learn much more about the instru-

Figure 5-1.

ments they play and reinforce vocabulary. Links can also be made to American and other world musics that are based on improvisation.

The unabashed pleasure on the faces of students involved in improvisation activities should be reason enough for providing these opportunities. However, because this activity is fun, it has been perceived by some as a filler activity and not a learning experience. *(Can't learning also be fun, and does having fun mean that learning isn't taking place?)* A casual observer might conclude that this is just so much noise-making. But if the students' efforts are treated seriously, self- and group evaluation will be a natural part of the process, and dramatic musical growth can occur.

Content Standard 4: Composing and arranging within specified guidelines

The process of composing can take any number of forms. For instance, a classroom project might be based on a five-note diatonic scale, or it might challenge students to compose a coda to a familiar song. For many in the class, their compositions may simply be improvisations that they remember long enough to record or write down. Whatever the intended product, the teacher's role is essential in helping students understand the process and encouraging them to go beyond their own expectations. Again, time is an essential element. Some students may

finish their compositions in a class period. Others will need longer. This requires great flexibility from the teacher in matters such as opening the music room before and after school or perhaps allowing a child to continue working on a composition during class time while the rest of the class moves on to something else.

Activities such as analyzing a famous melody of any style (for example, the theme from Haydn's "Surprise" Symphony or "Jingle Bells") for its repetition and contrast can show fledgling composers how simple a great melody can be. Students who can read music might begin by rearranging short melodic phrases from works they already know. Interestingly, the simple act of requiring an original composition at least once during the school year or grading period helps students understand that everyone is capable of this kind of creativity. It also can produce remarkable results. Placing student compositions on programs increases enthusiasm and attracts the interest of the adult audience in our product-oriented society.

Students in general music must have access to some kind of a medium to use in creating their compositions. Digital technology is becoming the primary medium for creating in many classrooms.[13] As with any high-tech process, fundamental knowledge is still the basis for success in its use. Although instant realization of an idea is the goal of today's computer-driven world, music students still need concrete, musically creative experiences, which take time to develop.

Content Standard 9: Understanding music in relation to history and culture

World cultures have an incredible richness of music to offer, and we as music educators simply cannot afford to allow Eurocentric training and opinions to deprive us and our students of the influence of a broad range of cultures. The world is changing and interconnecting faster than most of us are capable of comprehending. Communication around the world now occurs at the speed of light, and although technology can connect us with a place on the opposite side of the planet with the touch of a key, our understanding of other cultures remains surprisingly limited. Additionally, music education has often failed to provide enough avenues to prepare music teachers to meet the needs of their students when it comes to multicultural music. However, given current access to quality recordings and materials, workshops, public television and radio, as well as friends and neighbors from other cultures who are well versed in their heritages, there should be no excuse for ignoring this educational opportunity.

One thing to remember is that many students are uncomfortable with cultural differences or with being different themselves, and they often show this discomfort in ways that disrupt classroom routine and negatively affect instruction. Music opens the doors to the study of other cultures by presenting the differences abstractly and thereby helping us accept them at a less personal level. Students can examine the music of another culture objectively without the clutter of strong opinions or judgments based on physical differences such as clothing, hairstyle, or skin color.[14] The more students delve into the actual music, the more commonalities they are likely to find.

In addition to enhancing the understanding of other cultures, encounters with world music can actually validate the presence of representatives of different cultures in the classroom. Students who are interested in world geography and politics may also be validated by contributing facts they have learned.

Where Do We Go from Here?

In this chapter I have focused on the idea that *doing* is vitally important to learning, an idea that is well integrated into the National Standards and one that has been important in my own experience. It seems that much of traditional music education has had a limited impact on students, and I think the missing piece has been the focus on doing, on hands-on (and voices-on and fingers-on) contact with music. These activities, combined with knowledge gained through listening, will fill the gap and bring music into the totality of our students' lives. Classroom music will then no longer be an experience that is forgotten and left behind when the student moves on. Instead, it will become a link in a framework that pervades all parts of their lives and that leads to the next logical focus—the community.

As we assess where we are with music education and where we need to go next, it is clear that we have served only a small percentage of the community. Meanwhile, public scrutiny of music education practices has resulted in the elimination of music courses in many communities because of a seeming lack of student interest. The public has drawn the conclusion, based on a reality that has been difficult to deny, that music is an unimportant part of the curriculum and doesn't warrant support.

Here, some tough questions need to be asked:

- Why, when performing music programs became threatened by increased requirements for graduation and scheduling headaches, did our profession not take heed and seek additional avenues for reaching students across the entire student body spectrum?
- Why, when middle schools were being established, did the profession not aggressively offer retraining to performance teachers so that they would be more comfortable and effective in teaching an entire student body?
- Why did we ever assume that students who did not choose to be in

band, orchestra, or chorus would not wish to have an alternative means of participating in music-making experiences, such as experimenting with electronic composition or playing bass guitar?
- Why have we scheduled so many performances that our chorus, band, and orchestra students don't have time to come to a more comprehensive understanding of the music they are learning?
- Why have so few in our profession considered the possibilities of reaching beyond the student body and the school day to educate the community?

The nature of our rapidly changing society demands that we take a new look at all of our traditional institutions—how they function and whom they serve. Symphony orchestras are losing support, forcing symphony management to look for new programs and venues to attract audiences whose tastes are no longer limited to the Western European tradition of 1650–1900. Information is disseminated more and more by electronic means rather than print. The focus of computer games has been interactive and hands-on for some time. Yet so many institutions refuse to step out of the nineteenth-century traditions that control our national education system that alternatives to traditional public and private school programs are proliferating.

It seems clear that unless we come up with alternatives to traditional music teaching, the chances that music programs will be sidelined will increase. I feel strongly that those alternatives must focus on providing more opportunities for students to *sing, play,* and *create* music. From the work of Howard Gardner[15] and others, we now know that everyone has some level of musical intelligence. The extent to which musical potential is developed, however, depends upon many factors. The lack of opportunity should never have been, and cannot continue, to be a factor. We must offer *all* of our students equal opportunities to make music!

On the other hand, performance has been the traditional format of many school events, including not only concerts but athletic games, art shows, and plays. Such performances have long been the means of luring families from their homes and informing the community about students' accomplishments. As performance-oriented teachers, we are already accustomed to showcasing talent by putting a product on stage. This is a quick and effective way to inform an audience about the variety and quality of instruction. While parents in this information-oriented society are eager to boast about the showcased product, they also are fascinated by the process. Their understanding of what it takes to bring a group to performance level enhances their appreciation of the whole event. Putting more than just a product on stage—giving an "informance"—provides all kinds of opportunities, including the following:

- ear training or sightreading demonstrations
- singers accompanying themselves on guitars
- "guest" players from general music classes accompanying the chorus
- woodwind and brass players improvising in a percussion ensemble
- student demonstrations of specific challenges in the music being performed, such as polyrhythms or balancing the melody with accompanying parts
- demonstrations of electronic music compositions
- demonstrations of improvisational singing and/or playing

Realizing the importance of community contact and support, some school systems are opening their technology and music labs for members of the school community to use after school hours. Granted, this requires administrative cooperation and, on occasion, additional staff, but the resulting experience is well worthwhile. Opening labs to the public can give families quality time together as well as raise public awareness and generate funding.

Ultimately, the future of music education may well rest on the ability and desire of teachers to reach the whole public—to educate the community in much the same way the singing school master once did. We as educators must first believe and then act on the knowledge that music making is not just for the few who can afford private home instruction or those who join performing groups. Then we must inform parents, administrators, school boards, and politicians that *all* people have the potential to acquire the skills and knowledge that will help them enjoy a close association with music for the rest of their lives.

Armed with the National Standards and our vision, we must ensure that our convictions become the reality of the future. All of our lives will be the richer for it.

Notes

1. Music Educators National Conference, *The School Music Program: A New Vision* (Reston, VA: MENC, 1994), 13.

2. On one occasion, MENC hosted a panel discussion and demonstration of hands-on lessons for middle school general music programs that would focus on teaching to the Standards. At the end, a first-year teacher approached the panel. Puzzled, she said, "I don't really have a general music class. I teach music appreciation, and I don't know how to get them interested." Because of her lack of experience and training, she had difficulty assimilating what the panel was trying to explain about the nature of the middle schooler's need to be involved with active music making.

3. John Naisbitt, *Megatrends: Ten New Directions Transforming Our Lives* (New York: Warner Books, 1982), 36.

4. An elementary music teacher excitedly explained about a lesson that her fifth-grade students enjoyed. Yet, when she analyzed the lesson, she realized that it contained almost no music—it was basically a

creative writing project! Another elementary music teacher mentioned to me that the music book curriculum she was using allowed very little time for singing, much less ear training.

5. Many teachers work with administrators who judge a teacher's effectiveness by the noise level in the classroom. This is a problem that must be addressed with the administrator when implementing a more active, hands-on program.

6. The 4MAT System, by Bernice McCarthy (Barrington, IL: EXEL, Inc., 1980 200 West Station St., Barrington, IL 60010; telephone 800-822-4628), provides current information as well as a historical perspective concerning the way people learn. This system, which can be found on the World Wide Web (http://www.exel-corp.com), continues to gain favorable press from teachers who use it for developing creative, active lessons that teach to all learning types.

7. Music Educators National Conference, *Get America Singing . . . Again!* (Milwaukee, WI: Hal Leonard Corporation, 1996).

8. The use of Curwen hand signals provides an additional kinesthetic aid.

9. Adrian Legg records for the label Red House Records. His innovative approach to playing has made him a favorite among acoustic guitar fans.

10. A student from Holcomb Bridge Middle School in Atlanta was offered a job playing piano in a mall music store during the holiday season. When she drew a crowd by playing "Chariots of Fire," she had to explain to her audience that she had been

taking keyboard for only three weeks and it was the only song she knew. She went on to use her keyboard skills to help with choral sightsinging, arrange Christmas carols, and play by ear.

11. This exercise is patterned after the method used in Finland for teaching children scale tones and improvisation. Students use the five-string *kantele,* an instrument that can be tuned in different scales or modes. They strum chords by damping the strings they don't need or improvise melodies on the five diatonic strings.

12. Students in a seventh-grade chorus class were reluctant to take the solo measures in a twelve-bar blues. One student volunteered and then got cold feet when his turn came. When I assured him that anything he did would probably be okay, he started imitating animals. Soon the room sounded like a barnyard, and everyone laughed with the soloist (and the teacher). Eventually, many more students volunteered to be soloists.

13. This is true in visual art and industrial technology as well.

14. In my first year of teaching at a racially diverse school, an eighth-grade music class of about thirty students came into the music room yelling racial epithets at one another over an incident that had occurred on the way to class. I spent two days explaining to them why I had chosen to teach in the school and discussing the advantages we had over teachers and students in homogeneous situations. This was the same class that convinced me that we would have to go beyond our local differences so that we could see how insignificant those differences really were. This was also the year I changed the curriculum of eighth-grade general music to focus on world musics and began programming more world music in choral concerts.

15. Howard Gardner, *Frames of Mind: The Theory of Multiple Intelligences* (New York: Basic Books, 1983).

6

The Kinesthetic Connection in Performing and Understanding Music

Marvelene C. Moore

The Kinesthetic Connection: A Historical Perspective

For centuries, music educators and ethnomusicologists have acknowledged the importance of kinesthetic experiences in teaching and understanding the arts and subject matter in related disciplines. If we look back at the earliest cultures of the world, we discover that kinesthetic experiences were a major part of all aspects of life. Most often, it was dance and music that were inseparable. Together, they depicted and described tribal customs, ceremonies, religious rites, laws, and social life. In African cultures, for example, historian Lerone Bennett writes, "Whenever there was music, there was dance . . . men and women danced because dancing had both social and religious meaning. . . . Any event in the life of Africans, from birth to death, was celebrated by rhythmic movement because dancing,

to the African, was life itself."[1] Anthropologist Margaret Mead gives an account of a music and dance connection among the Manus people of the Admiralty Islands, north of New Guinea. "Whenever there is dance," she observes, "there is an orchestra of slit drums of all sizes played by the most proficient drummers in the village."[2] These two accounts describe the place of music in the lives of people who, though they resided on different continents, were united musically by their practice of performing music and dance as a unit.

The ancient civilizations of the Greeks and Romans provide further examples of the partnership between music and dance. In these cultures, music and dance occupied prominent places in the education of their citizens—music for the good of the soul and gymnastics (dance/movement) for the good of the body.

Moving into the Middle Ages, we discover the goliards, jongleurs, gauklers, troubadours, trouvères, minnesingers, and meistersingers carrying on this tradition of music and dance as a whole. The goliards were young poetic musicians who traveled throughout western Europe and sang Latin verses on a variety of subjects, including spring, drinking, love, morality, and immorality. Often during the songs, dance steps were used to depict the text. The jongleurs in France and the gauklers in Germany were often poor vagabonds who enlivened their music performances with animals trained to dance. They also played for weddings and festivals where people enjoyed music and dancing. In fact, their selections were often called "dancing-songs." The troubadours and trouvères in France and the minnesingers and meistersingers in Germany performed songs and "dancing-songs" that reflected the social and political climate of their times. They differed from the wandering minstrels, however, in that their ranks included princes, noblemen, and, often, ladies.

In the Renaissance, Baroque, and Classical periods, the educated and "cultured" upper classes danced the pavane, galliard, allemande, courante, minuet, and waltz, and they were also capable of actively making music by performing on keyboard instruments, composing, and arranging music. Some composers of the Romantic period—Mendelssohn, Schumann, Brahms, Tchaikovsky,

Dvořák, and, later, Bartók and Prokofiev, to name a few—often incorporated folk songs and dance tunes into their works; e.g., Bartók's collection of piano pieces "The Bagatelle," based on Hungarian folk tunes, and his "For Children" compositions, based on Hungarian and Slovakian folk songs and games. The inclusion of dance types and folk songs in these composers' works is indicative of the union of music and dance. For the Romantic movement believed in the anonymous origin and power of folk songs."[3]

One of the greatest influences on the music of the twentieth century comes from a folk culture—African American. Music and dance from this culture has been a significant source of inspiration for composers. Like their African ancestors, African Americans regard music and dance almost as a single art form. Consequently, when composers incorporate jazz, ragtime, cakewalk music, spirituals, blues, and gospel music into their compositions, they are being influenced by dance forms as well. In summary, when we view the historical development of music and its function in the life of man, whether in high society or among the common folk, the kinesthetic connection becomes quite clear.

The Kinesthetic Connection: Movement—The Key to Performance

Prior to the twentieth century, dance was the most common form of kinesthetic expression. In the 1900s, *movement* emerged as a different form of kinesthestic expression—a medium for enhancing music performance. Music educators who taught from this perspective made a clear distinction between dance and movement and their relationship to music. Anne Farber and Lisa Parker described this distinction as follows:

> The aim of learning to dance is to present and perform the artwork of the choreographer. To this end bodies are stretched and strengthened, techniques and styles of movement are studied and practiced, steps are learned. Music is usually present, and must usually be attended to—but not in an urgent, controlling way. . . . In the eurhythmics class, the body is trained to be the instrument, not of the performance of eurhythmics, but of the perception of music. The body is understood as the original musical instrument, the one through which everyone first *realizes* music in both its senses: apprehending and creating, and the primary, personal *trainable* utensil for musical understanding and production. The movements a student makes in a eurhythmics class do not have the essential purpose of training the body to convey a choreographic picture to an audience. Rather, their essential purpose is to convey information back to the mover himself.[4]

On the one hand kinesthetic participation was a means to an end (music performance). On the other hand, it was the end in and of itself (dance). It is the former position that many music educators of the twentieth century have adopted and implemented in their instruction.

Movement can be described as a physical motion that (a) prepares one for engaging in music, (b) aids in understanding music, and (c) accompanies performance of music. It can lay the groundwork for approaching a composition, help in articulating it, and serve as a companion in actual performance of the music. For example, a choral director might engage students in (a) executing physical motions that address specific rhythmic ideas in a piece of music prior to rehearsing the piece, (b) creating gestures during the rehearsal that represent specific articulations, such as legato and staccato, and (c) selecting specific gestures to be used to accompany the performance. Movements that directors can employ in these and other learning situations are classified in four ways: (1) gross motor actions, which involve use of large muscles (e.g., circling arms); (2) fine motor actions, which articulate a balance of time, space, and energy (e.g., clapping, snapping); (3) locomotor and nonlocomotor motions (e.g., walking, swaying); and (4) spontaneous responses to music, which result in creative expression.

The value of these types of physical responses in performing music in formal and informal settings cannot be overstated. Numerous benefits are derived from this approach to experiencing and expressing music, including development of cognitive, affective, and psychomotor skills. A number of scholars and researchers in education and music have conducted studies that document the relevance of movement in music education. D. M. Curtis and Martha Davis, in their research on movement and cognition and motor development, concluded that movement plays a role in developing the intellect.[5] Nell J. Sins, in researching the effect of a learning sequence that used movement on the ability of below-average middle school students to learn selected musical concepts, found that movement activities improved students' perceptions of form, sequence, and ostinato.[6] Helen Y. Cheek measured the effects of physical experiences on fourth-grade students' ability to perceive selected musical elements and found significant improvement in their understanding of some concepts and in their music reading skills.[7] Bryant J. Cratty's research revealed that movement contributes to self-confidence and a desire to succeed.[8] J. David Boyle conducted research revealing that locomotor movements greatly enhanced sightreading skills in junior high band.[9] L. Rosenbloom, in his study "The Consequences of Impaired Movement," tied much of the aforementioned research together with his findings on the importance of motor development to the development of the whole child.[10] The work of these scholars documents that kinesthetic experiences are essential for music learning, understanding, and performing.

Three schools of thought are noteworthy in their application of movement to music instruction. Educators from the first school, of which a leading proponent was Emile Jaques-Dalcroze, place emphasis on rhythmic movement as a means of learning and expressing music and developing musical sensitivity. They maintain the importance of four basic tenets that apply to all learning: (1) "perceiving and responding to music," (2) developing an "inner sensing of music: the inner aural sense and the inner muscular sense," (3) acquiring "sharper communication between the ear, eye, body, and mind," and (4) developing "a storehouse of aural and kinesthetic images that can be translated into symbols and, upon recall, be performed at will."[11] These educators believe that rhythm is the driving force in music, that it gives direction and strength to melody, aids in shifting harmonies, and adds color to sound. They hold to the theory that the basis of musical rhythm is found in the rhythm inherent in all human experience. Therefore, a physical response is required to truly experience all components of music. In such a response, the body becomes the bearer and source of musical sound.

Educators in this school emphasize that all music takes place in time (a determined period when musical events take place with no indication of spatial dimensions between the events) and requires energy (the force exerted to produce musical events). (See figure

6-1.) However, they view the contribution of space (distance, expanse, extent in which musical events take place) as providing the third dimension, which completes the balance in performance. (See figure 6-2.)

As students move and improvise in time with the appropriate amount of energy, they can become so absorbed in musical sound that they pay little attention to imitating others. Consequently, each person's creation can be original and authentic. The results are feelings of self-worth, confidence, and an appreciation for individual uniqueness. The final outcome is an increased comprehensive musicianship that promotes technical accuracy, sensitive expression, and the enjoyment and appreciation of music.

A second school of thought among music educators is the one that was advocated by Zoltán Kodály. Emphasis in this school is on (a) accuracy and quality in singing, (b) reading music, and (c) developing the inner ear's ability to identify pitch and reproduce it. Although these are the primary areas of concern, these music educators also employ movement as a means of attaining their goals. Locomotor movements are used to articulate rhythms, body percussion is often used to aid in rhythmic reading, and hand gestures (signals) are used to help with pitch accuracy.

A third school, based on practices associated with Carl Orff, focuses its attention on the concept of elemental music—rhythmic speech, rhythmic movement, singing and playing instruments—as essential to music learning. However, movement permeates every aspect of this approach as well. Body percussion accompanies rhythmic speech, locomotor movements aid in the interpretation of concepts and the expression of creative ideas, gestures add drama to singing, and nonlocomotor

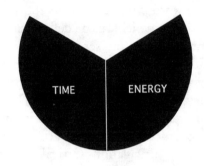

Figure 6-1. Diagram depicting time and energy with the absence of space in performing rhythmic movements.

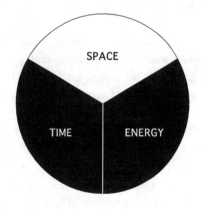

Figure 6-2. Diagram illustrating the balance of time, energy, and space.

movements serve as preparation for playing instruments. Improvisation is encouraged and is generally accomplished through preparatory movement exercises. Although the music educators in these three schools differ in the emphasis that they place on various components of music, they are unanimous in their belief that kinesthetic experiences (movement) are essential to performance.

The word *kinesthetic* has its roots in kinesthesia, which can be defined as moving, feeling, and sensing. In a kinesthetic experience the sensation of movement creates feelings that travel through the nervous system to the brain. The brain organizes the feelings into information on concepts (speed, accent, and direction), articulations (arrival and departure points; straight, curvy, or diagonal flow), and motion (arrangement and placement of arms, legs, and torso). Then the brain analyzes the motion and sends messages back through the nervous system to the muscles to correct the motion if necessary.[12] In other words, the student hears, moves, feels, organizes, analyzes, and moves with greater sensitivity and precision.

Rhythmic movement plays a major role in cognition. The Swiss psychologist Piaget was a leading proponent of this belief. He conducted numerous studies that documented the importance of rhythmic movement in acquiring knowledge and understanding concepts. He believed that there were four distinct phases of cognitive development: (1) sensorimotor, (2) preoperational, (3) concrete operations, and (4) formal operations. He also believed that, in the sensorimotor stage, movement played a major role in concept formation and problem solving.

Martha Davis, in her study "Movement and Cognition," cites research conducted with school-age children in London that suggests that each child possesses a vocabulary of movements that aid in the acquisition and manipulation of knowledge. Some students emphasize spatial directions, some stress force and weight, and some move rapidly back and forth from one movement to another. In all, the researchers found a parallel between the students' movement patterns and their intellectual functions.[13]

Rhythmic movement is also likely to have positive effects on musical memory. When a person moves, body sensations are stored and used as "pictures," which are then applied to similar experiences that are nonkinesthetic. In other words, an inner bodily image is formed when a person moves and is used as reference when performing another task. For example, students can clap their hands once at the beginning of an imaginary horizontal line and clasp hands toward the end of the line to represent movement of the phrase; or they can clasp hands at the beginning of the line and separate their hands gradually while moving toward the end of the line to represent a crescendo. The body then stores this movement sensation. When the student comes across this passage in a choral or instrumental piece, or in a song in the general music classroom, the movement sensation is recalled and enables the student to articulate the phrase appropriately—in proper time, energy, and space—resulting in an expressive performance. Music educators who have recognized this dimension of learning and expressing music include Carl Seashore, James Mursell, and Edwin Gordon.

Clearly, rhythmic movement can have a positive effect on music achievement. Students who experience music through body movement are usually more accurate in their performance of rhythms, more expressive of melodic line, and more confident as performers. Mursell particularly supported the use of muscular motor experiences in performing and expressing rhythms. He believed that rhythmic movement is necessary for students to become more secure in understanding rhythms.[14] This belief is ubiquitous among music educators at all levels and in practically all musical involvements.

The Kinesthetic Connection: Linkage to the National Standards for Music Education

The National Standards are guidelines for teaching and learning at all levels and in all areas of music. They identify the knowledge and skills that students should learn and then give direction for instruction: what teachers should teach and how they might teach it. The content standards are action oriented. They require a mindful response or reaction from the student that results in learning. That is, students are expected to demonstrate understanding, knowledge, and ability in the content areas by being actively engaged in the learning process.

Rhythmic movement is action-oriented. It requires the act of physical/affective doing in order to complete a task or assignment. It further demands absorption of the mind, body, and feelings in understanding and expressing music. Consequently, it forms a fitting union with teaching music based on the nine content standards. In the general music classroom, in performance group rehearsals, and in music methods courses at college and universities, rhythmic movement has proven to be an effective technique for specifically addressing Content Standards 1 (singing), 2 (performing on instruments), 3 (improvising), 6 (listening, analyzing, and describing), and 9 (understanding music in historical and cultural contexts).The following is a discussion of the application of rhythmic movement in teaching students competency in performance as described in these standards.

Content Standard 1: Singing, alone and with others, a varied repertoire of music. Whether the singing is in a general music classroom or in a choral ensemble, opportunities should be made available for students to sing alone and

Figure 6-3. Student rising from the floor to a standing position.

in both large and small ensembles. Regardless of the grouping, certain vocal skills should be addressed. Preparation for singing, proper breathing techniques, appropriate vocal placement, and desirable tone quality are a few basic vocal skill areas that should be considered. Rhythmic movement, when applied appropriately, can be a useful tool in achieving success in the development of these skills. Physical involvement through movement initially takes the focus from singing, an activity that frequently causes students to become tense and unsure, to movement, an area where students usually enjoy a great deal of success. This redirection of focus tends to improve their singing.

In preparation for singing, warm-ups for the body-instrument should be considered. Students can "take their instruments from their cases" by moving slowly from a crouched position on the floor, with head lowered, to a standing position. (See figure 6-3.)

The instrument (the body) can be "tuned" by rotating the head, rolling shoulders, bending knees, circling arms, swaying from side to side and back and forth, and, lastly, by stepping (walking) to a musical accompaniment. Students are now ready to begin "playing their instruments" by doing exercises in singing on the breath. Because singing on the breath involves motion and movement, rhythmic movement exercises are helpful in establishing this sensation. Performing gross motor movements, lowering arms and stepping with a balance of time, energy, and space, will visually represent the act of singing on the breath. More important, these movements will establish in the students' minds the sensation that is necessary for producing sound. Students can then internalize these physical sensations as they sing. The results are proper breathing and vocal production that is well focused. Until or unless the physical sensations occur and the experience is transferred from the physical to the internal, students cannot feel secure in their performances.

Gestures and whole body movements enhance understanding and performing of rhythmic and melodic concepts.

Rhythmic movement can be instrumental in articulating beat, note values, metric accents, syncopation, melodic phrasing and contour, musical nuances—crescendo/decrescendo, intensity, and many other musical components that may be present in vocal and instrumental music. As students perform musical concepts through rhythmic movement, they acquire greater skill and confidence in singing, alone or with each other, and therefore become open to exploring music of various periods and styles.

Content Standard 2: Performing on instruments, alone and with others, a varied repertoire of music. Playing a musical instrument requires a keen sense of timing, understanding of the relationship of timing to energy, and comprehension of the importance of space. For students to understand these principles and the necessity of balancing them in playing untuned and tuned instruments, experiences in rhythmic movement are essential. When students perform gross motor movements, such as walking, clapping, jogging, slapping, and stamping, and execute the appropriate spacing between each motion, it forces them to expend the energy required for accurate timing. Further, as students perform gross motor movements, they develop a vocabulary of neuromuscular traces that they can draw upon when performing on instruments that require similar motions. When they apply accent, intensity, dynamics, and other nuances to their

movements, they become prepared for the range of articulations that are necessary for performing expressively. The transfer of the neuromuscular sensations to specific instruments must be handled with care so that students do not lose their natural ability to express what they have experienced through rhythmic movement. Students need to understand that gross motor movements can be transferred to the smaller motions required for playing a variety of instruments. For example, when students perform short-short-long and long-short-short rhythm patterns in hands and feet, they should recall the neuromuscular sensation of moving to these patterns when asked to perform these rhythms on a hand drum or flute. The result is the transfer of muscular coordination from large muscles to finer motor movements.

Opportunities can be made available for students to perform movement compositions in large and small groups. For example, a group of students can perform two, three, or four simple movement ostinati simultaneously and transfer the ostinati to untuned or tuned instruments. Often younger students have difficulty playing rhythm patterns in compound meters. When students "skip" together in a group to a long-short (♩ ♪) rhythm or perform a "rolling gallop" to the short-long (♪| ♩) rhythm, they are able to transfer their whole body experiences and those they observed in other students to pitched and unpitched instruments. Further, as students perform locomotor and nonlocomotor movements with others, they acquire a greater sensitivity to their role when playing in an ensemble. These types of activities prepare students for performing in bands, orchestras, and chamber groups, and in the general music classroom. If students have numerous such experiences, they will have fewer problems playing in instrumental ensembles or performing alone.

Content Standard 3: Improvising melodies, variations, and accompaniments. Improvisation and movement form a unique partnership. In a music setting where rhythmic movement forms the basis for instruction, one does not exist without the other—to move is to improvise. When a student walks to music, the result is the creation of an individual motion that is predicated on his or her perception and reaction to a stimulus. The student does not think about how he or she will walk. Rather, the steps are a spontaneous response to the music. There is no time to think about the musical events that recently occurred or those that will happen in the immediate future. The student can focus only on the events of the present and respond accordingly.

To respond to present musical events, the improviser must draw upon his or her natural ability to perceive sound, to react emotionally, and to move appropriately. For those students who encounter some difficulty in improvising through rhythmic movement, numerous repetitions will increase their

skills. When students experience improvisation through rhythmic movement, they are learning to manipulate musical concepts—such as beat, meter, rhythm patterns, phrasing, contour, and chords—that are employed in creating original melodies and accompaniments. When applying these concepts they acquire a unique and powerful understanding of music.

Movement and improvisation are a natural alliance. Together they offer opportunities for students to create original works, to alter existing compositions (variations), and to invent appropriate complements to compositions (accompaniments). Further, when used in combination, they promote exploration and communication of musical ideas, contribute to developing skills in problem solving and cooperation, and encourage independence and a positive self-concept.

In the general music classroom, students can create improvisations by following a sequence of steps that yield immediate results. The key to success lies in structuring exercises that progress from the simple to the complex. For example, students might (1) perform a movement response to a call played by the teacher, (2) perform a response to a movement call improvised by a partner, (3) add vocables that complement their movements, and (4) sing vocables without moving. A similar procedure can be followed when using classroom instruments, both tuned and untuned. These exercises can also be extended to include the creation of complete melodies, variations of melodies, and accompaniments. The physical sensation derived from improvising through rhythmic movement first, allows students to gather, process, and respond to music appropriately and to transfer their experiences to singing and performing on instruments.

Content Standard 6: Listening to, analyzing, and describing music. When students are asked to move to specific elements in music—for example, dynamics, tempo, timbre, rhythms— they internalize their movements and may recall and transfer them to situations that involve listening only. Movement then becomes an important factor in the internalization of various styles through immersion in them by active listening, including movement as a very helpful component.

Standard 9: Understanding music in relation to history and culture. Singing, performing on instruments, improvising, and actively listening to a great variety of musics all provide a strong foundation for performing music from other cultures and periods with understanding. When we view music from a historical perspective and observe its role in the lives of individuals from various cultures, we find similarities in ways of conveying thought and feeling. We also find that movement and music are intertwined: movement accompanies many singing styles, and dance accompanies many instrumental music performances. In view of the linkage of move-

ment to music, it seems logical to employ kinesthetic skills that create conditions where students are immersed in experiencing all types of music from composers and cultures past and present. For example, because of the polyphonic nature of music of the past, like that of Bach (both vocal and keyboard), this music can be performed by students moving in groups to the subjects and answers. Likewise, melody with accompaniment, characteristic of Schubert's compositions, can be represented through the gestures and gross motor movements of a small group who performs the solo while a larger group moves as the accompaniment. Often, teachers and students avoid works of contemporary composers because of rhythmic complexities such as irregular meters and groupings. However, approaching these concepts initially through movement provides some familiarity with these musical features prior to a vocal or instrumental rehearsal.

It is possible to orient students to various styles of folk/ethnic music and dance by having them participate in preparatory movement activities that lead to the performance of folk melodies, instrumental pieces, drumming accompaniments, and ethnic dances. The body can be used as the instrument in executing these rhythms and melodies in rehearsal situations and in public performances. For example, in an African rhythm performance, numbers or letters can be assigned to different students who are then asked to create gestures appropriate for the overall sound of the performance when their number or letter appears. They are then asked to express the articulation of the rhythm as they move from one gesture to another. The same accurate timing necessary to move from gesture to gesture can be transferred to finer motor skills when applied to playing rhythm patterns on various instruments. The actual physical sensation of the rhythms, performed through kinesthetic exercises, causes the performance on instruments to become more accurate, energized, and exciting.

People all over the world have understood the relationship of movement to music and its place in communicating feelings; depicting social, economic, and religious life; and providing enjoyment. Recent research has reinforced the usefulness of movement in enhancing musical learning and experience. When movement is incorporated into the musical learnings stipulated by the Standards, those learnings take on deeper, more personally affective meaning. In performance, the kinesthetic dimension adds an essential component of musical understanding.

Notes

1. Lerone Bennett, Jr., *Ebony Pictorial History of Black America* (Chicago: Johnson Publishing Co., 1971), 44.

2. Margaret Mead, *Growing Up in New Guinea* (1930; reprint, New York: William Morrow Co., 1975), 43–44.

3. Alfred Einstein, *Music in the Romantic Era* (New York: W. W. Norton, 1947), 40–41.

4. Anne Farber and Lisa Parker, "Discovering Music Through Dalcroze Eurhythmics," *Music Educators Journal* 74, no. 3 (November 1987).

5. D. M. Curtis, "The Young Child: The Significance of Motor Development," *Journal of Physical Education and Recreation* 16, no. 3 (1971): 207–209; Martha Davis, "Movement and Cognition," *Theory into Practice* 16, no. 3 (1977): 207–209.

6. Nell J. Sins, "The Effect of a Learning Sequence Utilizing Movement on the Ability of Below-Average Middle School Students to Learn Selected Musical Concepts" (Doctoral diss., University of Georgia, 1976): 37.

7. Helen Y. Cheek, "The Effects of Psychomotor Experiences on the Perception of Selected Musical Elements and the Formation of Self-Concept in Fourth Grade General Music Students" (Doctoral diss., University of Michigan, 1979), abstract in *Dissertation Abstracts International* (1979): 40.

8. Bryant J. Cratty, *Some Educational Implications of Movement* (Seattle: Special Child Publications, 1970), 21.

9. J. David Boyle, "The Effect of Prescribed Rhythmical Movements on the Ability to Read Music at Sight," *Journal of Research in Music Education* 18, no. 4 (1970): 307–18.

10. L. Rosenbloom, "The Consequences of Impaired Movement: A Hypothesis and Review," in *Movement and Child Development*, ed. K. S. Holt (England: Lavenheim Press, 1975).

11. Virginia Hoge Mead, "More than Mere Movement: Dalcroze Eurhythmics," *Music Educators Journal* 82, no. 4 (January 1996).

12. Lois Choksy, Robert M. Abramson, Avon E. Gillespie, and David Woods, *Teaching Music in the Twentieth Century* (Englewood Cliffs, NJ: Prentice-Hall, 1986), 33.

13. Martha Davis, "Movement and Cognition."

14. James L. Mursell, *The Psychology of Music* (1937; reprint, New York: Johnson Reprint Corp., 1970), 59.

Selected Resources

Bachmann, Marie-Laure. *Dalcroze Today: An Education through and into Music.* Oxford: Clarendon Press, 1991.

Barrett, K. R. "Learning to Move—Moving to Learn: Discussion at the Crossroads." *Theory into Practice* 12, no. 2 (1973).

Boyle, J. David. "The Effect of Prescribed Rhythmical Movements on the Ability to Read Music at Sight." *Journal of Research in Music Education* 18, no. 4 (1970).

Caldwell, Timothy. "A Dalcroze Perspective on Skills for Learning." *Music Educators Journal* 79, no. 7 (March 1993).

Carabo-Cone, Madeleine. "Learning How to Learn: A Sensory-Motor Approach." *Music Journal* 31 (1973).

Cheek, Helen Y. "The Effects of Psychomotor Experiences on the Perception of Selected Musical Elements and the Formation of Self-Concept in Fourth Grade General Music Students." Doctoral diss., University of Michigan, 1979. Abstract in *Dissertation Abstracts International* 40 (1979): 2530A. (University Microfilms 79-25121)

Choksy, Lois. *The Kodály Method: Comprehensive Music Education from Infant to Adult.* Englewood Cliffs, NJ: Prentice-Hall, 1974.

Choksy, Lois, Robert M. Abramson, Avon E. Gillespie, and David Woods. *Teaching Music in the Twentieth Century.* Englewood Cliffs, NJ: Prentice-Hall, 1986.

Cratty, Bryant J. *Some Educational Implications of Movement.* Seattle: Special Child Publications, 1970.

Curtis, D. M. "The Young Child: The Significance of Motor Development." *Journal of Physical Education and Recreation* 16, no. 3 (1971).

Davis, Martha. "Movement and Cognition." *Theory into Practice* 16, no. 3 (1977).

Farber, Anne, and Lisa Parker. "Discovering Music through Dalcroze Eurythmics." *Music Educators Journal* 74, no. 3 (November 1987).

Findlay, Elsa. *Rhythm and Movement: Applications of Dalcroze Eurhythmics.* Evanston, IL: Summy-Birchard, 1971.

Gabbard, Carl P., and Charles H. Shea. "Influence of Movement Activities on Shape Recognition and Retention." *Perceptual and Motor Skills* 48, 116–18 (1979).

Gardner, Howard. "Children's Duplication of Rhythmic Patterns." *Journal of Research in Music Education* 19, no. 3 (1971).

Gilbert, Janet P. "Assessment of Motoric Music Skill Development in Young Children: Test Construction and Evaluation Procedures." *Psychology of Music* 7, no. 2 (1979).

Gordon, Edwin E. *Learning Sequence and Patterns in Music,* rev. ed. Chicago: G.I.A. Publications, 1977.

———. *The Psychology of Music Teaching.* Englewood Cliffs, NJ: Prentice-Hall, 1971.

Henke, Herbert H. "The Application of Emile Jaques-Dalcroze's Solfège-Rhythmique to the Choral Rehearsal." *The Choral Journal* (December 1984).

———. "Rehearsing with Dalcroze Techniques." *The Instrumentalist* (May 1993).

Holt, Kenneth S., ed. *Movement and Child Development.* England: Lavenheim Press, 1975.

Jaques-Dalcroze, Emile. *Eurhythmics, Art, and Education.* Edited by Cynthia Cox. Translated by F. Rothwell. 1930. Reprint, New York: B. Blom, 1972.

———. *Rhythm, Music and Education.* Translated by Harold F. Rubenstein. 1921. Reprint, New York: Arno Press, 1976.

Landis, Beth, and Polly Carder. *The Eclectic Curriculum in American Music Education,* rev. ed. Reston, VA: Music Educators National Conference, 1990.

Larsen, Ronald L., and Charles G. Boody. "Implications from Jean Piaget." *Journal of Research in Music Education* 19, no. 1 (1971).

Leonhard, Charles, and Robert W. House. *Foundations and Principles of Music Education,* 2d ed. New York: McGraw-Hill, 1972.

McCoy, Claire W. "Eurhythmics: Enhancing the Music-Body-Mind Connection in Conductor Training." *Choral Journal* (December 1994).

Mead, Virginia Hoge. *Dalcroze Eurhythmics in Today's Music Classroom.* New York: Schott Music Corporation, 1994.

———. "More than Mere Movement: Dalcroze Eurhythmics." *Music Educators Journal* 82, no. 4 (January 1996).

Pennington, Jo. *The Importance of Being Rhythmic: A Study of the Principles of Dalcroze Eurhythmics Applied to General Education and to the Arts of Music, Dancing and Acting.* Based on and adapted from *Rhythm, Music and Education* by Emile Jaques-Dalcroze. New York: G. P. Putnam's Sons, 1925.

Ristad, Eloise. "Musical Understanding through Movement." *Outlook* 32 (1979).

Rosenbloom, L. "The Consequences of Impaired Movement: A Hypothesis and Review." In *Movement and Child Development,* edited by Kenneth. S. Holt. England: Lavenheim Press, 1975.

Rowen, Betty. "Learning through Movement." *Teachers College Columbia Music Education Bulletin* 9 (1967).

Sins, Nell J. "The Effect of a Learning Sequence Utilizing Movement on the Ability of Below-Average Middle School Students to Learn Selected Musical Concepts." Doctoral diss., University of Georgia, 1976. Abstract in *Dissertation Abstracts International* 35, no. 5 (1976): 2708A.

Stauffer, Sandra L., and Jennifer Davidson. *Strategies for Teaching K–4 General Music.* Reston, VA: Music Educators National Conference, 1996.

Warner, Brigitte. *Orff-Schulwerk: Applications for the Classroom.* Englewood Cliffs, NJ: Prentice-Hall, 1991.

Teaching for Performing with Understanding in Band and Orchestra Settings

7

The Band and Orchestra Rehearsal
Toward Musical Independence

Patricia J. Hoy

Toward Refined Musical Experiences

For many years, scholars in music education have promoted the ideal that the role of music in education should be to create a desire in students to continue musical experiences as an adult. Another ideal is that of enabling the student to make sensitive choices regarding music performance based on musical knowledge and skill in listening. In order to accomplish these goals, the individual must have a need and desire for musical expression. Performing ensembles allow for group expression that sometimes feels profound; however, students do not often have an opportunity to experience expressive musical thought individually. Unfortunately, students in bands and orchestras often fail to develop understanding of music or, worse, they develop a distorted concept of its meaning. With careful planning by the director, students can have refined performing experiences that produce a love for music.

Such refined experiences flow naturally out of the study of musical elements. Directors can develop these experiences by teaching not only technique but character, mood, and message. Ensemble musicians are motivated to understand performance decisions when directors use a variety of methods, such as gestures, questioning and discussion, diagnosis with explanation, metaphors, and key words to stimulate student responses.

A rehearsal approach of this kind provides students with the appropriate vocabulary and framework for sensing and thinking about music. The director's ideas can stimulate a student's originality, helping it to blossom and continue to take shape. Ensemble musicians may realize their own individual responses to an idea by trying to find words to describe the message in the music. They need to identify with the emotions in the music and be able to make decisions regarding the skillful handling of elements to achieve the desired mood or character. Such a process is a delight for student musicians and provides a vital link to the essence of music.

By using an active approach to gathering, organizing, and assimilating knowledge, and by applying that knowledge toward revealing musical problems, students learn to support their own opinions intelligently and are less inclined to accept information passively and perspectives passed on through traditional diagnosis-remedy rehearsal situations. This kind of ensemble experience should encourage students to develop a deep, lifelong love for music.

In addition, ensemble members who experience intimate contact with the understanding, interpretation, and performance of quality music will most frequently choose to continue such experiences throughout their lives. Stimulating intuitive responses through carefully worked-out study of the music allows students to learn depth of expression, to think both analytically and creatively, and to communicate music persuasively. Refined experiences dealing with the essence of the music being studied in an ensemble allow students to better understand and participate in the interpretive decision-making process. These experiences also help students to devel-

op respect for the views of others and to better understand concepts such as compassion, trust, imagination, enthusiasm, and their application to the interpretation of music.

Understanding the essence of a work can provide the student with the ability to be a whole person, allowing ease and freedom of spirit along with the ability to look at all things with a fresh view. The degree of musical maturation developed may be measured by students' success in applying their understanding to new musical situations. Students who comprehend and conceive musical events with maturity in understanding and performance will be able to be musically independent performers.

The Musically Meaningful Rehearsal

Rehearsal techniques discussed later in this chapter may be used singly or in combination to engage students and, ultimately, empower them to enrich their lives through music. Such experiences can become important milestones in the development of musical maturity for student and teacher alike. Through rehearsals, an ensemble director must not only solve the technical problems but also stimulate and guide students to understand and participate in the decisions and processes involved in interpreting the selected music.

Directors must determine what methods and concepts will most effectively stimulate students and bring life to music. They must provide meaningful rehearsal experiences that will immerse students in the essence of the music in order to enable them to understand, create, and enjoy inspiring musical thought and performance. Through such rehearsals, images are enlarged by layering them gradually with more and more interpretive substance, creating and sustaining an exciting intensity. As directors learn to better organize their own thoughts about the inner workings of the music, these rehearsal procedures gradually become more intuitive.

When this type of teaching and learning takes place, understanding and realization of the expressive aspects of music enhance academic and technical musical study. This is the essence of successful teaching, serving to stimulate student imagination, personalize the response, and effect emotional involvement.

To help students understand a musical work and determine how best to recreate it, directors must guide them through meaningful inner experiences so students can better determine and understand information that is critical for making interpretive decisions. Directors who enable students to better conceptualize the music discover that students can perform difficult passages with ease as their individual and collective interpretive skills improve. Bands and orchestras often perform above the level of competence of individual players if each student is freely involved in the creative aspects of interpretation.

This will also allow students to better evaluate the whole performance and their own contribution to it.

Planning for Musical Understanding

Performance preparation must be taught and experienced carefully and intimately in order for students to become properly motivated. Concepts must be absorbed gradually, as students experience a variety of meaningful learning experiences that have been carefully orchestrated and presented by the director. This comprehensive education of the heart as well as the mind provides a lasting and positive effect on students' musical development and produces a healthy enthusiasm for each rehearsal.

The image that is built for any composition is enhanced by the director's communication with the ensemble. The director must undertake a comprehensive study of the music to determine what will facilitate the development of rich inner experiences. For students, this process will create a greater awareness as their imaginations stretch to understand and achieve the composer's intent.

Such an experience is most rewarding when the preparation as well as the interaction with the group allows directors to conduct both emotionally and intellectually with control and assurance. Although this type of preparation will eventually become automatic, directors may first need to practice some of the same basic techniques that artist-level performers use to connect with their audiences.

One technique that may promote eloquence in presentation involves directors imagining every aspect of the rehearsal as though the band or orchestra were surrounding them, sharing their ideas and thoughts. To better understand the effectiveness of their presentation, directors must attempt to see themselves through the eyes of band or orchestra members and sense what it feels like to be in the ensemble. Those directors who are able to envision themselves touching the group with what they see in the music will experience wonderful results.

The Role of Enthusiasm

Directors must also understand the importance of enthusiasm in their presentations. Filled with enthusiasm, the director's voice becomes richer, the whole expression is transformed, and those listening become completely immersed in the music. Eyes that shine or "dance" and raised eyebrows are much more effective than a dull blank stare or lack of eye contact. The face is the most expressive part of the body, and a vibrant face can help emphasize words or gestures. Other ways to show enthusiasm include body movement with the head, arms, or hands, changing the pace of body movements or speech, and moving around.

Highly descriptive words also offer great variety in a presentation, as do factors such as changing proximity to the students, using humor, and portraying a generally high degree of energy and vitality. This excitement must be sincere, with real love and enthusiasm for the work at hand. Presenting any work with enthusiasm is as vital to a band or orchestra director as it is to a performing artist who must connect with an audience.

Applying the Standards

The National Standards for Music Education provide a common agenda from which to build more refined musical learning experiences. As the director uses the various components of the Standards and weaves them together, greater knowledge of the function of musical elements leads students toward new goals and a new realm of understanding. Basically, the Standards deal with three factors: (1) the basic techniques of performance, (2) the use of musical elements in a composition, and (3) the skillful and expressive handling of those elements.

The most effective method of probing the complexities of performance is first to address each element separately. As students develop a greater level of understanding and depth of knowledge regarding skillful handling of elements in performance, the Standards offer them new goals and new possibilities for performance. Since the director's role is to foster an educated musical independence, those who approach rehearsals by engaging the minds of students through effective methodology, and who use the Standards developmentally, will be better able to guide students toward an understanding of the decision-making process and, ultimately, musical independence.

Parts and Wholes

There is great value in dissecting works, as well as an ease in learning smaller pieces of information through isolation. Understanding basic ideas well enough to project them persuasively so they may be performed with confidence requires this sort of thoughtful exploration of the individual elements. There must also be a process of reintegration so that when a director deals with individual elements, there is still an awareness that these smaller pieces of information actually fit back together to create a musical thought. As the work is reconstructed, students will be more capable of perceiving its overall architecture, emotional peaks and valleys, harmonic schemes, forms, unifying compositional techniques, thematic development, and artistic principles such as unity and variety, contrast, and stylistic consistency.

If students are engaged emotionally, perceive the energy and direction of the composer, and develop awareness of how the individual elements relate to the whole piece, they are more able to contribute through their own unique personal spirit. Well-integrated into rehearsals and individual practice, this long-term process, as opposed to a completely reactive or symptomatic treatment, will allow the resultant performance to be pleasing aesthetically for both the individual performers and the audience.

Clues to Expression

Students must become accustomed to finding musical clues that assist with performance decisions. They must accept the fact that the printed notes do not tell all there is to know about the music. Except for precision in correct note values and actual printed correct pitches, the elements are flexible. Using musical clues and taking a structured approach to analysis, with defined layers and categories, will further stimulate directors, encouraging precision in their comments and ensuring that they consider a variety of approaches to think about a particular musical idea.

The director's analysis might include the following steps: (1) determining the boundaries of musical ideas; (2) identifying the actual musical facts that come together to establish the idea, such as details of melody, rhythm, harmony, texture, and other elements; (3) determining the patterns that give life to these facts and those that create the musical events or lead to the discovery of the musical design; (4) stimulating the imagination and gaining a perception of the flow and momentum of these events to describe the dynamic energy of the idea; (5) developing a richer connection to an idea by finding words and images that epitomize its inherent character; and (6) relating the ideas to each other according to their function, continuing up to larger and larger structural areas to ultimately gain an understanding of the whole work.

Musical Energy

Along with providing a structured analysis, the director must lead students to an understanding of the music's physical presence. With effective methodology, students will find this sense of energy, flow, and momentum to be a stimulating way to examine music. The sense of the energy of a musical idea will be enhanced if thought is given to such properties as the shape, mass, texture, weight, tone color, tonality, articulation, range, repetition of notes, texture, speed, volume, and speed of ascent or descent. What impression does the phrase make on our consciousness? Awareness of musical energy, flow, and momentum makes it more possible to create imagery for musical ideas.

Leonard Bernstein stated this concept well in a discussion from his first Young People's Concert, *What Does Music Mean?* (January 18, 1958):

> The most wonderful thing of all is that there's no limit to the different kinds of feelings music can make you have. Sometimes we can name the things we feel, like joy or sadness or love or hate or peacefulness. But there are other feelings so deep and special that we have no words for them, and that's where music is espe-

cially marvelous. It names the feelings for us, only in notes instead of words.

Students in bands and orchestras become stimulated by the emotion created through various musical ideas and the skillful handling of musical elements to depict and portray them. Is a musical idea reflective, floating, oppressive, foglike, tragic, or brave? Personal background, mood, and maturity all affect one's perception. It is important for students to learn by hearing both the director's and fellow students' perceptions of a musical idea. When an audience hears a performance by an ensemble whose director has involved students emotionally with the music, they, too, enjoy a sense of energy.

Establishing Priorities

It is not always easy to prescribe appropriate remedies for performance problems, yet a director must not only evaluate rehearsal situations but also lead individuals to independence. The complex interaction between directors and ensemble members does not allow simple answers. It is essential that directors give deep thought to intercommunication.

In rehearsal planning, directors should set sequential performance goals in priority of musical importance, rather than reacting to perceived performance problems. This prioritization may vary depending upon the ensemble's skill and experience, the work to be performed, the director's familiarity with the ensemble, available rehearsal time, or proximity of a given rehearsal to performance.

Rehearsal Strategies for Developing Musical Understanding

The following rehearsal situations and methodology illustrate how the Standards may be employed to lead ensemble musicians to greater understanding and, ultimately, musical independence. The examples are organized by various musical elements or techniques. Ideas for developing rehearsal priorities at a variety of levels will also be presented.

In rehearsal preparation, the director should consider which components of the Standards deal with the musical elements or techniques being addressed. This analysis will help the director guide students in the decision-making process in regard to both technical and expressive aspects of their performance.

Knowledge of even the simplest skill or concept can grow and assume broader dimensions. Using various aspects of the separate elements allows growth in knowledge that is like a series of overlays on an overhead projector, each enriching the understanding of the original.

Melody. Melody is basically the horizontal organization of pitches as they coincide with rhythm. The following rehearsal sequence is the first of two final rehearsals prior to a performance. Since students have already achieved the expected level of accomplishment with

respect to tone quality, posture, breath control, stick control, or bow control, as well as accurate rhythms and technical proficiency, the director has determined that the priority for this particular rehearsal will be to do a final check of the major sections of the work that provide the character and atmosphere of the piece.

There has been a concern in rehearsals about the consistency of energy needed to effectively portray the contrast of melodic character. The performance factors stressed for achieving the desired energy in melodic performance have involved the skillful handling of dynamics, articulation, placement of weight throughout the length of the note, and changes in tone color. The director has made a point of reminding students that musical momentum is not a function of tempo; rushing and slowing down are not appropriate methods for achieving the character.

The students have studied important melodies in the score. They have listened to various recordings of the work while observing points in score sections that were printed out in multiple copies, projected from transparencies, or presented from computer displays, both in class and in outside assignments. In addition, they have all recorded the melody of various sections of the work on their own instruments, using appropriate expression for achieving the desired character.

A transposed melodic sheet has been provided to help students record improvised melodies in the style and mood of the work over the recorded accompaniment parts of the full ensemble. In rehearsal, students have had experiences to guide their understanding of how handling the elements in certain ways can help them reach the most effective level of performance of the work. This process has included direct involvement in the decision making, explanations of the director's decisions, and a sincere, enthusiastic presentation by the director regarding the performance factors. In addition, the director has used appropriate technical vocabulary to describe the music throughout the rehearsal sequence, explaining meanings as necessary, and students have been encouraged to use the vocabulary in their discussions. Through rehearsals, students have gained an understanding of how the elements of music were used in the construction of the melody in terms of expression and character, and of the compositional techniques used to create tension and release, flow, and momentum.

Example 1

Director (*With eye contact, facial expression, energy, and excitement about the section of music to be rehearsed.*) Let's remember what we need to do to create the feeling of intense heaviness and stress at Letter A. Does anyone remember the important points we must consider to generate this intense feeling in the melody and why we must consider these particular performance factors?

Student Yes. In order to have intensity and heaviness, we must slightly exaggerate the *crescendi* in the first two bars so the downbeat of the third bar doesn't suddenly come in *forte*.

Director (*With a smile.*) Yes! Prepare for that *forte* downbeat using the *crescendi* in bars one and two to create great heaviness and an oppressive atmosphere. Let's all sing the three bars at Letter A.

Director conducts the first two bars at Letter A to the downbeat of the third bar, with gestures and facial expression that convey great weight and heaviness, and sings with students.

Director Now, let's play it, please, at Letter A.

Passage is conducted and performed.

Director Yes! That's what we need to create the intensity and pressure of building to this *forte*. Now, remember to play *legato*—link the two *crescendi* and play with equal weight throughout the note, not tonguing heavily at the beginning. This will add to the feeling of pressure and heaviness—almost like clinging to a thought, like a burden, to the point of madness! Letter A again.

Director takes a moment to set the mood with face and body and maintains eye contact with the ensemble. All students are very focused while they perform from the first two bars at Letter A to the downbeat of the third bar.

Director Wonderful! You see how this creates that heaviness, stress, pressure, and oppression we wanted to achieve! Now, for those who enter in the third bar, we must remember to bring out exactly the opposite effect. Those who begin here are completely relaxed and light, giving relief to that stress we just created. Remember to play softly, with a much more transparent, hollow tone and with a short, very light articulation. Those who enter in the third bar only, please.

Passage is performed.

Director (*Director gains eye contact with students and smiles.*) Yes, this nine seconds or so of lightness is important for contrast because it then goes right back to burdened heaviness and stress in the fifth bar! Now, let's all please play from Letter A.

Students perform the section together, focusing on director.

Director Very good—now let's play from the very beginning, through this section, then all the way to Letter B.

This brief rehearsal sequence demonstrates the idea of allowing students to understand how a more effective performance of this melody results from decisions involving the use of dynamics, tone color, articulation, and weight. In addition, the enthusiastic presentation allows students to become more involved in the rehearsal. The order of musical importance set up in advance by the director takes priority over other performance factors that might arise. As problems are taken out of context and then reintegrated into the whole section, students learn why certain performance factors are necessary to perform

the piece effectively.

To analyze the music and establish rehearsal priorities regarding the performance of melody, the director might consider the following list of (a) questions for students and (b) statements to be generated in discussion.

Questions

1. How should the placement of dynamic accents be used to define the musical idea or to represent what the melody is saying?

2. When there are no dynamic marks, how is it determined which dynamic inflections should be used? Should all notes in a melody receive the same dynamic marking?

3. What is done typically with tone color or dynamics in a melodic line with several of the same pitches in succession?

4. How do large skips, mixed intervals, dramatic leaps, consecutive steps, repeated notes, scale segments, arpeggios, chromatics, or the predominance of particular intervals affect the performance of a melody?

5. What are the characteristics created by the presence or predominance of particular scale tones in a melodic line?

6. How is the relative volume of melodic sequences determined?

7. What is generally done with the last note of a phrase in terms of volume?

8. Where is a particularly important

note in the natural pulse, and how does this influence the volume?

9. Do all note values receive the same dynamic marking?

10. How do you determine the dynamics or tone color of various melodies in contrapuntal music? How do the melodies interact? Do they move in contrary motion or parallel motion? What intervals do they form conjointly? When do they create dissonance, and when do they create consonance? How do their individual climax points relate? How do you weave the melodies together most effectively?

11. Should the highest note in a melody always receive the most emphasis?

12. How do composers use melodic construction to create mood?

Statements

1. A *crescendo* is a common dynamic change that may be used to achieve momentum if the melodic line ascends.

2. A *decrescendo* is a common dynamic change that may be used to slow momentum if a melodic line descends.

3. The nature of the pitches (for example, starting a melody on the root, third, or fifth of a triad) affects the quality of a phrase.

4. The predominance of particular scale tones affects the character of melodic performance.

5. In melodic performance, we need to feel the importance of climax

notes, as well as the importance of those notes that help provide a sense of motion toward or away from the climax notes.

6. Experimenting with various versions of a melodic line helps lead to an understanding of the most instinctively satisfying interpretation.

7. All tones and rests are dynamically significant. Place all tones in a larger context.

8. Singing a melody can bring it to life, helping increase understanding of the needed voice tone quality and facilitating transfer to the instrument.

Harmony. Basically, harmony is considered to be musical sounds that are played simultaneously. The following brief rehearsal sequence is the second rehearsal of a work scheduled for performance at a later date. The director has established some priorities dealing with the basic concepts regarding the shape and overall mood of the composition. The focus is on the harmonic elements in various sections.

Example 2

Director (*With arms spread, less volume and intensity of voice.*) This work opened with a storm. Then came moments of calm. Here, the theme is major when it was previously in minor. The storm has cleared, and we start to see blue sky. Begin again, please.

Ensemble begins again.

Director Yes, but after this section, when we arrive at measure 52, it is full

. . . full. (*Rises to a more grand and dignified posture as this is stated, with arms spread in a great gesture of openness and acceptance.*) Like this. . . .Why must we consider this here?

Student   Because it suddenly goes to a major chord?

Director   Yes, it does. But what does this mean? How should the harmony affect our performance?

Student   The chord must be loud and ring.

Director   (*With pleasure, director changes voice quality and volume to reflect the message.*) Yes, the chord on this downbeat at measure 52 must be a radiant A-flat major—like the sun shining, and warm, full of resonance! What could the composer be trying to portray here? The beginning is a storm, then comes calm and blue sky, then the radiant warmth. What might be the message of the warm sun here?

Student   Joy, happiness?

Director   (*Eyes wide, jumps up, raises arms.*) Yes, maybe deep gratification and acceptance like this. (*Spreads arms out again in gesture of openness and acceptance.*) Now, let's all play this A-flat major chord at measure 52.

Conducting motions imitate the openness and acceptance shown earlier, and musicians play with glowing warmth, their capacity for expression suddenly enlarged.

Director   (*Speaking slowly in a deep voice.*) Wonderful! From the beginning

again, please. (*Face and body language immediately assume the image of a storm as they begin again.*)

This brief rehearsal sequence demonstrates the idea of connecting tone color, dynamics, articulation style, and relative weight of notes to effective performance of the harmonic elements of composition. In addition, the director's presentation allows students to become immersed in the concept of harmony as it might relate to the notion of a storm, calm, and radiant warmth. The predetermined priority of musical importance is maintained throughout the sequence, and students are led to a better understanding of the function of harmony as the chords are taken out of context and then reintegrated back into the whole section. Future rehearsal sequences for this section of music might deal with aspects of individual tone, intonation, blend, and balance, and how these create the desired warmth in the sound.

To analyze the music and establish rehearsal priorities regarding harmony in performance, the director might consider the following list of (a) questions for students and (b) statements to be generated in discussion.

Questions

1. How much is the understanding of music embodied in the harmony and enriched by it?
2. How do harmonic patterns affect dynamic evolution of music in different ways? Which chords—dissonant or consonant—could be con-

sidered to be more active or carry more weight?

3. How do basic harmonic progressions flavor the melody and define its color?

4. Which chords repeat or prevail, acting as poles or as a factor of organization for other chords?

5. There can be an exploration of the relationship between harmony and melody. Do arpeggiated melodies spell out harmonies? Do short scale passages outline a chord? Are certain tones in a line consonant or dissonant with the harmony?

6. Differentiate between such harmonic elements as rich chromaticism, pure triads, shifting tonal centers, polytonality, and atonality. What atmosphere, character, or mood do each of these create?

Statements

1. Harmony provides a tonal skeleton against which melodies develop, and it creates a pattern of motion that contains its own sequence of tension and resolution.

2. Emphasize harmonic progressions, repeating them, and listen to their particular sound quality as well as to the emotional suggestion of chords and chord changes.

3. It is much easier to understand one or two chordal concepts—such as F minor, C major seventh, or G dominant seventh—than to understand individual notes outside the concept of harmony.

4. Melody is simply harmony that is made more fluent. Compositional elements such as extension and embellishment have a function in this process.

Form. Form is the shape that results from the organization of the horizontal factors, vertical factors, and expressive qualities of music. The following rehearsal sequence is organized to demonstrate the development of concepts related to form and performance. Students have heard the director use appropriate vocabulary during the rehearsal and have been encouraged to respond with that vocabulary when appropriate. The director has prepared students for this sequence by having them read through a large section of the work and by making appropriate comments about intonation, improved fingerings, and other relevant matters.

Example 3

Director   If we as performers are to reinforce the form of a composition, we must learn to gauge the significance of each musical statement at every stage of its musical development. For example, a musical statement at the beginning of a piece is normally best shaped in a way that creates a feeling of suppressed dynamics that can be reinforced later in the piece. How can we do this in the opening of this work?

Student   Do all pieces have to begin with suppressed dynamics? The statement at the beginning of this piece seems to be very strong.

Director   It sure does seem to begin

strong. What do we do now?

Student Well, it seems that there's still a building to repeated statements later.

Director Yes! How does this happen?

Student Tension is created by several repetitions of the statement. It seems to gather force.

Director This is exactly what it does! Tension is created here by the accumulating thrust of the statement, which is so short that momentum is created by simple repetition. (*Sings the repeated statements.*) Let's sing it together.

Students sing opening repeated statements.

Director But we must be careful not to *crescendo* until one is indicated suddenly in measure 12 and grows to a *forte* in measure 36. If we avoid a premature *crescendo,* the form of the composition can be heard by the audience and the significance of these statements may be better judged. Let's play the opening sequence of repeated statements and the *crescendo* to *forte* in measure 36.

Students perform first 36 measures.

Director Now let's find other sections that have this same series of repeated statements. We must perform them the same each time, avoiding a premature *crescendo,* even though each section may be a little louder than the last. The statement appears a total of three times. We will now play all three of these sections, stopping momentarily

after each one, then skipping on to the next—reinforcing the second and third a little. The first statement at the beginning, please.

This rehearsal sequence allows students to better understand musical form and the importance of using dynamic shape in performance to create energy. It also helps students identify the fact that statements and sections in music often repeat.

To analyze the music and establish rehearsal priorities regarding musical form and performance, the director might consider the following list of (a) questions for students and (b) statements to be generated in discussion.

Questions
1. What are the relationships between the restatements of a theme?
2. How does a particular theme contribute to the development of the ongoing musical line?
3. What is the dynamic shape of the entire work? How do we reinforce consistently those aspects of the work that will enhance its overall evolution?
4. What section of the music gives the greatest intensity?
5. How are the main melodies structured? Why does this matter?

Statements
1. Determine the function of each pattern and the significance of each resolution, blending them all into a single cohesive musical statement.

2. A theme or motive at the beginning of a work is best shaped in a way that creates a suppressed dynamic tendency that can be expanded and reinforced later in the work, although works don't always begin with suppressed impulses.

Rhythm and texture are also elements of music found in the Standards and may be used to determine the musical importance and priority of rehearsals. Although no specific rehearsal sequences are illustrated here, the director may develop these using the methods of presentation discussed earlier, along with the questions and/or statements presented for each.

Rhythm. Rhythm is the durational division of sound and silence into long, short, regular, and irregular groupings. To analyze the music and establish rehearsal priorities regarding the performance of rhythm, the director might consider the following list of (a) questions for students and (b) statements to be generated in discussion.

Questions
1. Do the focal points of music always coincide with the strong beats of the metric structure?
2. Do the groupings of the notes match rhythmically the direction of a melody?
3. What is the role of silence?
4. What is the character of the rhythms? Are they galloping, solemn, dancelike, bold, majestic?
5. How does a particular rhythm fit into the rhythm of the entire ensemble?
6. Are the rhythms played accurately?

Statements
1. It takes imagination to perform rhythms vibrantly.
2. The metric structure of music is of major importance in determining its dynamic form. Meter provides a background series of pulses of different strength, within which, and against which, rhythmic patterns develop.
3. The metric framework enables the performer and the audience to time the evolution of the musical impulse and anticipate its moment of release.
4. Rhythm must be internalized rather than externalized. The performer must feel it with the whole body, understanding it, enjoying its particular nature, and projecting it with flexibility.
5. All notes barred together do not necessarily receive the same weight.

Texture. Texture involves vertical organization of sounds in a simultaneous unit, the qualities created by the density of the simultaneous pitches, or the accumulation of individual lines. Texture is determined by the composer's voicings, and each composer makes a unique choice in doubling and placing of overtones and color tones. To help students analyze the music and establish rehearsal priorities regarding performance factors in terms of texture, the director might ask the following questions.

Questions

1. Is the texture open or closed? How does this affect the mood of the work?
2. How are the various lines distributed among the voices? Does this weaving together of musical lines create music that is lacy, rough, woven, variegated, or homogeneous?
3. What are the relationships between various parts? Are they contrapuntal, homophonic, chordal, or melody with accompaniment?
4. What is the density of the voices? How much spaciousness surrounds them? Are they trellis-like, solid, or variegated? Are they transparent, opaque, diffused, or concentrated? What is the mood created by this density?

The following sections address some possible rehearsal priorities, based on basic performance techniques and concepts found in the Standards. Using the methods discussed earlier in this chapter and the questions and/or statements for each technique, the director can establish rehearsal situations that might lead to better understanding.

Tone quality. Sensitivity to tone should be established early. Listening to poor tone, whether self-produced or otherwise, will not create a desirable tonal image. To help students analyze music and establish rehearsal priorities regarding tone quality and performance, the director might consider the following questions.

Questions

1. What is the characteristic tone for a particular instrument?
2. How do you determine the appropriate tone color required by the music for a particular instrument?
3. Is the color of the sound the same throughout the entire work?
4. When, if ever, should one instrument or group of instruments in an ensemble attempt to match the color of another instrument or group of instruments?
5. Does a certain volume dictate a particular tone quality?

Style. Style is a combination of elements such as tone color, method of articulation, and dynamic interpretation based on the understanding of history and performance practice. To help students analyze music and establish rehearsal priorities regarding style in performance, the director might ask the following questions.

Questions

1. How should the tone begin?
2. How should the tone be sustained?
3. How should the tone be released?
4. Is there an emphasis of some kind at the beginning of a particular note? If so, what type?
5. How loud is *forte?*
6. Should the tone quality be bright, warm, focused, clear, or pure?
7. Should vibrato be used? If so, how

fast and where in the phrase or tone?

8. How is a particular twentieth-century technique performed?

9. How fast is *andante?*

Dynamics. Dynamics are the words, abbreviations, and signs that indicate relative degrees of volume in the performance of music. To help students analyze music and establish rehearsal priorities regarding dynamics and performance, the director might ask the following questions.

Questions

1. How do you determine the appropriate volume at which a particular *piano, forte,* or *mezzoforte* should be performed?

2. How do you make sure markings such as *sf* or any sudden dynamic change fulfill their function?

3. At what rate and what pace should the *crescendo* and *diminuendo* change?

4. Does the *forte* dynamic level remain the same for all instruments in all ranges?

Intonation. Intonation in ensemble performance is the ability of the performer to hear, adjust, and perform music in tune. The ears and minds of performers should be trained to hear exact tuning of intervals linearly and relationships vertically. Unison playing is an important method of developing discipline in terms of intonation. In addition, in unison playing the individual must submit to the group and still maintain the inspiration and freedom of a soloist. To help students analyze the music and establish rehearsal priorities regarding intonation in performance, the director might ask the following questions.

Questions

1. Are embouchure, air, hand position, posture, fingering, and tone color conducive for playing in tune in a particular spot?

2. What is the natural tendency of the instrument on this note?

3. Why is it important to play in tune linearly as well as vertically?

4. How does the color of the tone affect intonation?

Blend. Blend in musical performance is the mixing of tones to merge or unite them into one unique sound. To help students analyze the music and establish rehearsal priorities regarding blend in performance, the director might ask the following questions.

Questions

1. What is the timbral compatibility or tone color of those playing the same part?

2. Is each individual playing in tune with those who have the same part?

3. Is each individual playing the same dynamic level as those in the rest of the section who have the same part?

Balance. Balance in performance is the imaginary weighing of elements in the musical sound to provide a pleasing proportion among the various groups of instruments. To help students analyze the music and establish rehearsal priorities regarding balance in performance, the director might ask the following questions.

Questions

1. How do individuals determine how loud to play their parts?
2. How do individuals determine what function their parts play in the overall scheme (melody, harmony, accompaniment, etc.)?
3. What function does a particular note have in the harmonic structure?
4. What color should a particular tone possess to make its volume balance properly?

Technique. Technique means basic skills and the degree of expertise with which they are used in the performance of a musical work. In a rehearsal, the director, in effect, "practices the musicians" by leading them through a sequence of events that facilitate the correction and understanding of a specific problem. With a conscientious approach, the director can help students learn how to practice technique on their own. To help establish rehearsal priorities regarding technique in band and orchestra performance, the following statements might be generated in discussion.

Statements

1. Fingers must stay close to the strings, keys, or valves of instruments during a fast passage in order to make it sound as though it is being performed with ease.
2. The bow on string instruments or air on wind instruments must be used to reinforce other factors demanded by the performance of a specific work.
3. Increased difficulty of a particular pattern or rhythm must not dictate increased volume.
4. Practicing figures slowly, then gradually increasing speed, will help with the performance of awkward passages.
5. Practicing figures forward and stopping on each note several times before going to the beginning of the figure and moving on will help develop control of difficult passages.
6. Slowly work backward from the end of a figure, one note at a time, gradually adding notes as the beginning is approached, and then increase the tempo. This will help develop control of difficult passages.
7. Playing difficult passages using different rhythms will help develop control of these passages.

Discovery through Decision Making

Teaching methodology must include the ability to match knowledge and skill with the appropriate level of challenge. Guiding students to learn critical thinking skills and understanding requires that younger groups have a longer rehearsal time because of the developmental nature of this kind of knowledge. If approached appropriately, critical thinking skills and understanding become intrinsic as students gain more experience. Even when students with relatively different levels of knowledge and skills work together in an ensemble, it is still possible for each individual to reach a level of musical understanding that corresponds to his or her ability to conceptualize musically.

When students' knowledge and skills match a given challenge, they are able to reach the highest degree of understanding for their level of musicianship without becoming bored or frustrated. The director who has a performing group with a wide range of knowledge and skills must plan carefully. One student may reach only the correct note and rhythm stage, while another may be considering dynamic adjustment in a melodic line to give flow and momentum to the music. Discovery through decision making guides students to increased understanding.

By understanding or participating in the decision-making process, students can also learn to listen and monitor the sounds they produce and develop the potential to hear the music mentally. Intense personal and physical involvement through performance helps students feel and live the sounds they produce. Understanding the decision-making process and using individual musical elements for expression allows students to gain a sense of freedom and mold the performance intensity. When students are allowed to conceptualize these inner experiences, they respond with commitment and joy.

Students as Self Critics

One of the most important things that directors of bands or orchestras must teach students is the technique of good practice in the absence of the director. Consistency in the rehearsal process prepares students to evaluate and analyze on their own. Students must be able to observe and criticize themselves while practicing or they will continue making the same mistakes. The director works to nurture the decision-making process that students use for skillful handling of musical elements in performance. This allows them to see the individual elements without losing sight of the whole work.

The ability to conduct a personal critique is central to students' ability to experience a disciplined and effective performance process. Students who do not consider character and musical message frequently perform music in a sterile and unmusical manner and become easily bored and frustrated with the technical nature of the challenges that confront them. Furthermore, if the developmental aspect of understanding is emphasized, a reexamination of a work will invariably lead to greater depth of understanding. When students first begin to understand a musical idea, they respond with the excitement one feels in the presence of something new and beautiful. One of the greatest joys in performing is to return to a work performed in the past and discover new levels of meaning. This can be accomplished best by scheduling more than one performance of a piece or by revisiting a piece for future performance.

As educators, ensemble directors, and conductors, we must continually reevaluate and improve our teaching methodology to provide the most effective learning experiences we can for our students. At all levels we must become concerned with not only how we teach but what we teach, as well as with what the students learn. Students who choose not to continue to perform, even for their own pleasure, have not experienced rewarding rehearsals. Directors must love their work and be committed to developing students who will enjoy making music.

Music education applies not only to knowledge or technical skill but also to integrity, character building, and the appreciation of beauty. Music students who have enjoyed participating in a program that leads to musical motivation become nobler people. Playing an instrument in a band or orchestra in which the director facilitates the development of understanding and emotion in music puts students in contact with their physical and emotional being in a very powerful way. Pure technique fails if the emotional and expressive aspects of the music are not comprehended.

Using the methods discussed in this chapter, instrumental groups will improve greatly, and students and their directors will enjoy richer, more refined experiences. These methods facilitate the development of musical understanding and independence and develop a desire in students to continue quality musical experiences throughout their lives.

8

Making the School Orchestra a Treasure
Teaching Musical Understanding through Performance

Robert Gillespie

This is an exciting time to be an orchestra teacher in the schools. The Standards challenge us to create a new vision for string instruction: comprehensive music teaching through performance. This new purpose requires a change in focus. Rather than having our primary goal be that of producing a polished large-ensemble performance, we must focus on enhancing students' performance learning through singing, improvising, composing and arranging, listening, evaluating, and understanding music in relation to other disciplines and in relation to history and culture. These activities recommended by the Standards will give our students new insight into their performance. As a result, their orchestral experience will become an even greater treasure.

Implementing the Standards also give us opportunities to re-think our roles as orchestra teachers, allowing us to broaden our students' learning beyond performance technique and repertoire. We can become orchestra *generalists*, rather than only orchestra *specialists*. The Standards do not dismiss what is central to an orchestral experience for children in the schools—learning how to play orchestral instruments and performing the many great masterworks for orchestra; instead, they better equip us to give our students a more profound arts experience by implementing the Standards through the unique repertoire of orchestra. Incorporating the Standards into our instruction will not become a burden. Rather, it will be an opportunity to help our students appreciate and value orchestral performance as an art form more than ever.

Incorporating the Standards into our rehearsals and concerts requires a new way of looking at our teaching. Teaching our students to perform with understanding, as described in the National Standards, will require work, but the fruit of our labor will be a deeper experience in the art of orchestral music and of all music. And, after all, school orchestra teachers are serious about seeking new ideas to make their teaching and their students' learning more effective. Data from a recent study indicate that four out of every five certified string teachers have attended an orchestra teacher workshop during the last five years.[1] The National Standards for Music Education have given those of us involved in teaching orchestra in the schools an opportunity to reexamine our teaching strategies.

Applying the Standards in Rehearsal through Repertoire

One of the best ways to apply the Standards to our teaching is to select repertoire that lends itself to teaching toward the Standards. The following are some guidelines for selecting such repertoire:

1. Use only high-quality literature that is reasonably within the playing skills of students. If the music is too difficult to perform, it will become an obstacle to students' learning.

2. Select only music that is expressive. Literature that does not lend itself to musical expression is not worth our time or that of our students.

3. Select a wide range of repertoire, varied in genre, style, and culture.

4. Select music written by a compos-

er whose biography is available so that you can make correlations with historical events and artistic developments.

5. If you are considering an arrangement, be sure the score and parts of the original are available so that students can compare them to the arrangement.

Recommended Strategies for Integrating the Standards into Rehearsals

Evaluate how you are already teaching toward the National Standards, and use the achievement standards listed under each of the nine content standards to guide your teaching. Integrate them into your school orchestra rehearsals by using one or more of the following strategies in each rehearsal.

1. Discuss the life and contributions of the composer.

2. Provide the words to the melody if the work is based on a song. Have students sing the melody and discuss the difference they experience musically when they play it on their instruments as opposed to singing it.

3. Play recordings of different performances of the work, and involve students in evaluations of the quality of the performances. Use one musical aspect at a time: tempo, dynamics, intonation, phrasing, style, expressiveness, balance, and so forth.

4. Discuss important events that occurred during the life of the composer, and have students comment on whether there seem to be any relationships between these events and the composer's work.

5. Discuss important developments that occurred in music during the life of the composer, and have students consider ways in which these developments may have influenced the composer's work, or the role the composer played in these developments.

6. Discuss important developments that occurred in the arts during the life of the composer, and have students explore ways in which these developments may have influenced the composer's work.

7. Discuss developments that occurred in fields other than the arts (e.g., mathematics or science) during the life of the composer, and have students identify ways in which these developments may have influenced the composer's work.

8. Provide scores of the work so that you can effectively help students discern its form and structure, trace the development of melodies, and understand how their instrument's part compares to that of other instruments in the composition.

9. Play and have students listen to and discuss other works by the composer to help them gain an understanding of the sound unique to that composer's music.

10. Allow students to help determine appropriate tempi, styles, and phrasing for performance of the work.

11. Have students compare arrangements to the original. Provide recordings and scores of the original for discussion.

12. Teach composition by having students use parameters related to the work, such as meter, key, phrase lengths, characteristic rhythms and motives, and so forth in composing a melody for their

instrument. Have them improvise on a melody from the work, keeping the style consistent with it. Have students perform their solutions.

Suggested Rehearsal Strategies for Integrating the Standards with School Orchestra Repertoire

The following are nineteen selected works for school orchestra, along with practical suggestions for incorporating the Standards while rehearsing the works. After reviewing the compositions and their related teaching suggestions, you will see that incorporating the Standards into orchestral classes is possible, practical, and exciting.

Start by trying to include a few of the teaching suggestions in each class. You will find your students receptive, and you will still have time to get all of those "high twos and low twos" in tune. However, now your students will leave the rehearsal with a greater understanding (through performance) of the arts and how they relate to history and everyday life.

For ease of reference, the literature mentioned here is grouped by graded levels of difficulty and by instrumentation (string orchestra versus full orchestra): grade 1 string orchestra literature, grades 2 and 3 string orchestra literature frequently performed at the middle school level, grades 2 and 3 full orchestra literature common to middle school orchestra, grades 3–6 string orchestra literature typically performed at the high school level, and grades 3–6 full orchestra music common to the high school level. The music was selected because it is standard concert repertoire that is readily available for purchase or available in many school orchestra libraries.

Following each graded level is a list of additional repertoire that lends itself to integrating the National Standards. The music listed is of high quality and is musically satisfying. Various genres and styles are represented. Unfortunately, few examples of music from other cultures are included because, at present, that literature is neither standard nor easily accessible. It is hoped that as we incorporate the Standards into string/ orchestra classes, publishers will provide much more music from other cultures that is appropriate for school orchestra.

Be sure to involve students in making musical decisions during rehearsal. This gives students yet another opportunity to perform with deeper understanding. Also educate parents and administrators at performances by demonstrating students' work toward achieving the Standards. As they see students perform with greater understanding, their appreciation of the value of the orchestra as a part of the school curriculum will deepen.

Strategies for Grade 1 String Orchestra Literature

"Cripple Creek," arr. Siennicki, Highland-Etling/Alfred Publishing Company

Standard 3: Improvising melodies, variations, and accompaniments

Teaching strategy:

a. Discuss the concept of improvisation and how fiddlers frequently improvise while playing bluegrass music. Give an example of how to improvise on open strings by simply changing rhythms, dynamics, or articulations. Ask students to improvise on an open D and then an open A string by bowing different rhythms. Also, have one section of the orchestra play the "Cripple Creek" melody, followed by students improvising on open strings. Then have another section play the melody, followed by another section improvising.

Standard 6: Listening to, analyzing, and describing music

Teaching strategies:

a. Discuss the elements of bluegrass music and mention that it is based on blues scales and modes such as the Mixolydian, which has a lowered seventh scale degree.

b. Have students listen to a recording or perform for them other examples of bluegrass fiddle tunes such as "Old Joe Clark." Have them describe the similarities in style, tempo, and bluegrass sound.

c. Play a recording of bluegrass music that is performed by a bluegrass band. Discuss the instrumentation of a typical bluegrass band: banjo, guitar, mandolin, bass, and fiddle.

d. Have students compare the sounds of the "Cripple Creek" melody when it is played by the violins and violas versus the cellos and basses. Introduce the concepts of range and timbre.

Standard 7: Evaluating music and music performances

Teaching strategy:

a. Have students perform "Cripple Creek" in a legato style at a slow tempo. Ask them to evaluate the effect of that style of performance compared to a faster, dance-like style that is more traditional for bluegrass. Ask students which performance is more dance-like and why.

New World Symphony—Theme, by Dvořák, arr. Allen, in *Essential Elements for Strings,* Hal Leonard Corporation

Standard 1: Singing, alone and with others, a varied repertoire of music

Teaching strategy:

a. Have students sing the melody as you accompany them on the piano. Discuss the musical characteristics of the melody and how their expressive singing of it can be translated into expressive playing.

Standard 6: Listening to, analyzing, and describing music

Teaching strategies:

a. Show students one example from the score of the original symphony and discuss with them how it is different from their arrangement in range and instrumentation. [*Also Standard 5*]

b. Play excerpts of the melody from a recording of the original symphony. Have students compare the original melody to the melody in the arrangement and discuss the differences.

c. Play recordings of other Dvořák compositions, and have students compare them to the *New World* Symphony.

Standard 7: Evaluating music and music performances

Teaching strategy:

a. Play two different recordings of excerpts from the original symphony, and have students describe differences in the performances. Discuss the relative merits of the two interpretations.

Standard 9: Understanding music in relation to history and culture

Teaching strategy:

a. Discuss the life of Dvořák, particularly the time he spent in America. Explain why Dvořák gave this symphony the subtitle *From the New World.* Describe historical events that took place during Dvořák's lifetime, such as the completion of the transcontinental railroad and the American Civil War. Explore the ways in which Dvořák's symphony reflects both his nationalism and the spirit of nineteenth-century Americans who were part of a growing westward movement. [*Also Standard 8*]

"Happy Hoedown," by Chase, Hal Leonard Corporation

Standard 1: Singing, alone and with others, a varied repertoire of music

Teaching strategy:

a. Provide words to a hoedown song such as "Camptown Races," and have students sing the song. Discuss how their singing can emphasize its stylistic characteristics, and how their playing of it would also have to do so.

Standard 3: Improvising melodies, variations, and accompaniments
Teaching strategy:
a. By rote, teach the fiddle song "Bile Them Cabbage Down." Once learned, have students separately play improvisations, taking turns doing so. Then, while one student improvises, have another clap an improvised accompaniment.

Standard 6: Listening to, analyzing, and describing music
Teaching strategies:
a. Play recordings of selected hoedown songs (e.g., "Turkey in the Straw" or "Arkansas Traveler"), and have students describe the characteristics such songs have in common.
b. Play recordings of various fiddlers performing the same fiddle tune. Have students compare the performances and describe differences in melodic embellishments, style, and tempo. [*Also Standard 7*]

Standard 8: Understanding relationships between music, the other arts, and disciplines outside the arts
Teaching strategy:
a. Describe how traditional fiddle tunes and hoedown songs are passed aurally from one fiddler to the next. Discuss the aural tradition of folk songs and folk stories.

Standard 9: Understanding music in relation to history and culture
Teaching strategies:

a. Discuss life in the Wild West and how hoedown music was a part of it.
b. Have students dance a hoedown. Perform this piece in a concert with some students dancing a hoedown. Point out how the dancers move to the pulse, as do the string players' bows when students are performing.

"Ode to Joy," by Beethoven, arr. Caponegro, Kendor Music

Standard 1: Singing, alone and with others, a varied repertoire of music
Teaching strategy:
a. Have students sing the melody of "Ode to Joy," noting the musical demands it makes in order to achieve its powerful expressiveness. Discuss how singing the melody clarifies how it must be played, retaining the same spirit but without words.

Standard 2: Performing on instruments, alone and with others, a varied repertoire of music
Teaching strategy:
a. Have students play Caponegro's arrangement as chamber music with one student on a part. Discuss the difference between performing in a chamber group and in an orchestra. Show students the score of one of Beethoven's string quartets, and play a recording of it, asking students to listen for characteristics of chamber music performances that they identified in the discussion. [*Also standard 6*]

Standard 5: Reading and notating music

Teaching strategy:

a. Show students the score of the last movement of Beethoven's Symphony no. 9, in which the theme "Ode to Joy" appears, and play a recording of this movement. Discuss how Caponegro's arrangement is different from the original. [*Also Standard 6*]

Standard 7: Evaluating music and music performances

Teaching strategy:

a. Play two recordings of the last movement of Beethoven's Symphony no. 9. Have students compare the performances for qualities such as rhythmic energy, tone color, phrasing, tempo, balance and blend, and use of dynamics. Which performance has the more musically powerful effect? Why? [*Also Standard 6*]

Standard 8: Understanding the relationships between music, the other arts, and disciplines outside the arts

Teaching strategies:

a. Have students read the Schiller poem "Ode to Joy," which Beethoven used as his text for the choral movement of Symphony no. 9. Discuss other examples of texts that composers have set to music.

b. Discuss the life of Beethoven (1770–1827), and have students identify events occurring in U.S. history during his lifetime (e.g., Lewis and Clark reached the Pacific coast; Florida was purchased from Spain). Explore the relationship between the way Beethoven exalted freedom in his music and the independent spirit of a young nation, both signalling a change

toward human valuing of freedom as essential for a good life.

Selected Grade 1 String Orchestra Literature for Implementing the Standards

---

American Folk Song Suite no. 1, arr. Isaac, Kendor Music

American Folk Song Suite no. 2, arr. Isaac, Kendor Music

American Folk Song Suite no. 3, arr. Isaac, Kendor Music

"Cripple Creek," arr. Siennicki, Highland-Etling/Alfred Publishing Company

Famous American Spirituals, arr. Frost, Kendor Music

"Gavotte," by Haydn, arr. Abbot, Kendor Music

Handel Suite, by Handel, arr. Leidig, Alfred Publishing Company

"Happy Hoedown," by Chase, Hal Leonard Corporation

"Little Fugue," by Handel, arr. Siennicki, Alfred Publishing Company

New World Symphony—Theme, by Dvořák, arr. Allen, in *Essential Elements for Strings,* Hal Leonard Corporation

"Ode to Joy," by Beethoven, arr. Caponegro, Kendor Music

Schubert Suite, by Schubert, arr. Errante, Boston Music Company

Two Hebrew Melodies, arr. Niehaus and Leidig, Alfred Publishing Company

Ukrainian Folk Songs, arr. Dackow, Ludwig Music Publishing Company

Water Music Suite and "March" from

Joshua, by Handel, arr. Goehring, in *String Masters,* Book 1, Ludwig Music Publishing Company

---

Strategies for Grades 2 and 3 String Orchestra Literature

Brandenburg Concerto no. 3, by Bach, arr. Isaac, Highland-Etling/ Alfred Publishing Company

Standard 3: Improvising melodies, variations, and accompaniments

Teaching strategy:

a. Explain that the second movement of this work is printed only as two chords because performers on the harpsichord freely improvised based on the chords. Teach students how to improvise a melody using the D major chord as a basis for the improvisation.

Standard 6: Listening to, analyzing, and describing music

Teaching strategies:

a. Play recordings of two contrasting performances of this work—one that uses Baroque instruments and one that uses modern instruments. Have students identify differences and similarities. Also, ask them to identify their preference and explain the reason for their selection. [*Also Standard 7*]

b. Play recordings of the other five *Brandenburg* concertos. Have students identify differences and similarities in tempo, articulation, and dynamics.

Standard 7: Evaluating music and music performances

Teaching strategy:

a. Play a recording of the original concerto and ask students to compare it to the arrangement they have been rehearsing. Discuss similarities and differences, focusing on differences in amount of musical detail, complexity, demands on technique, tone color, and so forth. Emphasize that an arrangement approximates an original, but cannot substitute for it.

Standard 8: Understanding relationships between music, the other arts, and disciplines outside the arts

Teaching strategy:

a. Show and discuss examples of works created in the other arts during the Baroque period (e.g., paintings by Rembrandt and sculpture by Bernini). Have students identify Baroque characteristics in these works and compare their great attention to detail and complexity to the *Brandenburg* Concerto no. 3, which has three different violin parts, three diffeent viola parts, and three different cello parts.

Standard 9: Understanding music in relation to history and culture

Teaching strategies:

a. Show students a Baroque bow and explain that bows such as this were used during Bach's lifetime. Have students describe how its shape is different from the shape of their bows, which are based on a design developed in the nineteenth century by Tourte in France. Demonstrate and have students describe the different sounds produced naturally with a Baroque bow, such as the stopped bow stroke.

b. Discuss the roles of composers in Baroque society (e.g., church musicians or court composers). Compare these roles to those of present-day composers (e.g., university professors, commissioned composers, or TV and film composers).

c. Discuss historical events that occurred in America during the Baroque period (e.g, the arrival of the Pilgrims or the establishment of the thirteen colonies). Emphasize that by the time the United States was becoming a country, Europe had created a flourishing civilization with very complex music, such as Bach's, and a social system to support work such as his. The new United States imported the music of Europe, and, as time went on, developed its own musical culture. This culture was based on that of Europe and the musical cultures of all the peoples of the world who came here to live, as well as those native Americans who lived here before people in the rest of the world started to move here.

"Can Can," by Offenbach, arr. Isaac, Wynn Music Publishers

Standard 4: Composing and arranging music within specified guidelines

Teaching strategy:

a. Have students play other student orchestra arrangements of "Can Can" (e.g., the Dackow arrangement, which is titled "Finale from Orpheus in the Underworld") and note some of the differences between them and the Isaac

arrangement. Then have them notate the melody of "Can Can" and compose a different accompaniment for it. [*Also Standard 5*]

Standard 6: Listening to, analyzing, and describing music

Teaching strategy:

a. Have students compare "Can Can" to other dance music (e.g., ballet, Baroque dance, hoedowns, rock and roll). Discuss characteristics common to all dance music, as well as characteristics particular to each type.

Standard 7: Evaluating music and music performances

Teaching strategy:

a. Have students perform "Can Can" in a legato style. Discuss why it does not sound like the lively dance style that Offenbach intended.

Standard 9: Understanding music in relation to history and culture

Teaching strategy:

a. Define "musical theater." Explain that Offenbach composed "Can Can" for musical theater in Paris in 1858. Discuss the musical theater of today and of Offenbach's time, and have students identify similarities and differences.

Danza, by Nelhybel, E. C. Kerby Music

Standard 4: Composing and arranging music within specified guidelines

Teaching strategy:

a. Describe how Nelhybel composed

Danza, basing it on a five-note theme (A-D-C-B-A). Have students compose a melody using only five pitches, as Nelhybel did.

Standard 5: Reading and notating music

Teaching strategy:

a. Have students write out the five-note theme as it appears in their parts in the first movement, and then have them sing it. Play recorded examples of serialism (twelve-tone rows), and have students compare this compositional technique to Nehlybel's five-note compositional technique. Ask students to compose a tone row, following its rules, and then try to sing it. Note the difficulties, and compare it with the difficulty of Nelhybel's melody. [*Also Standards 1, 4, and 6*]

Standard 6: Listening to, analyzing, and describing music

Teaching strategy:

a. Play recorded examples and discuss the music of Nelhybel. Have students identify and describe characteristics of his music and compare it to music from other historical periods, such as Baroque and Classical.

Standard 7: Evaluating music and music performances

Teaching strategy:

a. Have students play each of the three movements of *Danza* at tempos different from those Nelhybel suggested. Discuss which tempos the students like best and why, as well as whether a composition should be performed only at the tempos specified by the composer, raising the issue of a composer's intention and the interpreter's freedom to alter that intention. Are there, or should there be, limits to how much an interpreter (performer/conductor) can do to change the original instructions given by the composer?

Standard 8: Understanding relationships between music, the other arts, and disciplines outside the arts

Teaching strategy:

a. Discuss how compositions are commissioned. Explain that *Danza* was commissioned for the Manchester College String Festival in Manchester, Indiana, and that it was first performed in 1971. Give examples of famous works commissioned in the other arts, such as Picasso's *Guernica.* Have students compare the role of a commissioned composer to that of artists commissioned to create works in other arts disciplines, focusing on the various decisions that might be involved for each art: length of the music, length of a dance, size of a painting or sculpture; different costs of producing a musical performance, a play, a drawing, or a poem; appropriate words in literary arts, appropriate mood/expression in music or a painting, and so forth.

"Mock Morris," by Grainger, arr. Dackow, Ludwig Music Publishing Company

Standard 2: Performing on instruments, alone and with others, a varied repertoire of music

Teaching strategy:

a. Have students study and perform music that has been written for string orchestra by well-known English composers other than Grainger (e.g., Vaughan Williams, Thomas Tallis, or Benjamin Britten). Ask them to describe similarities and differences between those composers' works and Grainger's. [*Also Standard 6*]

Standard 6: Listening to, analyzing, and describing music

Teaching strategies:

a. Explain that "Mock Morris" is based on Grainger's collection of short pieces for chamber music combinations of instruments. Discuss how a composer may take one of his or her earlier works and arrange it for a different publication. Show students the score of a string quartet version of Samuel Barber's *Adagio for Strings,* and have them compare it to his later arrangement of the work for string orchestra.

b. Have students discover, by looking at their parts and listening, where Grainger incorporates four different melodies into "Mock Morris." Use the melodies, rather than letters or measure numbers, as starting places during rehearsals.

c. Play recorded examples of Grainger's band compositions. Discuss how are they similar to and different from his string writing.

d. Point out how the violins are divided into three parts in "Mock Morris" instead of the traditional two parts. Play a recording and have students compare the score of this work to the score for *Brandenburg* Concerto no. 3, in which Bach divides all the string sections into three parts. Have them compare Bach's and Grainger's use of this technique.

e. Have students compare the Dackow arrangement to Grainger's original work. Discuss the similarities and differences.

f. This orchestral work is written in the style of traditional English Morris dance tunes. Play recorded examples of orchestral pieces that composers from other countries have written based on folk music (e.g., Copland's "Hoedown," from *Rodeo*). Discuss with students how the character of a melody may change depending on the way it is performed; e.g., legato versus staccato style, dance-like versus subdued, faster versus slower tempo, or Classical versus Romantic style.

Selected Grades 2 and 3 String Orchestra Literature for Implementing the Standards in the Middle School

---

"Ah, God from Heaven Therein," by Pachelbel, arr. Bender, MSB

"Air," from the *Peasant* Cantata, by Bach, arr. Gordon, Kendor Music

"Allegro," from Concerto Grosso, op. 6, no.1, by Handel, arr. Dackow, Ludwig Music Publishing Company

"Allegro for Strings," from Sonata, op. 1, no. 3, by Handel, arr. Frackenpohl, Ludwig Music Publishing Company

"Asia Minor," by Shapiro, Neil A. Kjos Music Company

"Beginning Bach," arr. Wieloszynski, Kendor Music

Bartók Suite, arr. Clark, Belwin/Warner Bros. Publications

Brandenburg Concerto no. 1, by Bach, arr. Leidig, Highland-Etling/Alfred Publishing Company

Brandenburg Concerto no. 2, by Bach, arr. Isaac, Highland-Etling/Alfred Publishing Company

Brandenburg Concerto no. 3, by Bach, arr. Isaac, Highland-Etling/Alfred Publishing Company

Brandenburg Concerto no. 4, by Bach, arr. Leidig, Highland-Etling/Alfred Publishing Company

Brandenburg Concerto no. 5, by Bach, arr. Isaac, Highland-Etling/Alfred Publishing Company

"Can Can," by Offenbach, arr. Isaac, Wynn Music Publishers

Concerto in D Major, by Bach, arr. Isaac, Alfred Publishing Company

Concerto in G: Allegro, by Vivaldi, arr. Franckenpohl, Ludwig Music Publishing Company

Corelli Suite, arr. Leidig, Alfred Publishing Company

Czech Folk Song Suite, arr. Isaac, Highland-Etling/Alfred Publishing Company

Danza, by Nelhybel, E. C. Kerby Music

"Farandole," by Bizet, arr. Isaac, Highland-Etling/Alfred Publishing Company

"Fiesta," arr. Conley, Warner Bros. Publications

"Finale," from Overture to *William Tell,*

by Rossini, arr. Dackow, Ludwig Music Publishing Company

"Finale from Orpheus in the Underworld," by Offenbach, arr. Dackow, Ludwig Music Publishing Company

"Flop Eared Mule," arr. Dabczynski, Boosey & Hawkes

French Renaissance Suite, arr. Leclaire, Warren Music

"Golden Slippers," arr. Rolland, Rolland Strings

"Hornpipe," by Handel, arr. Meyer, Highland-Etling/Alfred Publishing Company

"Korean Folk Tune," arr. Meyer, Highland-Etling/Alfred Publishing Company

"Meramec Polka," by Halen, Wingert-Jones Music

"Mock Morris," by Grainger, arr. Dackow, Ludwig Music Publishing Company

"O Mio Babbino Caro," by Puccini, arr. Heilmann, Heilmann Music

"Pezzo," from *Serenade for Strings,* by Tchaikowsky, arr. Del Borgo, Kendor Music

"Rondo in D Major," by Haydn, arr. Kaisershot, MSB

Symphony no. 1 in D Major: Second Movement, by Mahler, arr. Dackow, Ludwig Music Publishing Company

Symphony no. 15 in G Major: Finale, by Mozart, arr. Dackow, Ludwig Music Publishing Company

"Tango in D," by Albeniz, arr. Siennicki, Highland-Etling/Alfred Music Company

"Tennessee Waltz," arr. Rolland, Rolland

Strings

Themes from the "1812 Overture," by Tchaikovsky, arr. Niehaus and Leidig, Highland-Etling/Alfred Publishing Company

Themes from *The Moldau,* by Smetana, arr. Frost, Kendor Music

Theme from *Schindler's List,* by Williams, arr. Higgins, Hal Leonard Corporation

Themes from *Swan Lake,* by Tchaikovsky, arr. Halferty, Kendor Music

"Twist and Shout," by Russel and Medley, arr. Cerulli, Warner Bros. Publications

Two South American Tangos, by Villodo and Rodriguez, arr. Isaac, Alfred Publishing Company

Ukrainian Folk Songs: "Flirtation," arr. Dackow, Ludwig Music Publishing Company

"Vivaldi Magnificat," arr. Alshin, Kendor Music

"Waltz," from *Serenade for Strings,* by Tchaikovsky, arr. Del Borgo, Kendor Music

Water Music Suite, by Handel, arr. Etling, Highland-Etling/Alfred Music Company

---

Strategies for Grades 2 and 3 Full Orchestra Literature

"Hatikvah," by Ovanin, Ludwig Music Publishing Company

Standard 1: Singing, alone and with others, a varied repertoire of music
Teaching strategy:
a. Have students sing the first melody in "Hatikvah." Then have them perform it on their instruments, alone and with others. Discuss how the character of "Hatikvah" stays the same whether an instrument or voice performs it, and discuss the reason for this. [*Also Standard 2*]

Standard 4: Composing and arranging music within specified guidelines
Teaching strategy:
a. The form of "Hatikvah" is a fantasy variation. Have students notate a familiar melody and then compose a variation of the melody. Ask them to perform their variations. [*Also Standard 5*]

Standard 5: Reading and notating music
Teaching strategy:
a. Have students notate the old Hebrew melody that this composition is based upon. Then have them analyze the score to determine where the melody appears throughout the composition. [*Also Standard 6*]

Standard 6: Listening to, analyzing, and describing music
Teaching strategies:
a. Have students listen while following the score to determine how the composer varies the basic melody throughout the work.
b. Play recordings of other examples of Hebrew music. Discuss the music's characteristic sound.
c. Compare "Hatikvah" to other pieces based on Hebrew music. Discuss the similarities and differences.

Standard 7: Evaluating music and music performances

Teaching strategy:

a. Based on their evaluation of their performance during rehearsals, allow students to help make musical decisions regarding the many tempo changes throughout the piece. Ask students to explain their reasoning for suggested tempos changes.[*Also Standard 2*]

Standard 9: Understanding music in relation to history and culture

Teaching strategy:

a. Have students research the role of music in the life of the early Hebrew people. [Music was the center of their culture and everyday life, and all people in the Hebrew culture performed music daily.] Then have them contrast it with the role of music in American society today.

"Emperor Waltz," by Strauss, arr. Meyer, RBC Publications

Standard 4: Composing and arranging music within specified guidelines

Teaching strategy:

a. Ask students to compose and perform a simple eight-measure waltz-like melody in the style of Strauss. Then have them try doing it in a contrasting style—modern, or jazz-like, and so forth.

Standard 6: Listening to, analyzing, and describing music

Teaching strategies:

a. Have students define "waltz" and describe its unique characteristics based on waltzes they have heard. Then have them notate and compare the melody

of "Emperor Waltz" to the definition and characteristics of a waltz. [*Also Standard 5*]

b. Discuss the simple harmonic structure of waltzes. Have students compare that structure to the harmonic structure of popular musical genres such as rock and roll.

c. Play a recording of the original piece and have students compare it to the Meyer arrangement, discussing similarities and differences.

d. Play recordings of some of the many other waltzes that Strauss composed, and have students discuss similarities between them and the "Emperor Waltz."

Standard 7: Evaluating music and music performances

Teaching strategy:

a. Play several recordings of professional performances of the "Emperor Waltz." Have students evaluate the quality and effectiveness of the performances, explaining the criteria they are using to do so.

Standard 8: Understanding relationships between music, the other arts, and disciplines outside the arts

Teaching strategy:

a. Discuss other prominent composers and artists who lived at the same time as Strauss (1825–99), such as Brahms, Tchaikovsky, Monet, and Manet. Have students identify characteristics of their works and make comparisons between those works and Strauss's work.

"Hungarian Dance" no. 5, by Brahms, arr. Bauernschmidt, Wynn Music Publishers

Standard 5: Reading and notating music

Teaching strategy:

a. Show students the score to this arrangement of Brahms's "Hungarian Dance" no. 5. Have them determine how many different melodies there are [two] and mark them in the score. Ask them to describe how the melodies are different. Then have them sing one of the melodies. Discuss how Brahms changes the instrumentation, dynamics, and range of each melody as it appears throughout the piece. Have students listen for these changes as you play a recording or as they perform the piece. Make a list of all the changes students are able to identify. Use this list as one basis for an "informance," to demonstrate to an audience the analytic thinking musicians must do. [*Also Standards 1, 2, and 6*]

Standard 6: Listening to, analyzing, and describing music

Teaching strategies:

a. Play recordings of symphonic works by Brahms and of classical composers such as Haydn and Mozart, and have students describe the differences between Brahms's music and that of the classical composers.

b. Play recorded examples of Hungarian gypsy music, and have students compare the style of that music to the style of Brahms's *Hungarian Dances.*

c. Play recorded examples of Dvořák's *Slavonic Dances,* and have students compare them to Brahms's *Hungarian Dances.* Discuss the similarities and differences.

Standard 7: Evaluating music and music performances

Teaching strategy:

a. Show students the score of the original "Hungarian Dance" no. 5 by Brahms and play a recording of it. Discuss how it is similar and how it is slightly different from the Bauernschmidt arrangement. Based on criteria they develop, discuss the effectiveness of the arrangement.

Selected Grades 2 and 3 Full Orchestra Literature for Implementing the Standards in the Middle School

---

A Boyce Suite, arr. Benoy, Oxford University Press

"Carillon," from *L'arlésienne Suite* no. 1, by Bizet, arr. Stone, Boosey & Hawkes

Concerto in A Minor, by Telemann, arr. Errante, Highland-Etling/Alfred Publishing Company

"Emperor Waltz," by Strauss, arr. Meyer, RBC Publications

Finale from the *Surprise* Symphony, by Haydn, arr. Niehaus and Leidig, Highland-Etling/Alfred Publishing Company

"Handel Celebration," arr. Isaac, Warner Bros. Publications

"Hatikvah," by Ovanin, Ludwig Music Publishing Company

"Hungarian Dance" no. 5, by Brahms, arr. Bauernschmidt, Wynn Music Publishers

"Kalocsai Csardas," arr. Wilson, Kendor Music

"March Slav," by Tchaikovsky, arr. Herfurth, Carl Fischer

Midsummer Night's Dream, Selections, by Mendelssohn, arr. Meyer, Wynn Music Publishers

Norwegian Dances, by Grieg, arr. Isaac, Luck's Music Library

Peasant Suite, by Bartók, arr. Bauernschmidt, Wynn Music Publishers

Three Spirituals, arr. Elliot, Wynn Music Publishers

"Thunder and Lightning Polka," by Strauss, arr. Isaac, Wynn Music Publishers

Two South American Tangos, by Villodo and Rodriguez, arr. Isaac, Alfred Publishing Company

---

Strategies for Grades 3–6 String Orchestra Literature

"Allegro in D for Strings," by Vivaldi, arr. Frackenpohl, Ludwig Music Publishing Company

Standard 5: Reading and notating music

Teaching strategies:

a. Have students write out the opening melody of the "Allegro in D for Strings" and determine how many times it appears in the work.

b. Choose several simple two-measure phrases from this work. Notate them on the chalkboard or on an over-head transparency. Show them, one by one, to the orchestra, asking them to clap or sing what they see without your help. Then have them play the phrase to see how close they can get without your help. Then play the phrase on a recording while they follow the notation, clapping, singing, and playing, in turn.

Standard 6: Listening to, analyzing, and describing music

Teaching strategies:

a. Play recordings of other string music composed by Vivaldi. Describe his prolific concerto writing, noting that he composed more than four hundred concertos. Explain his important role in the development of the concerto form from the Baroque concerto grosso to the solo concerto.

b. Have students compare this string orchestra arrangement to the original Vivaldi concerto (Concerto for Two Trumpets in C Major, op. 46, no. 1) upon which it is based. Play a recording of the original concerto and have students evaluate the performance using criteria they have developed, related to technical ability, expressive power, imaginative interpretation, and stylistic appropriateness. [*Also Standard 7*]

Simple Symphony, by Britten, Oxford University Press

Standard 2: Performing on instruments, alone and with others, a varied repertoire of music

Teaching strategy:

a. Explain that *Simple Symphony* was

originally written for string quartet and that Britten added the double bass part when the work was published later for string orchestra. Divide students into chamber music groups and have them perform the work. Discuss how the experience of playing the work in an orchestra differs from playing it in a chamber group.

Standard 4: Composing and arranging music

Teaching strategy:

a. Explain to students that this work was based on music Britten composed between the ages of nine and twelve. Discuss the contributions of others who composed when they were children, such as Mendelssohn and Mozart. Have students compose one melody and perform it as their "serenade for strings" (see Standard 6 below). [*Also Standard 2*]

Standard 6: Listening to, analyzing, and describing and music

Teaching strategy:

a. Play recordings of other major compositions for string orchestra by English composers, and discuss similarities and differences. For example, have them contrast Elgar's *Serenade for Strings* with Tchaikovsky's or Dvořák's.

Standard 7: Evaluating music and music performances

Teaching strategy:

a. Play professional recordings of *Simple Symphony,* and have students discuss similarities and differences in style and interpretation.

Brazilian Images, by Diniz, Neil A. Kjos Music Company

Standard 2: Performing on instruments, alone and with others, a varied repertoire of music

Teaching strategy:

a. *Brazilian Images* is based on Brazilian folk music. Define "folk music" and have students play the melodies in the piece. Discuss how the melodies are similar to, yet distinctly different from, American folk melodies. Also have students compare the role of folk music in Brazilian culture to the role of folk music in America's culture. [*Also Standard 9*]

Standard 4: Composing and arranging music

Teaching strategy:

a. Discuss the structure of the first movement (a round) of *Brazilian Images.* Give students scores of this movement and have them mark the round's multiple appearances. Have them play this movement, while listening particularly for the appearances of the round. Then have them sing a familiar American round (e.g., "Row, Row, Row Your Boat"). Ask them to compose a simple four-measure round. [*Also Standards 1, 2, and 6*].

Standard 6: Listening to, analyzing, and describing music

Teaching strategies:

a. The third movement of *Brazilian Images* is based on a Brazilian dance. Discuss the melody and what makes it sound like a dance. For comparison, play recorded examples of American dance music (e.g., big band, country, and rock and roll), and have students discuss the similarities and differences.

b. Play recordings and discuss music by the great Brazilian composer Villa-Lobos. Have students compare his music to that of Diniz.

Standard 9: Understanding music in relation to history and culture
Teaching strategy:
a. Discuss the life and culture of Brazil and have students compare it to American culture. Also discuss the influence of Brazilian culture on Diniz's work.

St. Paul's Suite, by Holst, Edwin F. Kalmus & Company

Standard 2: Performing on instruments, alone and with others, a varied repertoire of music
Teaching strategies:
a. Define "suite." Have students perform and listen to recordings of other suites for orchestra, such as those by Bach. Discuss how the Bach suites are similar to Holst's *St. Paul's Suite.* Have students compare a Baroque gigue to the first movement ("Jig") of Holst's suite. [*Also Standard 6*]
b. Discuss Holst's dedication of his suite to the St. Paul's Girls' School orchestra. Have students play Holst's *Brook Green Suite,* another orchestral work he composed for the St. Paul's orchestra. Discuss how this suite is similar to and different from *St. Paul's Suite.* Point out that another well-known

string composer, Vivaldi, also wrote many works for a girls' school. [*Also Standard 6*]

Standard 6: Listening to, analyzing, and describing music
Teaching strategy:
a. Play a recording of Holst's transcription of *St. Paul's Suite* for band, and discuss how the same work can sound strikingly different when performed by a different instrumental ensemble. Have students compare recordings of orchestral works with transcriptions of these works for band or chorus (e.g., a choral performance of Barber's *Adagio for Strings*). [*Also Standard 7*]

Standard 7: Evaluating music and music performances
Teaching strategy:
a. Discuss the compositional technique that Holst used in the fourth movement of *St. Paul's Suite* (i.e., having two different melodies played at the same time). Have students compose two simple melodies, using the same key and meter for each, to be performed simultaneously. Pair up the students and have them perform their combined melodies for the class. Discuss and evaluate each of the pairings as to their musical interest. [*Also Standards 2 and 4*]

Australian Folk Suite, arr. Stephan, Neil A. Kjos Music Company

Standard 2: Performing on instruments, alone and with others, a varied repertoire of music

Teaching strategy:

a. Have students play each of the folk songs this suite is based upon. Then have them sing some American folk songs. Discuss how those songs are similar to and different from the Australian folk songs. [*Also Standard 1*]

Standard 4: Composing and arranging music within specified guidelines.

Teaching strategy:

a. Provide students with copies of the score for *Australian Folk Suite.* Select one of the three movements and ask students to find the melody. Have them study how the arranger changed the accompaniment throughout the movement. Have students write an accompaniment for a familiar folk melody (e.g., "Mary Had A Little Lamb"), using only I, IV, and V chords. Have students perform the solutions and assess their success in enhancing the melody. [*Also Standards 2 and 7*]

Standard 9: Understanding music in relation to history and culture

Teaching strategies:

a. Have students compare the last movement ("Bush Dance") of *Australian Folk Suite,* which is a native song favored by Queensland cattlemen, to American cowboy songs from the late 1800s (e.g., "Turkey in the Straw"). Discuss the similarities and differences among the melodies. Ask students what "lifestyle" difference of cowboys in the two cultures seem to be suggested by the songs.

b. *Australian Folk Suite* is based on three Australian folk songs. Ask students to select three American folk songs that they believe best represent America.

c. Discuss the culture of Australia, including why it is similar in many ways to American culture (e.g., both countries have roots in western Europe and they share similar folk song heritages through songs about cowboys and ranching).

Selected Grades 3–6 String Orchestra Literature for Implementing the Standards in the High School

---

Adagio for Strings, by Barber, Edwin F. Kalmus & Company

"Allegro in D for Strings," by Vivaldi, arr. Frackenpohl, Ludwig Music Publishing Company

"Ase's Death," from *Peer Gynt* Suite, second movement, by Grieg, Edwin F. Kalmus & Company

Australian Folk Suite, arr. Stephan, Neil A. Kjos Music Company

Barber of Seville, by Rossini, arr. McLeod, Neil A. Kjos Music Company

Brazilian Images, by Diniz, Neil A. Kjos Music Company

Brook Green Suite, by Holst, G. Schirmer

Capriccio Espagnole, by Rimsky-Korsakoff, arr. Dackow, Ludwig Music Publishing Company

"Choreography," by Dello Joio, Hal Leonard Corporation

Concerto Grosso, op. 6, nos. 1–7, 9–12, by Handel, Edwin F. Kalmus & Company

Concerto Grosso, op. 6, nos. 1–8, by Corelli, Edwin F. Kalmus & Company

Concerto Grosso for Piano and Strings, by Bloch, Broude Brothers Limited

Concerto Grosso for String Orchestra, by Vaughan Williams, Oxford University Press

Concerto in D Major, by Telemann, arr. Dowty, Wynn Music Publishers

Concerto in D Minor, first movement, by Bach, arr. Isaac, Highland-Etling/Alfred Publishing Company

Don Quixote Suite, by Telemann, Edwin F. Kalmus & Company

"Eine kleine Nachtmusik," by Mozart, Edwin F. Kalmus & Company

Five Pieces for String Orchestra, op. 44, no. 40, by Hindemith, European American Music Corporation

Holberg Suite, op. 40, by Holst, Edwin F. Kalmus & Company

"Hungarian Dance" no. 5, by Brahms, arr. Isaac, Highland-Etling/Alfred Publishing Company

Overture to *Lucio Silla,* by Mozart, arr. Isaac, Ludwig Music Publishing Company

Pastorale for String Orchestra, by Husa, Associated Music Publishers

Psalm & Fugue, op. 40a, by Hovhaness, C. F. Peters Corporation

Romanian Folk Dances, by Bartók, arr. Willner, Boosey & Hawkes

St. Paul's Suite, by Holst, Edwin F. Kalmus & Company

Serenade for Strings, op. 48, by Tchaikovsky, Edwin F. Kalmus & Company

Serenade in E Minor, op. 20, by Elgar, Edwin F. Kalmus & Company

Simple Symphony, by Britten, Oxford University Press

Symphony no. 8 in G Major, Finale, by Dvořák, arr. Dackow, Ludwig Music Publishing Company

Symphony no. 12 in G Major, first movement, by Mozart, arr. Dackow, Ludwig Music Publishing Company

Symphony no. 88, by Haydn, arr. Isaac, Wynn Music Publishers

Strategies for Grades 3–6 Full Orchestra Literature

Fidelio **Overture, op. 72, by Beethoven, arr. Isaac, Wynn Music Publishers**

Standard 6: Listening to, analyzing, and describing music

Teaching strategies:

a. The opera *Fidelio* was originally called *Leonore.* Beethoven typically struggled over his overtures, in this case writing four different versions. Play recordings of excerpts from his three *Leonore* overtures, and have students compare them to his *Fidelio* overture.

b. Play excerpts from a recording or video of the opera *Fidelio.* Have students discover how Beethoven summarizes all the principal themes of the opera in his overture. Have them compare *Fidelio* to an opera overture by

Mozart (e.g., *Don Giovanni* or *The Marriage of Figaro*). Are both composers successful in capturing a sense of the opera in their overtures? Discuss, having students explain the basis for their answers. [*Also Standard 7*]

c. Play a recording of the original overture, and have students compare it with the Isaac arrangement and describe the differences.

Symphony no. 12—First Movement, by Mozart, arr. Isaac, Wynn Music Publishers

Standard 2: Performing on instruments, alone and with others, a varied repertoire of music

Teaching strategies:

a. Have students perform excerpts from the other movements of Symphony no. 12 and discuss how they are related to the first movement. [*Also Standard 6*]

b. Have students play one of Mozart's early string quartets and compare it to this early symphony. [*Also Standard 6*]

Standard 6: Listening to, analyzing, and describing music

Teaching strategies:

a. Play a recording of the original symphony. Have students compare it to the Isaac arrangement and discuss the differences.

b. Play recordings of some of Mozart's later symphonies. Have students discuss how those symphonies are different from this early symphony.

Standard 9: Understanding music in relation to history and culture

Teaching strategies:

a. Play a recording of a Beethoven symphony. Have students discuss the differences between Beethoven's symphonic style in the Romantic period and that of Mozart's in the Classical period. Ask students what characteristics of the two different periods are exemplified in the two different musical styles.

b. Discuss the professional life of a composer during Mozart's time (e.g., that of a court composer) and contrast it with the professional lives of composers in America today. Invite a composer from the community to visit a rehearsal and present an explanation of this contrast.

The King's Musicians, by Lully, arr. Seay, Ludwig Music Publishing Company

Standard 2: Performing on instruments, alone and with others, a varied repertoire of music

Teaching strategy:

a. As a violinist in the court orchestra of Louis XV, Lully originated unison bowing among string sections, a technique that is used in virtually every orchestra today. Have students perform this piece with and without unison bowing. Discuss the differences in sounds produced. Also discuss why orchestras and conductors choose to use unison bowing today.

Standard 6: Listening to, analyzing, and describing music

Teaching strategy:

a. Select one of the five movements of this suite and have students study the score to determine how Lully treats the strings differently from the winds. Discuss how wind instruments were much different mechanically in Lully's lifetime (1632–87) than they are today; and discuss the implications of that difference for Lully in his writing for winds. Play a recording of an excerpt from one of Beethoven's later symphonies, and have students contrast Beethoven's wind writing with Lully's. [*Also Standards 5 and 9*]

Standard 9: Understanding music in relation to history and culture

Teaching strategy:

a. Discuss the life of musicians during Lully's time (e.g., how they were employed by courts, churches, municipal councils, patrons, or opera houses). Have students contrast this kind of life with that of today's professional string player.

Selected Grades 3–6 Full Orchestra Literature for Implementing the Standards in the High School

---

"Bacchanale," from *Samson and Delilah*, op. 47, by Saint-Saens, Edwin F. Kalmus & Company

Barber of Seville Overture, by Rossini, arr. Isaac, Wynn Music Publishers

"The Blue Danube," by Strauss, Edwin F. Kalmus & Company

Carmen Suite no. 1, by Bizet, Edwin F. Kalmus & Company

Egmont Overture, by Beethoven, Carl Fischer

"The Fair," from *Petrouchka,* by Stravinsky, arr. Isaac, CPP Belwin/Warner Bros. Publications

Fidelio Overture, op. 72, by Beethoven, arr. Isaac, Wynn Music Publishers

Fireworks Music, by Handel, arr. Gordon, Shapiro & Company— Educational

"Hoedown," from *Rodeo,* by Copland, Boosey & Hawkes

The King's Musicians, by Lully, arr. Seay, Ludwig Music Publishing Company

L'arlésienne Suite no. 1, Overture, by Bizet, Edwin F. Kalmus & Company

"Mexicana," arr. Bauernschmidt, Wynn Music Publisher

"A Mighty Fortress," by Nelhybel, E. C. Kerby Music

"Overture on Jewish Themes," by Gearhart, Shawnee Press

Pictures at an Exhibition, parts 1–5, by Mussorgsky, edited by Simpson, Masters Music Publications

"Russian Sailor's Dance," by Glier, arr. Errante, Alfred Publishing Company

"Sleeping Beauty Waltz," by Tchaikovsky, arr. Isaac, CPP Belwin/Warner Bros. Publications

Symphony no. 12—First Movement, by Mozart, arr. Isaac, Wynn Music Publishers

The Standards: A Blueprint for the School Orchestra Program

The National Standards are the blueprint for our orchestra programs. They give us benchmarks for assessing our instruction, rehearsals, music selection, and overall curriculum. None of us is qualified to teach all the Standards. Until very recently we were not prepared to do so in our college or university teacher preparation classes. However, we can use the Standards to help guide us as we continue our own education.

One of the best ways for string teachers to begin is by studying the American String Teacher Association publication *Standards for the Preparation of School String and Orchestra Teachers.* This publication is based on the National Standards for Music Education and describes the essential skills, knowledge, and concepts necessary for successfully teaching strings and orchestra in the schools. As you review the descriptions, select those areas in which you need additional training. Suggest those as topics to your school administrators for in-service meetings. Attend related sessions at your annual state music educator conference if they are offered. If they are not, consider contacting the conference planners and suggest that the sessions be offered.

Also, there are many summer workshops available for string teachers to attend sponsored by the American String Teachers Association, or by colleges and universities throughout the country. Use the Standards as your blueprint to review the content of the workshops and attend the summer sessions that best help you develop the skills necessary to teach toward the Standards. For example, if you need the skills to teach improvisation in your orchestra classes, attend a conference that offers improvisation experiences. In addition, review the many texts suggested as resources in the *Standards for the Preparation of School String and Orchestra Teachers.* The references include recommended pedagogical books, string class materials, graded music lists, videos, and a list of texts specifically written to help teach toward the National Standards in the school orchestra program.

As we look to the future of our standards-based profession, we should recommend to students interested in becoming string teachers that they enroll in those college and university degree programs that incorporate instruction for teaching toward the Standards in their preservice classes. Encourage the parents of these prospective string teachers to understand the Standards and see them as important criteria for evaluating the college or university their child may attend. *Standards for the Preparation of School String and Orchestra Teachers* describes the content of a string teacher preparation curriculum based on the National Standards. The document has the support of MENC and contains a statement from Carolynn Lindeman, MENC's immediate past president. In her statement Lindeman urges "those responsible for music teacher preparation programs to review and adopt these standards for successful string/orchestra teaching."[2] If our next generation of string teachers enters the profession prepared to teach toward the Standards, school string programs, and orchestras, will be strengthened in significant ways. The school orchestra will become even more of a treasure, where students will truly gain musical understanding through their performance.

Notes

1. Robert Gillespie and Donald L. Hamann, "The Status of Orchestra Programs in the Public Schools," *Journal of Research in Music Education* 46, no. 1 (1998): 84.

2. Carolynn Lindeman, introductory statement to *Standards for the Preparation of School String and Orchestra Teachers,* by the American String Teachers Association (Washington, DC: Tichenor Publishing, 1998).

Selected Resources

The following publications may be helpful in incorporating the National Standards into school orchestra rehearsals and tracing the development of historical, political, and artistic events.

Allen, Michael L. "The National Standards for Arts Education: Implications for School String Programs." *American String Teacher* 45, no. 3 (1995).

Allen, Michael L., Robert Gillespie, and Pamela Tellejohn Hayes. *Essential Elements for Strings: Teacher Resource Kit.* Milwaukee, WI: Hal Leonard Corporation, 1996.

American String Teachers Association. *Standards for the Preparation of School String and Orchestra Teachers.* Washington, DC: Tichenor Publishing, 1998.

Barber, David W. *Bach, Beethoven, and the Boys: Music History as It Ought to Be Taught.* Buffalo: Sound and Vision/Firefly Books, 1996.

Dabczynski, Andrew H. "National Standards for Arts Education: A Golden Opportunity for String Teachers." *American String Teacher* 45, no. 1 (1995).

Elledge, Chuck, Jane Yarbrough, and Bruce Pearson. *Music Theory & History Workbook.* 3 vols. San Diego, CA: Neil A. Kjos Music Company, 1993.

Grout, Donald J., and Claude V. Palisca. *A History of Western Music,* 5th ed. New York: W. W. Norton and Company, 1996.

Grun, Bernard. *The Timetables of History: A Horizontal Linkage of People and Events.* 3rd ed. New York: Simon and Schuster, 1991.

Hinckley, June, and Stephan Barnicle. "The Teacher's Guide to Classical Music for Dummies." Special insert in *Music Educators Journal* 84, no. 2 (1997).

Hoffer, Charles. *The Understanding of Music.* Belmont, CA: Wadsworth Publishing Company, 1989.

Jennings, Paul, and Teresa Jennings. *The Great Composers and Their Music,* vol. 1. Milwaukee: Hal Leonard Corporation, 1990.

Kjelland, James. "String Teacher Preparation and the National Music Standards." *American String Teacher* 45, no. 4 (1995).

Klevberg, Janet. *The Great Composers and Their Music,* vol. 2. Milwaukee: Hal Leonard Corporation, 1994.

Machlis, Joseph, and Kristine Forney. *The Enjoyment of Music*, 7th ed. shorter. New York: W. W. Norton and Company, 1995.

McLin, Lena. *Pulse: A History of Music.* San Diego: Neil A. Kjos Music Company, 1997.

Montgomery, June, and Maurice Hinson. *Meet the Great Composers.* Van Nuys, CA: Alfred Publishing Company, 1995.

Politoske, Daniel. *Music,* 4th ed. Englewood Cliffs, NJ: Prentice-Hall, 1998.

Schmid, Will. "Multicultural Music Education." *Music Educators Journal* 78, no. 9 (1992).

Straub, Dorothy A. "The National Standards for Arts Education: Context and Issues." *American String Teacher* 45, no. 3 (1995).

Straub, Dorothy A., Louis Bergonzi, and Anne Witt. *Strategies for Teaching Strings and Orchestra.* Reston, VA: Music Educators National Conference, 1996.

Volk, Terese. "Adding World Musics to Your String Program, Part 1: Chinese Folk and Thai Classical Music." *American String Teacher* 45, no. 3 (1995).

———. "Adding World Musics to Your String Program Part 2: Arabic Music." *American String Teacher* 45, no. 4 (1995).

Witt, Anne, Dean Angeles, Dale Kempter, and James Kjelland. *Teaching Stringed Instruments: A Course of Study.* Reston, VA: Music Educators National Conference, 1991.

9

Interview with Larry Rachleff
The Heart and the Brain in Performing

Catherine Larsen

Distinguished conductor Larry Rachleff is an articulate and devoted advocate of the idea that musical performance must be both heartfelt and aware. This interview with Arts-in-Education consultant Catherine Larsen is a fascinating glimpse into his deepest beliefs. It also contains powerful implications for the practice of music education.

Larsen: Larry, you've stated that you're committed to the idea of performing with musical understanding, to the idea that conductor, performer, and audience are equal parts of the musical equation. What do you mean by musical understanding? Why is it so important? And how do you know when the musicians have it?

Rachleff: Well, those are great questions. I think musical understanding is present when performing musicians are able to create something in which they comprehend the whole to which they are contributing their parts. So, in terms of a performing ensemble, it means the musicians understand how their parts fit into the entire composition—what makes up the whole, what the form of the piece is, how the components of the structure relate to the way their parts are to be played. It means that if the part just says *forte* for twenty measures, but in those twenty measures twelve are thematic material and the other eight are accompaniment, then, even though it just says *forte*, musical understanding tells the player, "Aha, these twelve bars I play stronger than the eight bars also marked *forte*."

Similarly, as a simple example of musical understanding, a brass player has a big *fortissimo* long note. He knows instinctively to "sing" the note beautifully at its start and to taper the note. He understands that this note isn't the most important thing going on, even though it's marked *fortissimo*. It's the musical context that provides the basis for "singing" the note and also for more or less getting it out of the way when that needs to happen. Musical understanding recognizes that context.

Another kind of musical understanding that's important is a knowledge of the appropriate style of a piece. A short note in Mozart is played differently than a short note in Stravinsky, for example. How do you teach performers the difference? Talk to them about the style of the period, the language of the music, the purpose of the note. You can tell when people play with musical understanding because, when you see it and hear it, it seems to make sense. It seems appropriate. The dynamics seem to be right. They don't seem too loud or too soft—they just seem to fit. The *forte* in Mozart is a sound that is more cushioned, more beautiful than the *forte* in Stravinsky, which would be a more strident, aggressive sound, for example.

These concepts are crucial. As the teacher, you don't need to teach the same concepts every time because the students can learn to transfer from one circumstance to another. You know they've got it when they demonstrate it. As we all know, great teaching is demonstrated in the students' execution of what we have shared with them. You

can give them the best explanation, with all the best analogies, but if they can't demonstrate it, they haven't learned it. So they've got it when, for example, in rehearsals the brass section has a figure that is written a certain way, and they instinctively know how to shape it because they're aware of its purpose and its function. The musicians in an ensemble need to know the function of everything they see on the page. Not that you will simply tell them; they will learn it—they will intuit and internalize it—according to how clearly you describe, verbally and nonverbally, what the piece requires.

Larsen: So you're talking about much more than reading the notes on the printed page in order to get to this musical understanding.

Rachleff: Yes. The notes on the printed page are no more than a structural guideline. We can take a poem and fifty people will read it differently. The notes on the page of music will be read differently by fifty performers. The objective issues, of course, will be the same. The right note value, the right pitch itself. But after that it's anyone's game, and it becomes a question of musical taste. The better the musician, the better the musical taste, and the more, if you will, reliable the performance—the more authentic, the more informed, the more appropriate. Just go back to the quarter note length, for example. A Stravinsky quarter note is short; it has a bit of an edge to it and is released very quickly. A Mozart quarter note has a bit of breadth, a good deal of beauty, and lifts and goes up into the air. The greatest musicians, when they play Mozart, give every note that kind of life. The notes on the page give you only the bare minimum of what has to be done. It's what we do beyond those notes that creates the music. If you're teaching music and you're not going beyond the notes, all you are teaching is the bare minimum of the "alphabet." You're not helping the performers put the letters together to make words and then, more important, phrases and sentences and paragraphs. A piece of music is not letters; it's paragraphs. And so performers have to understand how the letters make the words that make the phrases that make the sentences that make the paragraphs.

Larsen: In other words, many layers of meaning.

Rachleff: Yes. I think the layers of meaning in musical understanding are exemplified in how the music is performed, and these layers call upon *all* of our past experiences. For the teacher, this means you have to draw on all of *your* recollections in order for the students to feel the depth of what it is you're trying to create with them.

Larsen: In your mind, is it the conductor's obligation to engender or facilitate this musical understanding in his or her students? And along with that, are there special or specific rehearsal techniques that you use to bring this about? Are there things that you avoid doing? Are there differences in your approach

to teaching younger students as compared to middle or junior high students or high school kids and college students?

Rachleff: Regardless of the age—junior high, elementary, college, professional—it *is* the conductor's obligation to facilitate musical understanding. For example, I just had a rehearsal this afternoon with the players from the Lyric Opera of Chicago. The most important thing I can do is help them verbally and nonverbally understand what the point of their parts are and how they fit into the whole. I wouldn't necessarily rehearse them differently than a junior high band. My semantics might be different, and the amount of time it takes for them to get it is very different, you know—one hour versus one year! But the purpose is the same. What every performer needs to know is, how important is my part and how does it fit into what's going on?

Whatever rehearsal techniques you use to facilitate this, and whatever kinds of things you try to do or avoid doing, you must try to avoid giving the one "correct" answer. You want to try to find a way to get the musicians to be as independent as possible. Now that's really a hard thing for conductors because most musicians sit back and want the conductor to take them on the trip. And they *should,* in many ways. But the most important thing we can do is get the musicians to be independent of us.

How do you facilitate this? Ask questions in the rehearsal. Use imagery, for example: "Try to create the sound that you think is most appropriate to the mood that the composer is trying to create." "What kind of impact do you want the drama of the music to have here?" "In order for this to be together, who's got the fastest moving notes?" "Play these notes as pickups." Anything that will get the musicians thinking not of the spots on the page but about the musical purpose of where the notes have come from and where they're going.

You want to avoid a situation where the musicians are docile, uninvolved, and sit back and wait for your instructions and answers. This is a very difficult thing because we've got only so much time. We want to keep things moving, and we want the players to get it as fast as possible. But if they understand the concepts, they can transfer them to other situations and you won't have to reteach the same thing in a different guise; they can understand how a lot of what you do in X piece can work in Y piece. And to get that to happen, first of all, *you* need to understand it yourself. Secondly, engage their minds and imaginations, not by giving the answers as such but by trying to create a free environment, so to speak, where they can find the answers—create those sounds—themselves.

Larsen: Western classical music can be perceived as difficult to understand, particularly for people who have minimal experience with it. What kinds of musical understandings can the orchestra provide or create for its audience? How can it help bring the audience along? What do you see as your role in that process? What kinds of understandings do you hope your audience will get? What do you hope they will hear? And why is Western classical music an effective—perhaps the best—vehicle to create this kind of understanding?

Rachleff: Well, we could spend our whole time together, I think, just on those questions. Western classical music can be difficult for people to understand and engage with because it isn't necessarily the language that everyone is most comfortable and familiar with. When we were growing up, we could watch the Young People's Concerts with Leonard Bernstein on television. There isn't such a thing now, so it becomes crucial for orchestras of the world to take education as a primary role—to create concerts that young children and their parents can attend together.

How do you bring an audience along? No matter the age, from six to ninety, you talk to an audience at concerts. You let them know a bit about what they're going to hear. You help prepare them for what is going to happen in the music. This year in Rhode Island with the Philharmonic I've instituted postconcert discussions. I thought maybe ten, maybe fifteen people would stick around. Interestingly, about three hundred people have stayed after every concert to talk about the music we've just played. And these are not necessarily musicians; these are people who are somehow intrigued by what goes on. My point is that if we believe that Western classical music is too difficult for most people, then the audience will think that's so, too. We have to understand that it's something that isn't necessarily *for* everyone, but that you can make it accessible *to* everyone.

I think the best way to do that is to play the music superbly. Let the audience know and feel and see the great enthusiasm you have for it. Probably most important is to treat the audience with great respect—as if they were your children and you're bringing them along for the ride. The conductor's role in the process is as educator—conductor as teacher. There *is* no difference, and what we basically hope for is just that people will come away from our concerts having learned something and having been intrigued enough to come back and learn something more.

I don't know that Western classical music is the best vehicle for facilitating musical understanding. But I think Western classical music is a profoundly significant part of our civilization. It teaches us what it is to be civilized. It teaches us what beauty is. It gives us the deepest, most profound feelings about the human condition. When you have music that has depth, people are moved deeply. This past week in Rhode Island we did the Shostakovich Eleventh Symphony—a very long, difficult piece to play and to listen to. It's sixty minutes without a break between the movements. I mention it here not for self-promotion but to point out that the members of this audience, who were mostly nonmusicians—as every audience is—rose to their feet at the end because they could relate to what the composer was trying to say. Before we performed the piece, I chatted a bit with the audience about it, and in the postconcert discussion several nonmusical folks in the audience said to me, "Are you going to perform other Shostakovich Eleventh–type pieces?" I truly believe that audiences can touch, relate to, and feel what we do if we give it to them with the greatest sincerity and depth.

Now, what does that mean? It means that, as the conductor, you have to be completely prepared. You have to know your scores very well, and you have to teach, train, share, and inspire your groups to know their purpose—their function—so that they play the music with this kind of deep musical understanding; so that when they play this motive, they know it signifies gunfire or whatever. Or they see this motive and they know it's the theme, such as Alma's theme in Mahler's Sixth Symphony, dedicated to his wife. I mention this because I'm studying Mahler's Sixth right now, but it could be any piece. I'm also doing Copland's *Appalachian Spring,* in which some tunes signify the bride and the groom. Every piece, whether it has a program or not, has a strong dramatic point of view. Whether it's the march "The Liberty Bell" or Pachelbel's *Canon,* it doesn't need a story to have drama. It's our mission to find our relationship to, as we say, what's behind the notes—the drama, the point of view, the profile of the piece of music. And if we do that, an audience with no experience will engage itself in what we're doing. They will see it, they'll feel it, and they'll hear it.

Larsen: Do you think that this kind of experience with something dramatic, with something profound that touches people—although they don't know the formal terms for what they just heard—creates a desire to know more? That engaging people in the factual then helps them get back into it in a different kind of way?

Rachleff: That's interesting. I think people want to know more about something that has moved them. I think they're intrigued by why it moved them. My sense is that people who have some sort of experience that touches them will want more like it, because, frankly, it just *felt* good, and if it feels good, do it! So, basically, if people go to a concert, a museum, dance, or a theater and are turned on by something, I think it's only natural that they will want to see it, hear it, taste it again. If you have a rehearsal with youngsters that's inspiring and positive and challenging, those kids will want to come back the next day, not for the exact same experience but for more of that kind of experience.

Larsen: Can you talk about the application of the National Standards in helping make the music come alive for performers, and, as a result, for audiences, too? How do you get the printed page to allow the kind of freedom of expression and interpretation that you described as necessary for performers who are engaged? What are some of the obstacles that the printed page presents?

Rachleff: Well, the National Standards describe things that people have probably been doing for years, and now that they're codified, it's certainly helpful. I think music comes alive for performers mostly when they feel free. So, as a musician, how do you get to feel free? Well, obviously you've got to be able to sing or play with some degree of facility. You've got to be able to deal with other people, also, because it's the spontaneity and the freedom you feel with one another—that you play off with one another—that creates that energy. A duo has a certain energy, a string quartet has a certain energy, and a marching band has another kind of energy.

Improvisation has its own kind of energy. The ability to improvise, or to develop the ear, allows you to create this kind of freedom, allows you to be more involved in musical possibilities. People who are able to create improvisations are people who are hearing what they are doing while they are also hearing all of the other possibilities of what they can do. They have to hear the melody in their heads while creating all of the variations or other options at the same time. So improvisers hear two things at once. That creates a kind of freedom and imagination.

Composing and arranging music is not quite related here because it doesn't have as much to do with performing. Clearly, though, the ability to create, compose, write something—from your ear to your head, through your heart to the page—means you're being musically free to be expressive, because you're letting out something that's inside of you. Personally, I feel that reading music is not a deterrent to being free to play, to be expressive. The reading of music, as I said earlier, is just the beginning.

There is no question that the more we feel about the relationship between the other arts and music, the deeper our experience will be with the music that we have. Of all the National Standards, I think the most profound are the eighth and ninth—the relationship that music has to the other arts and to the world. What we're able to do in some way when we teach music is to show our students what part of human nature the music relates to—what connection it has to what was going on in the culture at the time that the piece was created. Why are Mahler's tempos what they are? Well, he was a big walker, and in that day and age, that's how people got from place to place. That's why his music can't move quickly. It moves as fast as someone who would walk graciously, generously, and comfortably. It isn't the speed of someone walking downtown in New York City.

All of these little things have to do with what goes on in the civilized world and the way that relates to how we create music. Knowing the history not only tells us the right style in which to play the piece but gives us a sense of the culture at the time. The ninth standard is so essential because it relates to all the aspects of the language of music. You don't articulate Aaron Copland's music like that of Richard Strauss. Why? Because you're dealing with the language of Germany versus the language of America. The languages sound different, so the manner of articulating musical sound must be different. When you talk about the music of Maurice Ravel or Claude Debussy, you ask what it means to sound French. Well, the music must have the sound of the language. It is much the same when you hear Russian music. Why does it sound so deep and rich and heavy? It's because that's what the language sounds like. The difference between saying *bonjour* and *zdravstvuite,* both of which mean hello, is obvious. I think these are things we have to share with our students.

So, in many ways, all of these standards help free musicians from the page, allow them to hear more independently, and give them a greater opportunity to interpret the music. What are some of the obstacles the printed page presents, you ask? I think the only obstacles are the ones that we put there. We must help musicians understand that the printed page is just the beginning of the information; it's just the menu, not the meal. It's just the recipe, the set of words. The printed page gives us freedom if we can get past the literal notes. And how do we get past the notes? We do it by getting musicians to become independent and free of the notes. How can they do that? We make sure they have the skills on their instruments, and we teach with the kind of musical imagination that engages the students' own imaginations.

Larsen: Many music educators believe that the emotional, "feelingful" response is the most important aspect of the performance experience. Do you agree? How does the value of this type of response relate to the importance of technique in the rehearsal? Can you comment on the relationship of cultural and historical information about the music to the depth or the quality of the emotional response?

Rachleff: Well, I think the *only* reason to play music is for its emotional and feelingful responses. I can't imagine that there would be any other purpose. The reason we make music is because of its beauty, because it makes us feel a certain way. Without that you don't have music; you just have notes. So I completely agree with that statement.

How does this relate to the importance of technique? Well, fortunately or unfortunately, in order to create an emotional, feelingful experience, we all must possess certain skills. If your students are not able to achieve this emotional experience, I daresay they might be playing music that's simply too difficult for them. You need to pick repertoire in which players spend most of their time—80 percent of their time—not on chasing the notes but on listening and hearing musically. Listening and hearing musically leads to feeling. If they spend 80 percent of their time just trying to find the notes, that leaves only 20 percent for expressive listening and hearing. So, if you're not getting into the emotional stuff, check out the repertoire you're doing. How many fast pieces do you have versus slow? And don't tell me that they just don't like to play slow because it's hard. Well, it is hard. You show them where the beauty is in the music and how to go from note to note; how making a phrase is an experience—more important, it's an event.

Cultural and historical information, as I was speaking of before, is essential to musical expression. Knowing the world as it was at the time a composition was created relates significantly to how we look at a piece of music and interpret it. We can help our students understand what that world was like by reading accounts to them and having them study what was going on at that time, reading letters of the composer that express the sentiment of the society at the time, and so forth. Read to them the reviews of the first performances of Beethoven's Fifth Symphony, which referred to it as something like "cacophonious garbage." That gives them a perspective on what Beethoven achieved.

There's another aspect of feeling and its centrality in music that needs to be mentioned. That's the importance of the words we choose to use as teachers. The more you can connect the symbolic, creative, imaginative relationships of the music to the performer, the more the musician, no matter the age, will relate and be inspired. Musicians will connect more with "Make this a glorious sound" than with "Play louder here." They will connect more with "Make your rhythm feel urgent" than with "Don't slow down." They'll connect more with "Violins, take a bit more poise here, be a bit more dignified," than with "Don't rush." I think anything that connects to the spirit produces a deeper meaning. The words we use should connect with the spirit of the music.

Larsen: You've stated that you regard programming, or selecting repertoire, to be of great value as a teaching tool. I'd like you to talk about the function of repertoire selection. Why is this so important? And what is your opinion as to the usefulness of repertoire selection in addressing the National Standards with regard to the performance experience?

Rachleff: Yes. I was mentioning that just a bit earlier, when I talked about the Shostakovich piece. Music that has depth—it doesn't have to have length; it just has to speak to the heart and the soul—is music that's going to inspire the most people. So the music we pick, like the literature the English teacher

picks, is of the highest importance. There's a reason that we read *Hamlet* and not comic books in school. And there's got to be a reason we show the kids great art. What is great art? Well, maybe it will mean something different to different people. I think most everyone will agree that Mozart, Beethoven, Bach, and so on, created great art. And you want young children of all ages to experience great art. It's something they will always remember.

I would suggest that when you pick repertoire for your groups, you have in mind a sense of how much time they will need to run around for the notes and how much time they'll be able to just experience the spirit of the music. Try to find the right ratio. How do you know what that ratio is? Well, you develop it over time; it's a sense you have. One way is by examining your rehearsal—how many minutes you spend talking about technical issues versus subjective issues; how many minutes you spend talking about getting notes lined up versus the meaning of this *crescendo.* Hopefully, the percentage is balanced in favor of the spirit rather than the fingers.

You might start every program with a project piece, which is usually a work of some length that will require both some fingers and some heart—a piece that will give them a feeling of accomplishment. It probably will be the longest selection on the program. The students should learn its form and structure, where the piece comes from, and what its style is. It's a piece you really do in the greatest depth—something that you treat like a project. For band, it could be a Holst suite. It could be a symphony for orchestra—whatever seems appropriate to the age level. And then I think it's probably important to have one piece that's just for the heart—something short, slow, perhaps Bach—something where finding the notes is not the issue but finding the meaning is.

And then it's good to have one piece that stretches your audience as well as the people on stage—something, as we approach the end of the millennium, that really requires some sounds that are a bit unusual or unique. Maybe it's some improvised music or maybe it's some aleatoric or free chance music; music where maybe the players read graphic notation rather than just regular Western notes. This piece asks the players and the audience to experience something that otherwise they might never have the opportunity to do.

I think that in schools, basically, the relationship between the audience and the literature is rather small. You properly pick your literature for the students in the group. You help the audience learn about it, you help the audience like it, you keep them informed—particularly the parents—of what you're doing and why you're doing it so that they feel part of the learning curve as well. But, generally, unlike in the professional orchestra business, you don't have to worry about the audience. All

you need to worry about is changing the lives of every student in your group—not a small worry, of course. The way you do that is by picking repertoire that inspires their hearts, their brains, and their fingers, probably in that order.

Larsen: The National Standards call for experiences in music of many cultures. Can an orchestra play music from other cultures while remaining true to that culture's traditions? Does the fact that the orchestra is a most obvious example of the Western classical tradition become problematic here?

Rachleff: Well, the issue of many cultures is a bit vague because that could mean German, French, Italian, and so forth. Of course, orchestras do that all the time. You do a concert where you have an Austro-Hungarian focus featuring music of Bartók and Kodály—or a concert featuring music of French culture. But I think what they're probably referring to in the National Standards is something called world music. Can an orchestra function with one foot in Mozart, if you will, and one foot in African drumming? The answer is probably yes and no. The greatest aspect of an orchestra is that it represents a cultural tradition. That's not something that should be apologized for; it's what it is, and thank goodness for that. It's a tradition that has survived and that will continue to survive because of the great art that has been written for it.

At the same time, I do think that orchestras should be investigating opportunities to collaborate in a world of cultural sensibility that does involve, say, the commissioning of a work for your high school orchestra and for African drummers—or for "anybody" drummers playing African drumming style. Let's say the city you live in has a large Japanese population. Maybe you can commission someone to create a piece that calls for original Japanese instruments and Western instruments, combining them in an orchestral piece. The only limitation here is one's imagination. If you're in a school district that has a large African American population, why not have a piece for your school orchestra or band complete with a narrator reading the words of some significant African Americans? It could be danced at the same time in a multimedia way by a solo dancer while, above the dancer, an overhead projector presents photographs that relate to this. So, yes, I think an orchestra can and should involve itself with all of these varied cultures.

But we must not relinquish the power of what an orchestra is. We must not turn our backs on its tradition. We can incorporate these other world music cultures into the orchestra, but at no time should we feel that such music should replace the traditional repertoire. In my opinion there still is nothing like seeing gifted, if you will, high school orchestra musicians, on stage playing with all their heart some music that was written two hundred years ago. It's such a fabulous way for us to continue this lineage of what we have in common

with what has come before. There is a profoundly important depth to that as well.

Larsen: And also a culture.

Rachleff: Right. Clearly it keeps you in touch with a society, with a history, with a civilization that occurred before. Kids at the dawn of a new century can relate to kids at the turn of the century two hundred years ago. We can appreciate and still find meaning in the same experiences. Science has created ways for us to move in all of these remarkable new paths, and so has music and music technology, and that's fabulous. Still, the acoustic performance of classical music is wonderful.

Larsen: Is the orchestra an anomaly in today's world? Is it a viable experience? Is there room in the orchestra rehearsal for the musician's imagination? How can this imagination be cultivated in the orchestral environment? You've talked about the functions of listening and discussing as part of the rehearsal, which could be viewed as kind of an unusual use of a conductor's time. How do you find it useful, and why do you think this imagination stimulation is important?

Rachleff: I don't think an orchestra is an anomaly in today's world, any more than a museum is an anomaly. An orchestra is a spiritual institution that must stay in touch with both what has come before and what will come in the future. If an orchestra does not participate in where the world of music is going, is not aware of the trends, it won't be viable. Its viability lies in both its celebration of what was and its willingness to move forward.

Obviously, I feel that the orchestra rehearsal not only has room for musicians' imaginations but that it's essential to engage them. The only trick is, how do you do it? As we discussed earlier, it's so much in how you describe what you want—how you try to perform the composer's music, not yours. I mean, you are there only as the spokesperson, the conduit. It's not that *you* want them to play shorter, it's *Beethoven* who wants them to play shorter! The imagination is cultivated in any environment when that environment feels free—when players feel that they can be right, but it's also okay to be wrong. The National Standards are there not as a taskmaster but as a guide—not something that creates anxiety, but something that creates some structure.

Is it a waste of the conductor's time to talk about listening? Well, maybe it takes less time just to say "Violins, longer" than "Now, violins, listen to the sound that the *celli* are making. How can you best fit the length of your notes into their sound so that it seems appropriate?" Yes, that takes longer, but the point is that they will have learned something—that listening to the *celli* provides the answers to several similar questions in five thousand other pieces. So my answer is, really, how can you afford *not* to use that time? It's important because this is what gives musical

understanding. Sure, you can tell them just to play longer, and they will dutifully do so. But you need to show them why they have to play longer. For example, "Violas, play the F-sharp full value here. Why? Because the end of your note is the beginning of the next passage for the second violins." So you've told them not only what you want but why. You've given a purpose. Next time you come to something like that, maybe you say to the violas, "Here comes that elision again." So now they've learned a little vocabulary along with a little function. Next time it comes, you don't say anything; you just look at them with that gesture that looks like an elision gesture. Pretty soon they've learned about ten things, unwittingly, through their own imaginations and your patient, persistent teaching.

What makes an orchestra so relevant today is the energy of the performances, the spirit of what happens. You still cannot replace ninety musicians giving it everything they have for the same goal. There's basically nothing else in the world that happens like that. In a sporting event you've got some people rooting one way and some rooting the other. But in an orchestra, chorus, band, or jazz ensemble, everyone's got the same purpose. We're going to make something great—we're going to head for this destination and "take no prisoners." It's total freedom with appropriate total commitment. When it works, there's nothing else quite like it. Why? Because you have so many people's energy symbiotically cooking up something, and the result is breathtaking.

Larsen: Your focus as a conductor is on the music-making experience. Do you feel that the presence of the National Standards is encouraging? Do you think that the Standards can or will enhance the music-making experience?

Rachleff: I think the Standards will enhance the creativity and understanding of the students—by getting them to improvise, to do some composing, and to improve their ability to describe and analyze what goes on; by getting them to look at music from an angle that isn't necessarily performance-oriented; by getting them to see the relationships to history, culture, and the other arts and disciplines; by allowing them to find a point of view, a reference, a sense of the meaning of where these composers lived and where *their* creativity was coming from. Getting people to sing and make music with understanding is something that will energize all of these other Standards.

The question of whether the presence of the Standards will have an effect on the excitement of music making remains to be seen. No number of standards is going to make music teachers feel inspired by what they do. No list is going to make music teachers deeply love the music they're teaching. However, having these Standards does provide an avenue whereby these issues of composing, arranging, creating, listening, analyzing, describing, evaluating, and relating will remind teachers of

where we need to take our students. We don't need to take them to perfect performances; we need to take them to performances that have meaning. And what is something that gives meaning? It's something in which you understand what you're doing. If you're also interested in a really good performance, which of course I am, then you have to find a varied enough repertoire that's germane to your group so that they can experience this meaning. The title National Standards is, of course, a bit daunting. I'm sure that most people have been doing the things the Standards require in one way or another, where appropriate, for years and years.

The most crucial thing to remember is that, for all of us, the most important thing we can do with our teaching is get children to feel something—to feel that what they've just accomplished was important and significant and, therefore, that *they* are important and significant. Great music teaching all comes down to one thing, I think, and that is how students feel about the experience they're having with you and with the music. Is the environment engaging, is it imaginative, is it stimulating, is it challenging, is it positive, is it probing, is it alive? Is it always changing, is it varying, is the repertoire fascinating? Do you challenge and reward? If you're doing those things, the National Standards can be a great partner for you. The National Standards *without* those things will not accomplish what you want. You need both sides—the

heart and the brain—to make this
work. Sure, we need the Standards as
guidelines. But most important, we
need love for, and a commitment to,
great teaching and great music making.

Teaching for Performing with Understanding in Choral Settings

10

The Challenges of Performing Choral Music of the World

Mary Goetze

Standard 1 in the National Standards (Singing, alone and with others, a varied repertoire of music) challenges music educators to present choral music from diverse cultures in classrooms and performing ensembles. There is nothing new about the inclusion of music that originates outside the western art tradition in the choral repertory. Even before the current emphasis on multicultural education, numerous choral publications were based on folk songs from international sources. Choirs are traveling abroad with increasing frequency, and choirs from around the world appear regularly at American choral and music education conventions. These appearances have sparked an increased interest among American choir directors in singing non-western music. In this chapter, I will discuss issues that emerge when choirs incorporate music from unfamiliar traditions into their repertory.

I will discuss vocal music from outside the western art tradition—music that is not traditionally included in music history courses in most music schools or conservatories. This category will include both folk and composed music from international sources as well as European and American popular and folk music styles. Within its culture of origin, this music may be notated or transmitted aurally. Rather than referring to this music with the cumbersome phrase "music from outside the western art tradition," I have opted to call it "international music."

While I fully support teaching students a rich array of the world's music, I believe we achieve the intent of Standard 1 and multicultural education only when we perform the music with integrity. I believe this requires

- accurately recreating the music—that is, to the degree possible, learning it and singing it the way it is learned and sung within the culture from which it comes; and

- leading students to develop an understanding of the music, its function, and how it reflects that culture.

First, I will discuss the challenges that I have encountered in carrying out an exploratory project with a choir that specializes in the performance of international music. Next, I will share the procedures I have developed in an attempt to present and recreate this music with integrity and understanding. Finally, I will report on the outcomes of this project, both for the college-aged students and for myself.

Challenges of Including International Vocal Music in the Choral Repertory

Acquiring choral repertory. The first and most obvious challenge of incorporating international music into the choral repertory is finding literature to perform and collecting information about it. While available for decades, most publications of international choral music are aptly described as "arrangements based on international material." Regardless of the voicing of the individual or group that performs the music within the culture, the octavos are typically written for SATB or SSA ensembles. Editors or arrangers often provide minimal or no information about either the music or the culture.

Professional periodicals have not filled this void. Except for some features on performing African American music,

articles in the *Choral Journal,* the journal of the American Choral Directors Association (ACDA), or MENC's journals rarely address performing international music with integrity. Most articles that do address international music focus on studying it in general music settings rather than performing it in choral ensembles. The paucity of articles on international music stands in stark contrast to the number addressing the performance practices of early music. With the surge of interest and research in early music, choral conductors have become increasingly knowledgeable about performance practices of the Renaissance, Baroque, and Classical periods. Over the past two decades, exhaustive research and insights into pre-nineteenth-century music have yielded performances that conform to musicologists' understanding of the practices of the period. The music is often performed on carefully constructed replicas of the historical instruments.

It is unnecessary for performers of international music to hypothesize from historical documents about such matters as style, tempo, or timbre as performers of early music do. International music and musicians are accessible to us by means of recordings, television, and live performances. Furthermore, the artists are no longer necessarily far across the globe but within the bounds of our country or even our communities. It is time to apply standards of scholarship, integrity, and authenticity to the performance of international music—music that is of our time and increasingly of our country.

Establishing authenticity. This leads to a second challenge: identifying the authentic style or version of the music. Western musicians assume that it is possible to determine one traditional form of a song in the same way we can determine the definitive version of, say, a Bach cantata by examining the score in the composer's collected works. However, music that is not notated is dynamic and responsive to numerous influences upon the makers of the music. People were making musical exchanges even before television and recordings carried western music to remote areas of the world. For example, most travelers to New Zealand are likely to hear the song "Hoki, Hoki" performed with the swinging of poi. The familiar melody is the one we know as "Little Brown Jug," which the Maori learned from soldiers in World War I. Singing the melody with their own text, the Maori have fully integrated it into their culture for more than seventy-five years. Is it an authentic Maori song if it is based on a song we recognize as an American fiddle tune?

With the kind of cross-fertilization that is now happening so readily around the world, continuous intermingling of musical styles is inevitable. I propose that we accept a broader definition of authenticity that accommodates the numerous forms in which a selection of music exists: Authentic music is that which is made by natives within their own culture, regardless of the source of the musical material. Although some versions may more clearly be traced to their origin than others, no single version of music that meets this criterion is more authentic than another. If a song is being performed in a particular way within its culture of origin, it should be considered a legitimate version.

Inappropriate uses of music. When I visited New Zealand/Aotearoa in 1995 to study Maori culture and to collect song materials, Stuart Manins, from Auckland University, led me to recognize the necessity of having permission from the Maori community to sing their songs. He recounted stories of other western researchers who had taken ownership of music that is sacred to the Maori, teaching it to others and even publishing it. We have assumed that we can transcribe, arrange, and share international music without respecting its connection to particular societal functions. We have not considered it important to obtain permission to perform the music outside the culture. Recently, Native Americans have spoken out about the special function of their sacred music as related to particular ceremonies. Their protests have led us to recognize the inappropriateness of using chants that are reserved for their sacred rituals as listening material in classrooms or performance material in concerts.

In light of this, we must reexamine the materials that are currently in our libraries and catalogs. We should consult with ethnomusicologists and natives to ensure that the music is appropriate for performance by non-natives and in contexts different from those within the culture. Those who collect music from other cultures must first get permission to share the music with others and to have it performed outside its cultural context. If we perform this music, it serves to represent that culture to our students. Certainly, individuals from the culture, preferably elders, should be consulted about the selections that serve to represent them.

Transmitting music with integrity. Assuming that a song is freely given for performance with our choruses, how then is it transmitted so that it retains its style and integrity? I will begin with a discussion of the text because that leads us to recognize another western assumption and practice: making the sounds of the language and music conform to those with which westerners are familiar.

Problems in symbolizing the text. In earlier American publications of international music, editors included only an English text, loosely translated for singability. In some later examples, some editors included a non-English text along with a singable translation. If the song was not in a European language, they most often presented a transliteration (which provides the closest English equivalent for the sounds of the original language), rather than the orthography (the characters or letters of the original language). However, even

within European languages there are sounds for which there are no English equivalents, such as the German "ch" or the French "y." Linguists addressed this issue by developing the International Phonetic Alphabet (IPA). IPA is a single system of symbolizing the sounds used in all languages around the globe. While some choral directors use IPA effectively for German and the Romance languages, choral publications are only beginning to include IPA for other languages. Even with IPA, however, a problem still exists: It is impossible to interpret the symbols for sounds we have not heard. The obvious solution is for publishers to provide an aural model of the sounds of the language. For example, the compact discs (CDs) accompanying *Share the Music,* Macmillan/McGraw-Hill's elementary music series,[1] include a recording of a native speaker reciting the text for each non-English song.

Problems in symbolizing the musical sounds. A similar problem exists for the representation of musical sounds. We have traditionally operated on the assumption that there are "equivalents" in western notation for all musical sounds. Western notation evolved to symbolize music that is consistent with the way we conceptualize rhythm and pitch. We sometimes fail to recognize that there might be ways of thinking about music other than our own. For example, the five-line staff was devised to notate subdivisions of an octave into eight pitches. Even the notation of chromatic music is cumbersome on our staff. Clearly it fails to accommodate the division of the octave into quarter tones, or the complex scales of Indian music. Western composers in the twentieth century, encountering this same limitation of pitch notation, turned to more graphic forms to represent various pitch effects. Similarly, western symbolization of duration does not accommodate music that is organized in ways other than meters of two, three, or four beats. Some African music is organized around groupings of the micropulse, a smaller subdivision than beats within meters. Scores attempting to notate this music are awkwardly riddled with dotted rhythms and ties.

Furthermore, when western musicians read notation, they automatically apply the conventions of western performance to the notated score. For example, our traditional training informs us how to approach the performance of each of three quarter notes within a measure of 3/4 meter. Even though the symbols look identical, our training has led us to accent the downbeat and imbue the final one with motion that leads into the next measure. When we do this with international music that is inappropriately represented by notation, we may further compound the inauthenticity of that music.

More important, representing international music in western notation may filter out the actual sounds that contribute to the uniqueness of the music, and to that which makes it expressive and meaningful within the culture. If notation is the sole means for transmitting the music to a choir, it is unlikely that the singers will experience the essence of the music or be able to convey it to an audience.

In recognition of this problem, a few editors and their publishers have begun to make recordings available with the sale of octavos of international music. However, the recordings are only occasionally of native choirs. Furthermore, western singers are unlikely to be able to capture details of the musical and vocal style of the culture because they have been trained to employ traditional western choral intonation, tone quality, and blend. Again, we may filter out the essence of the musical expression when we change the vocal timbre and the tuning and perform it with a conventional western choral blend. In western musical practice, we would not take the liberty of substituting the composer's choice of, say, a tenor for a soprano, an oboe for a clarinet, or a women's chorus for children. Yet even if an authentic model is available, many choral conductors would not hesitate to change the vocal timbre of international music to a western sound.

For many, any change from the accepted western vocal timbre of our choirs is unthinkable. Conductors and voice teachers who question even the appropriateness of singing in popular vocal styles cannot fathom imitating the vocal timbres of more remote styles. For example, music from the Balkan region requires a high instead of a lowered larynx, and some African styles make extensive use of the chest instead of the head voice. Opponents argue that such singing would threaten students' singing technique and vocal health. There is no evidence or research to suggest that this assumption is correct.

These issues have led me to some perplexing questions: Are we really exposing our students to international music when they sing with compromised pronunciation of the text? Can they savor the special flavors of the music if the pitches and rhythms are fitted into western notation and "straightened" out to conform to western concepts of tonality and meter? What kinds of ethnocentric assumptions lie behind our inability or unwillingness to sing with non-European vocal timbre? Can we justify avoiding these styles for reasons of vocal health when people within entire cultures have sung that way for centuries?

To respond to these questions, I have explored alternative means of introducing international vocal music to my college-aged choir. I turn now to the procedures that have resulted from this exploration.

Recommendations for presenting international music

In the fall of 1995 I founded the International Vocal Ensemble (IVE) at Indiana University. The group meets four hours each week and presents an "informance" each semester. Most of the students are music majors, and approximately one-third to one-half are planning to be music teachers. In order for the students to become acquainted with a broad range of music, I divide our study into two parts. In one, we focus on becoming acquainted with one culture in depth. In the other, we learn a selection of pieces from two or three other cultures. Within the rehearsals, I introduce them to people who are natives of each of the cultures they study. In this section, I will describe some of the methods that have been effective in teaching these students to sing music in the native style.

Utilizing published music effectively. It is informative to consider the typical ways international music is presented in octavos. Here are some categories into which most published international choral octavos fit, arranged in order from the most to the least westernized:

1. A composition by a western composer who incorporates a text or uses a melody from an international source as a theme.
2. An arrangement of a song by a western arranger, written with conventional choral voicings.
3. An arrangement by an international arranger, written with conventional choral voicings.
4. A transcription of a song as sung in the originating culture.
5. A transcription of a song that is learned with an audio recording of a performance by a western choir.

6. A transcription of a song accompanied by an audio- or videotape of a native group.

For your students to have an experience that provides them with the full flavor of the music, the type described in number six is best. For any of the others, the experience for the students should be supplemented by playing recordings of native groups. Among the numerous CDs in the world music section of most audio stores or catalogs you are likely to find examples of other songs in the same style by native groups, and occasionally a rendition of the published song.

In order to authenticate materials that are not well documented, consult ethnomusicologists and people who are natives of the culture from which the music comes. Consider posting a request for information on-line, using the Web sites hosted by ACDA or MENC. Alternately, doing a search on the World Wide Web can put you in touch with others who may be able to assist you. If you are performing a folk-song transcription or arrangement, seek out natives and ask them if they are familiar with the song. If they know it, ask them to translate the text and sing the melody without looking at the score. From this you can discern whether the song is part of a common repertoire within the culture, and how the published transcription or arrangement differs from the informants' versions. Compare the versions and adapt the arrangement as necessary.

I recommend choosing octavos that provide the original text as opposed to only a translation. In a few recent publications, the editor provides the orthography that allows students to see the original letters or characters. If you have natives of the culture in your choir, ask them to share their knowledge with the choir or bring in members of their family or community to assist the choir with the language.

Nearly all published international music includes some form of pronunciation guide. Transliterations into English equivalents are common, but I believe that it is preferable to teach students IPA. Regardless of the method of symbolization, it is essential for the students to hear a native speaker pronounce the sounds with which the symbols are to be associated. If possible, ask a native speaker to sing the song text as well.

Most often publishers of octavos include only performance suggestions and transliteration guides to assist with pronunciation. A few recent octavos include information about the music and the culture. By choosing scores that have more detailed information, conductors will encourage publishers and editors to recognize the importance of making space for documentation in future publications.

Developing aural and video resources. In the choir I am now conducting I have developed procedures that do not depend upon published scores. The students learn from native informants who are residents or visiting artists in my community. I have also been privileged to travel to countries where I can observe the music making, study the context, and record the performances myself.

I have been surprised at how feasible this kind of exchange is. It would be so even if I were to limit myself to the region within which I live. Here are recommendations for collecting your own material.

The arts listings in newspapers can lead you to discover performances by local folk artists. In some cities, ethnic groups maintain a culture center that serves to perpetuate their cultural traditions by offering classes and other activities. Once they see that your interest is sincere, most groups are willing or even eager to share their material and information about it. These contacts will inform you of native groups that may be touring and performing in your region.

If possible, make contact with touring groups before they arrive in your area. Find out if they would be willing to meet with you. If their schedule allows, invite the performers to come to your rehearsal so that the students can learn the music directly from them. With their permission, make a videotape of the session. In addition, conduct an interview with the artists for the videotape. Ask them to explain how they learned or wrote the song, where it would be performed in their country, and who would sing it. Be sure to ascertain whether the song is appropriate for a non-native group to include in its

choral repertory. Ask the performers to write out the text and to pronounce the text slowly for the videotape, allowing time for the group to repeat each phrase on the tape. Give them an opportunity to view the videotape you make.

It is important to communicate explicitly how you intend to make use of the music you collect. If you expect to show the tape outside your rehearsals or share copies of it with other directors, be sure to get the performers' permission and have them sign a release form. If you ever sell copies of the videotaped material, it is appropriate that the original performers receive part, if not all, of any profits that result. (Traditionally in western culture we have taken ownership of such materials, and this has included banking the profit. I encourage rethinking this practice.)

Presenting unfamiliar languages. In teaching my choir to use IPA, I ask a linguist to explain the system to the students. Students need help recognizing and producing consonants and vowels that are not used in English, particularly those that require unfamiliar lingual and labial coordination. As students learn to associate the symbols with the sounds of the language, they become more proficient in producing sounds accurately. Their ability to aurally discriminate subtle differences in vowel and consonant sounds will increase markedly as well.

Presenting non-notated materials. The use of video and live models calls for different methods of teaching the music. As for visual representation, students in my choir have in hand only the text, accompanied by IPA and a translation. It is essential to play the recorded video materials repeatedly over time in rehearsals, even after the students have learned the material. With more familiarity, the choir will hear details they missed in previous hearings and confront the limits of their aural perception. What may appear as a simple song upon first exposure unfolds into more than the right pitches, rhythms, and words as they become conscious of additional details and subtleties. For instance, students will soon perceive accents in Latin American music or improvised vocables in African music—musical details that would not appear on the score if it were notated.

In learning a homophonic song with tertian-based harmony, have the choir first listen and reproduce the melody with the text. They should sing both after and with the recorded model. Next, have all singers listen for the bass line and sing it with the text. Finally, they can fill in other pitches that are present in the harmony.

If the students are not accustomed to improvising harmony by ear, the following exercises may assist them in hearing nonmelodic tones. Play two pitches simultaneously, and ask the students to sing from the higher to the lower pitch. Repeat, beginning with the lower pitch. Similarly, ask them to sing the pitches in sonorities of three and four pitches as an arpeggio. Play a chord and ask them to sing the lowest and then the highest pitches; then require them to find an inner pitch. You can repeat these exercises with short progressions of two or three chords.

Live or video modeling is essential for learning music that is integrated with movement. Students learn choreography best by watching and simultaneously imitating the steps. As students master the choreography, allow them to view repeatedly and help them focus their attention on details of the style. I ask the choir to face a partner as they move, and to compare the partner's movement with that on the video. The entire process speeds up as the students become more keen in their observations.

Developing rhythmic skills. In preparing songs that require stepping a pattern in three against the duple feel of the song text, we practice interlocking rhythmic exercises that result in polymeters.[2] For instance (using western terminology), students clap on alternating pulses, represented here by eighth notes. One-half of the choir claps on the first, third, and fifth eighth notes, and so forth, and the other on the second, fourth, and sixth eighth notes, and so forth.

♪ ♪ ♪ ♪ ♪ ♪ ♪ (♪ = group 1, ♪ = group 2)

This leads to sensing the inner subdivision of pulses, called micropulses.

Next each group claps this pattern of three pulses:

♪ ♪ ʼ

Both groups perform the pattern, offset by the duration of one eighth note.

Group 1

♪♪ʼ ♪♪ʼ ♪♪ ʼ

Group 2

ʼ ♬ ♬ ʼ ♬ ♬ ʼ ♬ etc.

When this three-pulse pattern is stable, have the students clap it while singing melodies, such as "Jingle Bells" (see figure 10-1), that are in duple meter. (One measure of duple meter = ♪ ♪ ♪ ♪)

Such exercises lead students to feel patterns of two and three in relation to the micropulse, rather than to quarter notes and the intellectual construct of

meter. The goal is to feel

rather than

3 ♩ ♩ ♩ ♩ ♩ ♩

for example, which allows shifting freely from two-pulse to three-pulse patterns, as in the following:

Outcomes of the Project

At the end of each semester, my IVE students respond to questions about their experience in the choir. From the comments students wrote in the first year I prepared a list of statements with which students in the second year were asked to agree or disagree on a five-point scale. The questionnaire was com-

Jingle Bells

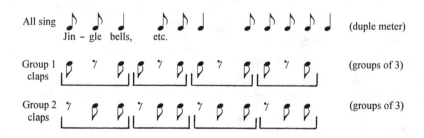

Figure 10-1.

pleted by fifty-nine of sixty-three ensemble members. (They were not asked to identify themselves.) In this section, along with my own observations, I will report the responses to the items that are pertinent for this chapter.

Effect of the project on students' musical skills. Through learning music aurally, we exercise aspects of our own musical potential that may go undeveloped in traditional western musical training. Students agreed (66.1 percent) that their "tonal memory and rhythmic abilities have improved" through the ensemble experience. An even larger number (74.5 percent) confirmed that "picking out harmony parts helped with aural skills."

I have observed that students perceive differently when they are listening with the intent to reproduce the musical model. Recreating music accurately requires more active and intense attention than other modes of listening. In fact, watching a score may inhibit attention to details of style. Let me illustrate by recounting an experience from the first semester of this project. The choir was learning a South African song exclusively from a video of the Pretoria Youth Chorus. To prepare myself for this experience, I had used a transcription of the song given to me by Erica Swart, the director of the choir. Much to my surprise, the students added lip trills and improvised vocables that did not appear in my notated version and that I had missed when viewing the video! Even in the presence of the

sounds, I was aware only of those that were notated. My own perception was limited by watching the score. I had experienced what James Froseth (University of Michigan) calls being "eyebound."

An outcome of learning music aurally is that the students simultaneously commit the music to memory. Over 70 percent of the students reported that they encountered more difficulty in memorizing music learned from notation than recalling music presented aurally. An even larger number (87.8 percent) felt that in performance, they communicated "a greater sense of the music when singing from memory." In addition, their retention of the music over time exceeded my expectations. Even after months had elapsed, students were able to recall all aspects of songs learned, including the movement, with surprising clarity. With the statement "When we learn without a score, I feel we truly possess the music instead of it being merely paper and ink," 74.1 percent were in agreement. This has reminded me that, despite our propensity to refer to the notated score as "the music," music is sound. Furthermore, international musics are often much more than *only* sound.

Certainly the process of learning international music described here addresses content standards from the National Standards other than number 1. There are abundant opportunities to improvise (Standard 3); listen to and analyze music (Standard 6); integrate this music with other arts, most often dance (Standard 8); and understand music in relation to history and culture (Standard 9).

The aural approach recommended here need not hamper students' reading skills (Standard 5). Keen aural discrimination is an important part of being musically literate. Listening to a recording of a native group and following the notation can enhance reading skills. Comparing the recorded model with the score reinforces the association of sounds with symbols. Students may also become conscious of discrepancies when the score and the recording do not match. They may discover details that are not indicated in the notation, such as subtle slides between pitches, bending of pitches, or ornamentation. In conjunction with a methodical approach to sightsinging, these experiences can reinforce students' ability to read music.

Students' attitudes toward singing international music. The student response to learning music hitherto unperformed in the Indiana University School of Music has been overwhelmingly positive. As objective evidence, I can cite an increased interest in the ensemble in terms of the requests for admission, the number of singers who return, and the size of the audience. On the questionnaire, 80.1 percent of the students agreed with the statement "I encourage my friends to join IVE." The primary reasons given for leaving the ensemble have been schedule conflicts, graduation, internships, or student

teaching off campus.

More important would be the effect of this project on students' attitudes toward music (and people) of other cultures. While positive comments they have made to me about their feelings cannot be considered a totally reliable means of assessment, their behaviors have revealed the impact of their experience. A student who participated last year, now teaching in a public school, chose to teach her middle school students several selections from our repertory. In her unsolicited comments she reported that her students had been successful in learning the music and that they enjoyed it. Many IVE students have brought in CDs they have found with examples of the kind of music we are learning or examples of particular styles they find intriguing. One composition student who loaned me her CD said, "As a result of [the choir], world music has become my passion. Sometimes I go hungry in order to have money to buy CDs." Her recent compositions reflect the influence of the international music she has learned. Eighty-nine percent agreed that the experience has made them "more open-minded about music of other cultures."

Because our university has numerous international students, I have been able to provide IVE students with an opportunity to interact in rehearsals with people who are natives of a culture we are studying. When the choir members have encountered other natives on or off campus, they have been delighted that they are able to sing a song the native recognizes. The benefit has been reciprocal: Natives who visit the choir articulate their pleasure in hearing their music sung in the School of Music and in being asked to teach it to the choir. One choral conductor from Brazil said, "I have been here five years studying your choral music, and for the first time I am reminded that I am an expert in my own music." Other natives have demonstrated an obvious emotional response to hearing their music while being far from their homeland.

Understanding how music functions within another culture also leads us to become conscious of the way music functions in western culture. Through the IVE experience students may recognize the subtle and complex ways our music reflects the values and the assumptions by which we live. For example, Manuke Henare, a native Aotearoa/New Zealander, was describing the Maori's circular view of time to my group. He drew a spiral figure in a horizontal position on the board, to illustrate that when contemplating the future, the Maori look to the past. I asked the students how they might characterize time in western culture. Quickly a student responded by drawing an arrow pointing to the right. A second student improved upon this and drew the arrow with an upward slant to symbolize the idea of moving ahead and progressing. We noted how our musical terminology reflects this teleological

notion. We describe harmony in terms of "progression" toward a point of resolution—a characteristic western way to think that, we often forget, is culturally determined rather than universal. Recognizing assumptions other than our own opens our eyes to human diversity.

Conclusion

This chapter has presented challenges, procedures, and outcomes of teaching students to recreate music from outside the western art tradition with integrity and understanding. I have advocated holding ourselves to the same high standards in performing international music with integrity as we do with western music. We are seeing this quest for authenticity in other aspects of American life today. There was a time when eating Italian or Chinese food meant opening a can. Today, we can savor these foods cooked freshly by chefs who grew up in the culture, and we may have only to go around the corner to find them. When teaching our students music from around the world, why should we not provide them with the real thing? Performances from around the world are accessible to them on radio, television, and CDs. Why should they be satisfied when the music is served to them in a westernized can?

As we look to the future, we can anticipate that performances by natives will become increasingly accessible to us in our schools. Ethnic populations within our communities are likely to continue to grow. Distance education can make it possible to interact with artists on the opposite side of the world. Video and audio models can be found on the World Wide Web. The CD-ROM, satellite linkups, or other emerging technologies may become more effective ways of transmitting international music than a choral score. The prospects are both exciting and challenging.

The essence of the approach I have presented is (1) to learn and to sing international music *their* way rather than our way, and (2) to develop an understanding of how the music functions within its cultural context. Traditionally, we have adapted diverse music to fit the characteristics of our own musical perception, conception, and musical and pedagogical styles. Regardless of the setting from which the music sprang, we have taken the liberty to alter its function to serve as music sung for an audience, as westerners do. Performing international music with integrity requires conductors and students to adapt to the demands of the music, to learn how and why the music is made, and to learn something of the people who make it. To the degree that is possible, we must share this experience and information with our audiences as well. Our musical skills and knowledge, as well as those of our students, will be enhanced by our participating in this exciting process.

In making a sincere effort to accurately recreate international music, we inherently honor the cultures and their musical traditions. In our naive ethnocentrism, we have thought it was respectful to notate their music in our way, to tune up their "primitive" scales, and to sing their music with a more "refined" vocal quality. Intended or not, this has communicated to them that we believe that our music is superior. As we weternize international styles, so also are the new generations of native musicians. As a result, some musical traditions are dying out with the elders. Perhaps if we value other traditions, we can contribute to the preservation of all musical styles so that we and our children can enjoy the rich variety of music our world encompasses.

The process of recreating international music has educational and musical value, but I believe it may have a more profound value as well. Through this experience, students can identify with the makers of the music; that is, they can sense the emotions that are embodied in the music. They are able to partake of the essence of the musical expression on its own terms. The insights students gain into culture and humanness through making music with integrity and understanding are knowledge that is not attainable through verbal conceptualization alone. And of course, that is the ultimate reason for educating our youth in music and all of the arts.

Notes

1. Judy Bond et al., *Share the Music* (New York: Macmillan/McGraw-Hill Publishing Company, 1995).

2. These exercises were presented by Alain Barker, a former Indiana University student from Durban, South Africa, in a 1995 African music workshop at Indiana University.

The Standards and Performance in the Context of Culture

11

Ethnomusicological Musings

Contemplating the Standards as Agents of Cultural Transmission and Change

Bruno Nettl

Culture, Competence, and Standards

"Culture," so said an anonymous academic wit, "is what people [in a society] agree upon." I have been tempted to counter that culture is what people argue about. But in any event, the oldest of the influential definitions by anthropologists, that of E. B. Tylor, suggests that common knowledge and the acceptance of common principles, rules, and interpretations of the world are what binds a society. "That complex whole, which includes knowledge, belief, art, morals, law, custom, and any other habits and capacities acquired by man as a member [or humans as members] of society"[1] tells us that the people

in a society share a fund of knowledge, a way of interpreting and representing the world, and a group of rules and principles to govern behavior. In other words, in order to be a member of a society, there are certain things you must know; if you don't, you are only marginal to the society. The definition of culture does not suggest that all knowledge and all of the rules found in a culture must be known equally to all of its members. But the implication would be, I think, that for a society to exist, there are certain things that all or virtually all of its members must understand.

This premise is not difficult to accept when considering small, perhaps tribal or village societies—of the kind that hardly exist today, to be sure. In large, heterogeneous societies such as American society, Western society, the society of a particular city, or even of a particular School of Music, it is much more difficult to find things on which all agree. There may be some: certain principles of dress that distinguish genders and age groups; one drives on the right; red means stop, green means go; everybody should know how to read; it is normal for children to live with their parents (not a cultural universal, I assure you); it is normal to sleep about eight hours a day, in one stretch (also not a universal); or, normal music is music in which you hear more than one pitch at a time and that is based on the system of functional harmony. Maybe also: all humans should be treated more or less equally; it is possible for humans to own things and animals but not other people; some people are better than others at doing certain things, and this is a result, in part, of "talent."

However tenuous the validity of this miscellany of beliefs for contributing to a definition of a culture, one is then tempted to ask whether all members of a society must also possess certain skills. Well, there certainly are some: certain basic skills in personal hygiene; eating with utensils; reading and writing; some simple arithmetic; memorizing some precomposed texts—prayers, poems, psalms. Many skills that are clearly part of the culture are not shared, however: dentistry, piano virtuosity, plumbing, electronics; to be a member of American society, you need not master

them, but you must, I would assert, know that they exist and when to turn to their specialists for satisfying your needs.

So it is reasonable to suggest that in order to be a member of a society, you must meet certain standards of knowledge and behavior. Western societies have elaborate school and certification systems to guarantee compliance. Older tribal societies had rituals to enforce them. Asian societies have complex codes and treatises as well. The handing down of tradition through oral and visual means is shared by both complex and simpler societies.

Well, here we are contemplating the desirability of teaching all members of American society certain principles and certain skills in music. We are suggesting—I realize I am putting this somewhat extremely—that in order to be a proper member of American society one must possess certain minimal musical skills and understandings. Or at least one must have the opportunity to learn them.

Are there already certain of those musical skills and understandings that virtually all members of American society possess? Let me suggest that these do exist in two areas: performance of a limited repertory, and ability to discern certain styles. I suggest that there are a few songs that almost everybody can sing, if imperfectly. Among them might be "Happy Birthday," "Jingle Bells," and perhaps a few patriotic songs. And I think people can roughly identify musical genres after a few seconds of hearing them, distinguishing classical music from popular, jazz from country, Western from non-Western. Perhaps that's all, and the categories are rough, but I would suggest that being able to do these things makes one legitimately a member of society, and lacking the ability makes one marginal—perhaps a foreigner recently arrived, a member of an out-of-the-way minority, or someone tone-deaf or aurally impaired.

With the National Standards for Music Education in place, ideally, the basic musical skills and understandings of Americans, those necessary to be full-fledged members of this society, will increase—they will change from what they have historically been. To be a musically educated American, according to the Standards, one will have to acquire a more comprehensive set of skills and understandings than has generally been expected heretofore.

Education: A Domain of Culture or the Mechanism for Cultural Transmission?

Anthropologists sometimes divide culture into "domains," which include social structure, subsistence, religion, art, politics, and technology. The adherent of Tylor's definition might maintain that all of these constitute "a complex whole," and thus are interrelated so that all are affected by the same guiding principles; as one changes, all may change. Some might also include language and perhaps education as domains of culture, but others would maintain that these are, in a sense, not separate domains but rather, as it were, what one "does" culture with. Education, particularly, seems to me to have an important role in the shaping of culture.

Actually, education has two important roles. It is what people use to transmit culture, to keep it, as it were, intact; and it is used to change culture. In American society of recent times, emphasis has been placed on both functions. The educational system has been used to effect major changes in American culture—for example, through the integration of public schools and the manipulation of school populations, or through the introduction of the concept of multiculturalism. At the same time, the education system has been urged or even required to support and rebuild a traditional body of knowledge and values in the American population.

In the world's cultures, it is the latter—the maintenance of a canon—that has usually been the task of the educational system. (By "system" I mean any of a great variety of processes, from formal schools to the transmission of family traditions, from a guru-disciple relationship to permission for children to sit by and watch as important knowledge and skills are exhibited.) The formal teaching of music in the world's societies has ordinarily involved the maintenance of a system, the passing on of received knowledge and established art.

Ethnomusicologists, to the extent that they have been concerned with the study of teaching and learning, have usually been concerned with these processes as a way of transmitting culture, not *changing* culture. There has usually been emphasis on the reliability of oral tradition and on the importance that non-Western societies place on the undisturbed transmission of cultural materials.

Several examples might be mentioned of formal institutions whose purpose has been to teach an unchanging culture. In India, the *gharana* system, described among others by Daniel Neuman and James Kippen,[2] is an institution that fulfills such a function. The educational system ties a student to one teacher exclusively for a number of years, seeking to assure that the teacher's style, approach, and repertory are passed on without change, completely, and without being disturbed by outside influence. One might, therefore, see a gharana as an educational system with certain standards enforced by the authority of an ancestor with a reputation that has become in part mythical, such as Tansen or Amir Khosrow, or in South India, the nineteenth-century composer Tyagaraja.

From this example it would appear that if there are standards of some kind in the musical education system of traditional India, they concern primarily the population of professional musicians. To be sure, music schools modeled on Western conservatories have developed in India in the twentieth century, as has the concept of amateur musicianship and the desire of many middle-class families to have their children become somewhat conversant with classical music. Although the music schools provide a very demanding curriculum and all students seem to master important rudimentary, though complex, areas of Indian musical theory and technique, the degree to which the music schools explicitly maintain standards valid for all of their students is questionable. It would seem that the personal approach of a student's major teacher would be most influential, and a group of students surrounding one teacher—something like the Western concept of the "studio"—might be seen as a kind of modern-day and microscopic gharana.

"Standards" in the Teaching of Persian Classical Music

The concept of standards, of requirements imposed on all, is more explicitly illustrated in the system for teaching Persian classical music in the twentieth century. We are not talking about a music education system valid for all students, or all children, such as the U.S. system is intended to be, but one which attempts to unify what is expected of all who try their hand at instruction in classical music. The "educational system," if you will, is the Persian *radif,* a body of music organized in the late nineteenth century, consisting of between two hundred and three hundred short and largely nonmetric pieces that one learns in order to provide a basis for improvisation, the principal form of music making in the classical system. The concept of individual repertories and approaches, perhaps similar to the Indian gharanas, which probably characterized the system of teaching music in the Middle East for centuries, was replaced by the notion of a radif that everyone was to learn. Each teacher, even now, has his own version, but the versions have much in common and there have been attempts at standardization, as in the publication in 1963 and 1978 of the radifs of certain authoritative teachers and the adoption of certain masters, and their radifs, by important educational institutions. Despite the clearly personal aspects of an improvisatory musical system, and the maintenance of some individuality of the various masters, we have here the concept of a commonly held repertory that serves as the point of departure, and thus the idea of a standard to which everyone who claims to be involved in Persian classical music must adhere. To a large extent, Persian classical musicians are judged by the degree to which they have mastered and continue to adhere to the radif.

The idea of knowing the radif is to provide the student with a basis for both content and style. The structure of the radif is such that it includes themes that may be used in improvisation, and these themes must be memorized. But also, it presents these themes in multi-ple versions and variations, to show the student that each of them can be presented in many ways. The student is thereby encouraged to improvise more and more varied versions. Also, the radif includes a great deal of thematically inconsequential material that is developed in various ways—repeated, varied, subjected to melodic sequence, made the point of departure for new melodic flights, contracted, expanded—again to show the student how to use techniques to improvise. So, the radif gives content—the twelve modes and the tunes associated with them—and style—techniques to be used in music-making.

The radif also teaches values: the tension between hierarchy and equality—hierarchy in traditional political and social structure versus the equality of all before God in Islam; the importance of unpredictability and surprise, of individualism (and the lower value, though also the obligatory presence, of the predictable); the difference in the order of events in informal and formal situations. These values can be abstracted from the music and from the way it is discussed, but they can also be observed in social behavior and discourse. The musical system, as in all cultures, reflects important aspects of the social system.

Thus, in traditional Iranian culture, it makes sense to consider the radif as a "standard" for the student of classical music. It is what every musician must know, and it is the basis for all music that is considered properly part of the classical system. It is also the canon of the musical system, and perhaps we could regard the issue of standards as somehow related to the concept of canon. If the concept of standards in education means learning a kind of canon, then surely education is a way of transmitting the culture, faithfully.

Certainly this is the case in the Persian classical system. But the learning is done by students who wish to be specialists; one cannot maintain that a person must know the radif to be a competent member of Iranian society, only to be a competent musician.

Transmission of Culture and Culture Change

The notion of standards works well in a system that purports to transmit a culture intact. What of the situation in which the purpose of education is to be a device to implement cultural change? Let me again turn to my experience in Iran for an example. In the first three decades of the twentieth century, it seemed to some Iranian musicians that the system of Persian classical music would be crushed by the increasing interest in Western music. The responses to this danger could be grouped into three categories: (1) maintaining the classical system unchanged (adopting, as it were, a siege mentality); (2) allowing Persian music to become more like Western music by the adoption of central elements of Western musical culture, such as functional harmony, emphasis on the composed piece and

de-emphasis on improvisation, and realignment of the scales so that they would fit the Western conception of the diatonic scale and, where needed, of tempered quarter tones (half of a tempered half tone); and (3) trying to maintain the traditional sound of the music by permitting change in the music's social contexts and functions. Although a mix of elements of all three responses characterized the subsequent history of Persian music, the third one, which we might call modernization, has been dominant. The person most responsible for this balance of responses was Ali Naqi Vaziri, a military officer who became interested in both Persian and Western music, studied in Europe, and was determined to bring various technologies of Western music to Iran specifically in order to modify the Persian musical system so that it could survive.

Among the reforms brought about by Vaziri were aspects of education. Vaziri insisted on the importance of notating Persian music, which materially changed the way the music is transmitted (i.e., taught) and changed substantially its improvisatory and individualistic aspects. He established conservatories of music in which people of all ages might learn to perform Persian music. He instituted a separation of study of the radif and learning the techniques of instruments, something again new to a system in which musical repertory and techniques of performance were combined; and he also was responsible for the separation of radifs by instrument, teaching different versions of the radif for violin, plucked instruments, and *santour* (a hammered dulcimer)—something that changed the system to being much more instrument-specific than it earlier appears to have been. He instituted theory classes separate from performance lessons. In general, he wished for a much larger proportion of the Iranian population to have an understanding of their music than was the case before, and he wished to permit many people to have a chance to study performance, not in order to make them professionals but to build educated and appreciative audiences. In addition to music schools, Vaziri established music clubs for sponsoring performances, and he took special care to provide opportunities for women to enter the musical culture by permitting young girls to study in the music schools along with the boys, by establishing a women's music club, and in general by urging the participation of women on a par with European practices.

Can one say that Vaziri was introducing something like standards for Persian music in the musical culture of Iran? Certainly not in the public schools, which avoided music. And certainly he had no expectations that every Iranian would have a certain level of musical education. But his work seems to hold up the ideal that in order to be a proper member of Iranian society, a certain kind of musical competence is required. It is hard to know how well he succeed-

ed. In Iran, since the death of Ayatollah Khomeini, Persian classical music is flourishing, in part because popular music is disapproved, and in part because the classical tradition is pointing in a religious direction. But it seems unlikely that a larger proportion of the population understands classical music than before.

There is one area of Iranian culture in which music plays a greater role than before, and it is not because of Vaziri's reforms but because of the close association of music and ethnicity in situations in which a society is put in a position of cultural stress. I am speaking of the musical culture of the emigré communities of Iranians—those Iranians who have moved to the United States and who have rekindled their interest in their homeland as a way to cement their ties to one another.

Musical Competence and Musical Standards in Ethnic Minorities

According to Alan P. Merriam, music contributes to the integration of society and validates social institutions; these are among the principal functions of music. Becoming acquainted with members of Iranian immigrant groups in American cities, one quickly draws the conclusion that the two principal domains of culture (plus, of course, language) that the society draws on to underscore its ethnicity are cooking (folklorists prefer the term "foodways") and music. Interviewed about their interest in music, Persian classical music in particular, a good many immigrants indicated that when in Iran, they had taken little interest in Persian music, but after coming to the United States, they began to listen to recordings of it, to go to Iranian music concerts, and to learn something about its theory. It helped them reconstruct memories of Iran, and it made them feel that they were part of an Iranian society even though abroad. And indeed, Iranian ceremonies such as the New Year's celebration "Nowruz" are more often accompanied by musical performances in America than they were in Iran (at least in the 1970s, the period for which I can speak). Iranian music concerts play more of a role in America than they did in Tehran of that time. They share characteristics of many ethnic music concerts: the audience dresses up quite formally, and people come very early in order to engage in socializing for half an hour or more.

Now, it would not be reasonable to say that knowledge of Persian music—that is, understanding the radif to some extent (recognizing the principal modes, perhaps) and the main genres of classical music—is essential for being a member of Iranian society. That kind of musical competence is not a standard of membership in the culture. And yet in my experience, Iranians in the United States tend to claim this kind of knowledge more readily than did the people whom I knew in Iran around 1970.

The use of music by minorities to integrate society is well established, of course. Italian-Americans, Greek-Americans, Swedish-Americans have all used music and dance—and food—to indicate to each other and to the outside world that they are members of a distinct ethnic group, and proud of it. Children in some of these societies have been told, in effect, that they must learn the songs and dances in order to be members of the ethnic group. They may dress like mainstream Americans, have jobs of all types, even forget the traditional language, and they may diverge in terms of religion, economic status, and social beliefs, but what will tie them to their ancestors is likely to be music and dance more than anything else. There is something about these tendencies related to the concept of cultural competence—something that brings us near to the idea of standards in music education.

Music as Emblem of Culture in Native American Societies

If music is used as an integrating force by Euro-American minorities trying to keep their cultural identities intact while also joining the mainstream, it has also been a major factor in reconstructing the cultures of Native American peoples, some of which have been virtually destroyed. Traditional culture (hardly the "stone age" ways of life in the imagination of some white people, but probably eighteenth- and nineteenth-century practices) had substantially disappeared in the twentieth century. Older practices and traditions came to be unknown to the majority of the members of many tribes, but they continued in the minds of a few individuals, often perhaps in fragmented form. The first half of the twentieth century may be characterized by the development of intertribal or pan-Indian practices whose purpose was to integrate Native American society as a whole. But after 1950, there came increased interest in tribal practices, and the idea of reestablishing tribal identity became a major task of the leaders in society.

This was true in the society with which I have some acquaintance, the Blackfoot people of Montana. In the 1960s, after periods of extreme poverty, some natural disasters, and widespread cultural malaise, several individuals began to believe that the knowledge of tribal traditions, kept by a few older men, should become more widespread. This included informal and eventually formal movements to teach the Blackfoot language to young people who had grown up speaking only English. More important, an annual tribal powwow was established, at which Blackfoot people from the American and Canadian reservations and elsewhere gathered for several days to rekindle cultural traditions. Most significant, some tribal leaders, including Earl Oldperson, later the long-term chairman of the tribal council, began to teach young children songs and dances. The implied basis of these activities was the belief that to be a proper member of

Blackfoot society, certain competencies were required; certain standards were held up as ideals.

These teachings of the Blackfoot elders were not very different from those of the Iranian Ali Naqi Vaziri. They put into practice the definition of culture that requires that members of a society agree on certain values and be able to do certain things. Education thus fulfilled its two missions: transmitting the traditions of a culture, and effecting cultural change.

An Ethnomusicologist Contemplates the Standards

In a way, this is what the National Standards for Music Education seek to achieve. It appears to me that the notion of standards in music education, the notion of cultural competence, the relationship of music and ethnicity, and the anthropologist's definition of culture have a lot to do with each other. Looking at the Standards from an ethnomusicological perspective, it seems clear to me that something rather unprecedented is being attempted. We are a culture in which most musical activity has been carried out by specialists. Even the notion of general participation, a hallmark of our conception of folk culture, has turned out to be an oversimplification. Even in European village societies there have been specialists in the knowledge and practice of music. Nevertheless, the Standards propose that each student should, as it were, have a crack at each of the musical activities recognized in society—performance, composition, improvisation, and various kinds of perception and reception. There are elements of this approach in the Iranian and Blackfoot models, to be sure. Vaziri thought that for Persian music to survive it had to become more widely understood in its own society and it had to achieve the kind of status that is enjoyed by music in Western societies. The Blackfoot elders wanted children to learn music from human teachers, not exclusively through visions, the traditional way of acquiring music. Both models involve transmission as well as change.

To me, however, the Standards seem to have the purpose of changing musical culture very substantially. To the side of the ethnomusicological mind interested in broadening musical understanding by providing intercultural and multimusical experience, and by looking at music as an aspect of culture, the establishment of the Standards is a promising development. To the other side, which observes events and analyzes them without involvement, their implementation will provide a fascinating study of transmission and cultural change, to be compared with the many other different ways in which musical culture has been transmitted and changed by human societies. The Standards intend to make available to all children of America the broad range of musical involvements this culture provides, so that all may be full members of their country's musical community. It will be fascinating to see whether this admirable and ambitious hope comes eventually to be realized.

Notes

1. E. B. Tylor, *Primitive Culture,* vol. 2 (London: J. Murray, 1871), 1.

2. Daniel Neuman, *The Life of Music in Northern India* (Detroit: Wayne State University Press, 1980), and James Kippen, *The Tabla of Lucknow* (Cambridge: Cambridge University Press, 1988).

The Ideas in Action

12

An Agenda for Teaching Performing with Understanding

Bennett Reimer

During the course of the 1996 Northwestern University Music Education Leadership Seminar, the attendees generated a set of ten guidelines relating to the cultivation of musical understanding through and in performance. These guidelines, embedded in the discussions of chapters 3–10, provide a powerful and practical agenda for action. Here they will be made explicit, as a summary of the book and as a source of insights all music educators can employ as they attempt to infuse their teaching with opportunities for their students to grow as understanding performers.

Guidelines for Teaching Performing with Understanding

1. **Performance can and should be an important means for achieving significant learnings in all nine content standards. All nine must be included as learning goals in all performance settings.**

As briefly mentioned in chapter 2, the Standards can be fulfilled in both general music settings and in a variety of special-focus settings. In the former, all nine standards would be represented in age-appropriate and learning-objective-appropriate balances. Overall, for a general education in music, the intent is to introduce students to all the learning/experiencing aspects of music as the nine standards delineate them, rather than to focus on any particular one(s) with the others being supplementary.

In the latter case—that is, for special-focus settings in which one particular musical dimension becomes the focal point for all learnings—the balance shifts, so that one standard becomes primary and the others become supportive.

Performance has traditionally been the dominant special focus in American

185

music education; hence the need for a book like this to help guide the profession to more effective practices that infuse performance with all the learnings contained in the other standards. But performance need not be the only special focus for musical involvement and musical learning. Improvising (which, of course, requires performance but in a substantially different way than does the performance of composed music), composing, listening, analyzing and describing, musical criticism, interdisciplinary learning, cultural and historical studies, all can be the primary focus of instruction, with the other Standards areas conceived as contributory to that focus. Providing such expanded opportunities may well be the major thrust of a renewed music education profession in the future.

The performance opportunity, however, will continue to be an important aspect of the total music program, because many young people will no doubt continue to desire to be involved with music through a performance perspective. So our professional obligation to continue to offer strong performance programs remains pressing, now reflecting our increasing awareness that "strong" means, in large part, programs devoted to fostering understanding performers.

As this book has attempted to make clear, performance learnings readily, naturally, and productively incorporate learnings from all the other Standards areas. The understanding performer is one who, while approaching music from the particular perspective of a performer of it, is able to incorporate within that musical role a host of relevant connections to the wider musical/cultural world in which performance resides. With performers no longer conceived as only skilled technicians dependent on others for creative decisions, the development of understanding performers is an ideal we can now back up with action—with specific teaching/learning strategies based on a clear set of principles for what achieving musical understanding requires. We have no excuse, if we ever did, for approaching performance teaching as anything less than a powerful modality for nurturing creative, independent, understanding performers. Such a goal not only transforms our contribution to our students; it is also worthy of our professional expertise. A primary agenda for the music education profession at this time in its history is to conceive performance as a powerful context within which all musical learnings entailed in the Standards can be assimilated, and to ensure that such learnings actually take place by regarding the Standards as a practical guide and source for learning objectives in performance settings.

2. Rehearsing and performing music are likely to lead to performance with understanding and significant learning, as described in the Standards, when there is a planned effort to achieve these outcomes.

It is one thing to give intellectual

assent to the need for infusing all the Standards within performance programs; it is another to actually do so. While some performance teachers have already adapted themselves to standards-based teaching, and others have done so for a very long time before the Standards appeared in their present form, still others—perhaps most others—will need time and practice in order to learn how to enrich their teaching with far more subject matter than traditionally has been included.

For standards-derived learnings to become part and parcel of the performance experience, specific, careful planning will be needed to make those learnings authentic, relevant, and effective. The preceding chapters in this book offer a host of ideas and examples as to how that can be accomplished. But no book can substitute for each teacher's decisions, in the particular context in which she or he works, as to which learnings need to be incorporated at which specific points in the performance teaching-learning continuum.

Such decisions, Guideline 2 insists, cannot be left to the spur of the moment. While there is an important "improvisatory" dimension to effective teaching, in which decisions on-the-spot are called for, there must also be a dimension of careful, reflective planning to insure that those on-the-spot adaptations will in fact occur across the broad spectrum of learnings the Standards exemplify. More than ever could have occurred pre-Standards, performance

teachers, and general music teachers when they are teaching performance, must now consciously and carefully plan their programs, repertoire, teaching strategies, rehearsal procedures, and even public performances with the learnings in the Standards front and center in their consciousness. What learnings need to be incorporated in the next class or rehearsal? How do they connect with the piece(s) we are preparing? How do they connect with and expand previous learnings? What further learnings do they open themselves to? In short, how does performance become a curriculum—a planned, sequential, comprehensive, balanced progression of developmental learnings such as every subject studied in schools is required to be?

We should not deceive ourselves into thinking that the task of transforming performance into a full-fledged curriculum of musical learnings will be easily accomplished. It will not be easy because (1) we have little experience at it, and (2) it is among the most complex endeavors in all of education. Musical learnings from all the Standards, remember, must, in genuine performance, become embedded as an ingredient in the performer's actions. The learnings by themselves, as awarenesses or understandings not yet infusing the artistic decisions performers must make, are not, for performers, sufficient. The teacher's guidance toward transforming a wide spectrum of understandings into the actualities of musically expressive sounds is the special contribution such a teacher makes—a contribution involving every student's mind, body, and feelings in concerted, unified action. No wonder this will not be accomplished effortlessly. No wonder the entire profession of music education will need to work together to fully develop its considerable capacities to meet this challenge.

3. When performers have been helped to gain insight into the structure, context, significance, and relative merits of the music they are studying/performing, in addition to the technical facility to perform it adequately, both musical understanding and the quality of performance are enhanced.

For performers, the payoffs of achieving deeper and wider understandings of the music they are encountering are twofold. First, they become broadly educated about music, a goal worthy of pursuing in and of itself. But in addition, and specifically related to the performer's role, their performances become better. How better?

Few experienced music educators can have escaped hearing performances of school groups or individuals whose playing or singing has been technically adequate or even impressive while the musical values beyond technique have been painfully shallow. While nonspecialist audiences may miss this perception (although they are certainly not incapable of gaining it), professionals can spot the situation readily. We can excuse it, knowing how much effort

and time it takes to get the technical demands fulfilled, or assuming that school-age children can't be expected to bring musical maturity (understanding) to the task except superficially. But neither of those excuses holds water.

In regard to technical demands, repertoire so difficult as to require extraordinary efforts in order to bring it to even a barely adequate technical level for public performance is repertoire inappropriate for the students in question. That point has been made, over and over, by many music educators. Learning a piece, we are likely to agree, goes far beyond getting the notes in working order. If that were not the case our jobs could essentially be regarded to be of a technical nature, and musical performance a matter of technical training. As musicians we know better. We know what artistry requires, including highly developed technique as an essential ingredient. When we settle for teaching at the level of training, or are forced to do so by improper repertoire combined with inadequate preparation time, we denigrate our professional role, our students' needs, and the music we are performing. The Standards are a clarion call to abandon that unfortunate tendency in school performance programs.

As to musical maturity, are students in K–12 grades capable of the insightful musicianship genuine performance requires? The only adequate answer to that question is "yes—to the degree reasonable for their age and experience."

Whether the students in question are very young or high school seniors or college students, they are all, by virtue of their humanness, capable of being mature performers—*mature for who they are at their particular stage of development.* Maturity, after all, is always relative. Musically mature first graders are those capable of performing as insightfully as one can hope first graders to be. Maturity is not something one awaits in the future. It is the achieved depth of understanding one demonstrates at every stage of one's life.

Regarded this way, effective performance teaching is that which aims toward cultivating maximal musical maturity for all student performers at every stage of their development. Maturity, here, is synonymous with the achievement of musical understanding in the mode of performance. That is, the students' maturity, or level of understanding, must be displayed *in the act of performing.* When it is displayed by, say, a class of first graders singing a song, we recognize it immediately. While we can expect that one dimension of that display will be technical accuracy, we also recognize that every student has internalized—has accommodated within his or her singing as integral components—the melodic/rhythmic/dynamic/stylistic/cultural awarenesses that transform the song into an artistic utterance. Yes, they are just first graders. But they are *musically artistic* first graders. When we encounter their artistry we are inevitably deeply touched musically. We know that they are as well. And we resolve never to settle for anything less, no matter the age of the young people we are teaching to perform.

Performances infused with musical understanding, including contextual influences on the music, are, by definition, of better quality than those devoid of such understanding. Quality performances, to be artistic rather than only proficient, *require* that breadth and depth of artistic understanding be demonstrated to the degree the youngsters in question are able to do so. All such demonstrations of musical/artistic understanding demonstrate that musical performance manifests human intelligence at the highest levels of its potential. Regarding performance as one important way for humans to understand—to exemplify intelligence in action—transforms the role of the performer from recreational to foundational. Performances infused with understanding integrate, in a single, extended act, complex, higher-order thinking capacities; skilled bodily control over the transformation of thought into meaningful sounds; and the shaping and molding of those sounds in affectively moving ways. Helping young people achieve such artistry is the foundational obligation of performance teachers in every setting in which performance takes place.

4. Developing musical understanding through and in performance is most effectively accomplished when

responsibilities for planning, selecting, rehearsing, practicing, and making musical decisions are appropriately shared among students and teachers/directors.

Teachers, of course, are responsible for making substantive decisions about, and exercising significant control over, the whys, whens, whats, and hows of education. But we know that education is most effective—that it deeply changes students in positive directions—when many responsibilities are distributed among students and teachers in an atmosphere of cooperative pursuit of mutually desired ends. Students cannot simply be "given" the understandings of their teachers. They must be helped to reconstruct within themselves, through their own acts of appropriation and transformation, the understandings being sought. Ownership of the process of education, while influenced by teachers, must also be achieved by students, who are most effectively involved in learning by being partners rather than only recipients.

The performance culture of the Western world, especially in large-group contexts, has often been based on a leader-follower dynamic. That arrangement of responsibilities is built into the way much music has been conceived in Western music history. That conception depends on the "concerted" efforts of a large group of people to achieve a largely predetermined musical end ("the work") as guided by the unifying vision of the person responsible for "direct-

ing," or "conducting," the process of realization. The roles of leader and follower are well-defined in such a structure of creative endeavor.

Given this inherent dynamic it is quite natural for directors of large musical ensembles in the schools to assume the mantle of leadership and to act out its many responsibilities, such as for choosing music, planning rehearsals, carrying out each step in the process of learning the pieces through direct instruction, making and imparting all major and even minor decisions about how to properly interpret the pieces, planning and conducting the concert with all its associated details, and on and on with all the very real and quite necessary steps to comply with this kind of musical performance expectation. One can only be enormously impressed with the diversity and depth of challenges fulfilled by competent school music ensemble directors. Such people truly deserve a great deal of genuine respect.

Directors who provide all the required leadership for successful performance of concerted Western music, and who also succeed in imparting to their students a sense that they, too, are owners of both the processes and products of performing, are models of what effective performance instruction can be. In such situations the directors are able to balance their own necessary leadership with the active, creative, respectful involvement of their students in all the many musical decisions and solutions required to bring a convincing performance into being. They demonstrate, at every step along the way, that performing is a genuinely creative act requiring the full responsibilities of all involved. In such situations students are allowed to—*are required* to—be genuine musicians; that is, creative artists in the particular role of musical performance. The gift of experiencing artistry as a musical performer is the greatest a director/teacher can give to students. That gift can be and should be given to children of all ages, no matter how young, and in all situations in which performance takes place. The foundational understanding that performing is a personally creative act then powerfully underlies and enriches all the other understandings required for successful performance.

5. An important outgrowth of musical understanding is musical independence. All performance experiences should have as a major goal the nurturing of musical independence.

The culminating outcome of achieving Guideline 4 above is that doing so cultivates every student's musical selfhood—the qualities of musicianly creativity particular to each student's unique personality. This kind of artistic independence tends to be subjugated within the demands of the concerted/collaborative/self-subordinating role musicians must play in large-group contexts, especially for those who are not able to occupy solo chairs, which provide for a high degree of individuality.

The key point here is that no matter how coordinated the playing/singing of ensemble performance must be, all involved in it must at the same time feel that their individual performance retains its selfness—its genuine personhood—while also being integrated with those of others. This paradoxical task—the achievement of selfhood and partnership simultaneously—lies at the heart of all group artistic performance. Perhaps the best term to describe that experience is "communion." Here, in musical communion, individuals participate in joint, creative, self-combined-with-others experience, in which neither individuality nor community is sacrificed. The power of such experience is so great that all who achieve it are touched forever. It is among the greatest values of group performance.

Achieving such experience requires each participant to be able to bring his or her genuine personhood to the task. Independence as a musician means the ability to apply one's musical understandings to the musical problems and challenges one faces, whether performing alone or with others. Independence conceived this way becomes synonymous with freedom. One achieves the freedom to be, musically, who one is, with all the challenges, satisfactions, and responsibilities this entails. To cultivate this sense of freedom in all one's students, through the challenges, satisfactions, and responsibilities one presents to them, is a basic obligation of every performance teacher.

6. The broadest possible array of performance opportunities should be made available to all students.

For a very long time in the history of music education in the United States, and in other countries especially in the Western world, performance beyond the exploratory or introductory experiences offered in general music settings has been limited to three basic Western ensemble formats—bands, orchestras, and choruses. Each of these ensembles fits well with the large-group Western ideal, satisfying both musical values and also the practical value of including as many students as possible with a minimum investment in faculty. Each ensemble represents a broad, diverse literature of worthy music, ranging across the spectrum from quite easy to very difficult. Each lends itself to a variety of associated smaller ensembles and associated genres, expanding musical possibilities beyond full-group, standard repertoire. Each has its particular attractions both for students and audiences. For these and other reasons the band-orchestra-chorus format of school performance programs has been and remains dominant.

The number of students electing to become involved in performance programs so conceived, has, over the past several decades, begun to decrease. There are probably many reasons for what seems to be a declining interest, or, at least, no discernable growth in interest, in traditional school performance electives. The one reason of concern here is that the musical experiences attainable within the band-orchestra-chorus format are gradually becoming less attractive or compelling as compared with a great variety of other musical experiences available in rich, diverse ways outside traditional school music settings. Music is certainly not decreasing as a potent force in the lives of school-age children; if anything it is burgeoning as a source of pleasure and satisfaction in all of American culture, including, very prominently, the culture of young people. The power of music in youngsters' lives is as great or greater than it has ever been, especially in light of its increasingly easy availability to all. The attractiveness of traditional school performance programs, however, has dwindled.

There are several possible responses to this situation. One is to change nothing except the level of advocacy efforts for what we now offer. We are presently witnessing an unprecedented investment in advocacy initiatives on the part of all who have a vested interest in maintaining bands, orchestras, and choruses as they have traditionally existed. These initiatives intensify in direct proportion to the decline of interest in these programs. They may stem the tide, at least for a while, but they are likely to fail in the longer run. Musical culture has changed and is continuing to change in ways causing bands, orchestras, and choruses to be less and less relevant to the musical satisfactions sought by increasing numbers of people.

Rather than frantically advocating for the status quo, it is becoming clearer that what is called for is a serious reconsideration of the nature of the performance program in schools. While maintaining the benefits of important traditional opportunities, we must also face squarely the need to rethink how we can better serve the musical needs of a culture no longer devoted to or limited by the musical opportunities schools continue to rely so heavily upon.

The key to our continuing relevance to the musical interests of those who choose to learn to be performers is not to abandon the excellent opportunities we have made available in bands, orchestras, and choruses, but to encourage and hasten the already existent movement toward adding a greater diversity of performance opportunities reflecting a more accurate representation of the musics thriving in contemporary American culture. This means much more than the (healthy) use of more small-group literature as related to the repertoires of bands, orchestras, and choruses. It means, also, an expansion of musical literatures far beyond those school-sanctioned styles to the diverse domains of popular styles and styles related to cultures from around the world.

We must not underestimate the revolutionary nature of this challenge. Not only will it rebalance school performance programs in significant ways, it will require important changes in musical attitudes and values by the music education profession; in recruitment into teaching of many young people whose performance experiences and commitments are outside the band-orchestra-chorus milieu; in reconstructing school music facilities and schedules; in rethinking appropriate performance settings and events; in reconceiving what constitutes a viable faculty of school music teachers and what constitutes a viable college/university faculty capable of preparing the diversity of performance teachers that will be required; in enlisting non-music education college/university faculty members to supply the needed preparation of performance teachers whose specializations are outside the Western concert tradition; and on and on with all the ripplings outward of a breakthrough from our singular focus on Western concert music to a better alignment with the diversity of the musical culture that actually exists in the world in which we live. Make no mistake: what might sound like a modest proposal to provide an increased array of performance opportunities will, if it is not to be window dressing, have profound implications for changes in the music education profession and all the supporting professions on which it depends.

Is the profession capable of this level of redefinition? Without it, will it be doomed to eventual extinction, at least in the form in which it has so far existed? These are questions deserving whole-hearted, honest, and widespread debate by all devoted to the music education endeavor. In the meantime, the Standards require that all possible efforts be made to expand performance opportunities in the direction of genres and styles heretofore unrepresented or only marginally represented in traditional school performance programs. Each such expansion is likely to involve in performance a segment of the student population that would have never been involved otherwise, thereby enhancing the musical experiences of a broader representation of students and strengthening the contribution and security of the profession as a result.

7. **High-quality literature, as defined within each genre, style, and culture, provides the greatest opportunity for genuine, satisfying, and educative musical experiences for performers.**

A major argument for the primacy of the traditional performance ensembles in school programs has been that the literature for these groups is of high quality, while that of other groups is necessarily of lower quality. This argument reflects a long-standing and widespread bias in Western musical culture, based on the idea that musical quality is a zero-sum game. That is, if one particular style or type of music is considered to be good, or "high," others must then be considered to be comparatively less good, or "lower." The judgment that the classical music performed by orchestras and choruses represents the highest level of the musical hierarchy, followed by the lesser but still respectable music

of bands, then followed by the ragtag assemblage of musics of low quality represented by various popular styles and by various "foreign" musics, has held sway, and to some extent continues to be exercised, in a great many college/university music departments in which music educators obtain their education. Given that students accepted into higher education music departments are those who have become immersed in, and who have been successful with, the musical values represented by bands, orchestras, and choruses in schools, and whose college education further reinforces those values, it is no mystery why the hierarchical idea of musical value has persisted for so long.

In recent years, as Western culture has been subjected to reappraisal from a great variety of sources exploring and debunking long-standing attitudes, a spirit of rejuvenation and open-mindedness has been manifested in many aspects of social values. In music the realization has spread that artistic/aesthetic value, rather than being competitive or hierarchical, is demonstrated in all musics of the world, each contributing its particular musical values to people's potential satisfactions. This does not mean that every instance of music is as "good" or "valuable" or "excellent" as every other, in a kind of extreme egalitarianism that avoids any and all judgments of quality. It does mean that each musical practice develops its own, internal criteria of quality, and each instance of music must be judged according to the criteria relevant to it. Every music in the world is likely to have instances of highest to lowest quality, including Western classical music, and each music should be judged according to its particular, culturally determined criteria of goodness.

As this more tolerant value orientation continues to expand we are witnessing more acceptance in school music programs of musics previously shunned as being "lesser" in value or even devoid of value. We are even beginning to witness a shift in that direction in the hallowed halls and rehearsal rooms of those bastions of conservatism called college and university departments or schools of music, where innovation often requires infinite patience in the face of fierce opposition. In this matter of movement toward a more liberal value system, school music teachers have been, and, it can be argued, must continue to be, in the forefront, exerting continual pressure on colleges and universities to keep up with, or at least move in the direction of, needed changes.

In this time of reorientation from a single criterion of musical quality to a more open acceptance of quality as situated in particular musical practices, music educators must be willing to explore musics with which they are not entirely familiar, and to seek, within each such music, guidance toward including the best possible examples according to the particular musical practices in question. This makes great

demands on teachers. After all, it is much more comfortable and secure to deal with what one knows, and do it well, than to stick one's neck out into unfamiliar, puzzling territory in which success is uncertain. The requirement in the Standards that a broad array of musics be included, and that the highest quality examples of each be chosen for performance, will call on all the courage professionals are capable of demonstrating, along with patience and tolerance as the entire field of music education struggles to rebalance its long-standing values and practices.

8. Improvisation provides a powerful opportunity to develop musical independence, higher-order musical thinking, understanding, and personal creativity for every performer. All possible opportunities to develop improvisation abilities should be provided students in both general music and elective settings.

While expertise and interest in improvisation were represented by the attendees at this leadership seminar, it is clear that the special nature of this musical endeavor, and the complex issues surrounding it, require a separate seminar devoted to it. A few comments will have to suffice at this point.

Performing composed, notated music and performing improvisations share the requirement that the basic technical skills for musical expression through performance be in place. Beyond that similarity there are fundamental differences in the musical thinking and understanding each calls upon. Performing composed music entails an interpretive ability—the expertise to translate notation into sounds, to create those sounds as appropriate for the composer's intentions while also bringing them to life with imagination and personality, and to do so either by oneself or as a partner with others in a shared interpretation, a shared attempt to represent the composition authoritatively and vividly. Interpretation, to be successful, requires a great deal of relevant musical understanding in addition to the skill to accomplish what is required by the technical demands of the music one is performing. It also takes a particular mind-set—a mind-set of devotion to the composition as one's foundational artistic obligation.

Improvisation, unlike performing compositions, entails the making of substantive decisions about what to perform while engaged in the act of performance. There are many constraints on what one can properly improvise, provided by the musical content of the piece serving as the basis for one's improvisation, by its historical-cultural-stylistic expectation system, by what others are doing in a group improvisation, by the breadth and depth of one's imaginative repertory of musical gestures, and by one's individuality as a musician at the time one is improvising. (In so-called "free improvisation" the first of these constraints—a pre-set piece providing a basic structure within which one improvises—is missing, but

all the other constraints apply). Within the context of all these constraints the goal remains, nevertheless, to create an original event every time one improvises. To do what improvisation requires demands the craftsmanship that allows one to do what one chooses to do, the musical understandings related to the contexts that make one's improvisation authentic, the imagination to be both original yet grounded every time one improvises, and a mind-set of devotion to generating fresh musical insights in the immediacy of the performance act.

Learning to perform compositions, or to improvise, does not prepare musicians to do the other, except insofar as some basic technical abilities may apply to both. Each entails a complex mode of musical being with its own goals and challenges. Many argue that the two actually are incompatible, and that the more one is steeped in the musical thinking/doing one of them requires the less likely one will be able to accomplish the other successfully, accounting for the rarity of musicians who are excellent in both. Whether or not this position is convincing it is clear that enabling performers to improvise requires specific, focused, intentional instruction relevant to its unique demands.

Who is capable of supplying this instruction? Music educators whose entire experience as performers, and whose entire training to be teachers of performance, has been limited to the performing of composed music, are singularly unequipped to do so. Some music educators have had a good deal of experience improvising in the most well-known style of music in our culture dependent on improvisation—jazz—and, if they have been lucky, have been trained to teach it effectively as part of their studies in music education. The proliferation of jazz offerings in the schools, taught by experienced improvisers, has been a major advance in our profession's ability to serve the musical interests of a significant segment of the student population.

But much remains to be accomplished if this powerful way to understand musically is to be nurtured as part of the education of all students, at least some of whom are likely to want to continue to improvise as a major way to be involved with music. In general music, in addition to the improvisational activities offered in Orff and other experiences, far more can be done to insure that all students are enabled to understand and create in the challenging, satisfying mode of improvisation, including jazz styles, world music styles in which improvisation is the basic way to perform, popular styles that incorporate improvisation, and the infusion of improvisational thinking into a broad range of exploratory performance experiences. Each of these lends itself to electives in which further expertise can be developed for those choosing to do so.

The stipulation in the Standards that improvisation in its many manifestations should become a basic component of all music programs challenges the profession to develop its expertise in what has been a neglected aspect of musical creation. Adding this kind of performance creativity to the kind required for composed music will significantly enrich the creative musical opportunities for all students.

9. To fulfill the intent of the National Standards, expectations for performance must reflect that the students have been successful in achieving musical understandings.

As with all learnings, the attainment of understanding in and through performance requires ongoing assessment of whether and to what extent it is being accomplished. Such assessment can take many forms, including tests and other formal evaluation modalities, and also through providing appropriate opportunities for demonstrations of understanding in auditions, assignments, contests and festivals, public programs, and so forth. Understanding cannot simply be hoped for. It must be expected, and looked for, in all aspects of instruction. That will require that students demonstrate, as an essential dimension of their learning, their level of achieved understanding. How can this be accomplished?

Teachers of performance must remember that understandings expressed verbally, while helpful and revealing, are insufficient. As explained in chapter 2, understanding, consisting of the forming of relevant connections, must, in performance, be demonstrated in the relevance of musically informed performance decisions each student is able to make. While verbal explanations can help clarify those decisions, pointing out the connections being brought to bear on them, the proof of the "performance pudding" is always in what the student(s) actually are able to do with those connections in the performance act.

This suggests that in any testing for performance understanding, challenging problems be presented, dealing with interpretation, analysis, technical demands, ensemble issues, cultural/stylistic veracity, imaginative exploration, all requiring student-determined decisions to be made. Those decisions can be illuminated by verbal explanations, but such explanations cannot substitute for performance demonstrations. Verbal tests must not be equated with tests of understanding when performance understanding is being assessed. There is a strong tendency to do so, because of the traditional but misguided notion that understanding is always verbally (or numerically) expressible. That this is an error is made clear by performance.

Movement toward valid assessment of performance understanding has been dramatic since the publication of the Standards and the follow-up publication of Standards-related materials. MENC's *Strategies for Teaching* series and its publication *Performance Standards for Music* go a long way toward providing guidelines for and specific examples of the many ways understanding can be culti-vated and demonstrated. If practices based on these examples become pervasive in performance teaching the profession will have achieved a maturity and relevance it has long sought. The long-standing attitude that performance is not and cannot be a genuine curriculum of learnings, and that the only valid assessment is a rating of a finished, polished performance, will finally have been replaced by the realization that assessment is ongoing, multidimensional, and obligated to focus as much on the qualities of what has been learned as on the flawlessness of a teacher-determined end product.

When this attitude, backed up by action, pervades all performance instruction, students, parents, communities, and other education professionals will soon take it as a given that performance is a multichallenging endeavor with its own, special, artistic demands on minds, bodies, and feelings. All stand to gain by this (accurate) perception, including, not least of all, music education professionals, whose contributions to human understanding will be more clearly perceived than traditionally has been the case. Indeed, the overt expectation that performance must always be infused with understanding will insure that attitudes toward performance will shift in the direction of recognition of performing as an important way for humans to be intelligent. When understanding is lacking in performance, overshadowed by technical training of a convergent nature, it is reasonable for people to regard it as essentially an "activity" rather than a "discipline." The movement toward performing with understanding will strengthen the status of and respect for performance in schools as a genuine subject with its particular demands on intelligence.

A necessary aspect of this movement will be the recognition by all professionals involved in teaching performance (which means practically all teachers of music in the schools) that understanding must occupy a far more visible, more proactive place in instruction than has typically been the case.

10. In addition to the development of expertise in teaching the unprecedented depth and breadth of musical learnings the Standards embody, the preparation and continuing education of performance teachers must be founded on their personal experiencing of excellent models of how performing with understanding is nurtured.

The responsibility for teacher education that is Standards-based and aimed toward fostering musical understanding rests largely on college music education faculty. They must introduce undergraduate and advanced students to the Standards and develop their competence to become teachers able to apply the comprehensive learnings the Standards entail, including all the learnings that enable performers to acquire understanding. That is perhaps the most pressing agenda at present for music teacher educators, an agenda filled with

both challenge and opportunity.

But music education specialists at the college level are not generally expected to provide the substantive theoretical, historical, cultural, and general learnings essential for music teachers, and they are often not the ones responsible for offering performance training in studios and rehearsal halls (depending, of course, on the size and diversity of particular college music departments). Whoever does offer that performance training, whether non-music education specialists or music educators who also teach performance, must be able to immerse their students in experiences that are as rich with the development of understandings as those students will themselves be expected to offer when they become teachers or return to teaching. Without internalized models for fostering performance understandings, gained in all dimensions of their performance experiences, students are unlikely to be able to foster their own students' understandings or even be interested in doing so. To the extent their own performance training has been focused on achieving an optimum balance of technique with understanding, they are likely to regard this as the normal and desirable way to teach performance and will willingly follow that model in their own teaching, aided and refined by their music education specialization learnings.

Unfortunately, much music teaching experienced by music education majors, in theory, history, literature, and performance, including conducting, is focused heavily toward the preparation of professional performers rather than professional school music teachers. In both private lessons and ensembles the goal is often to produce performance excellence far more narrowly defined than the Standards conceive it. When private teachers and ensemble directors follow the professional musician model, the students assimilating that model are likely to regard it as gospel, especially given the high regard students often have for their performance teachers. Such students then become school performance directors who try as hard as they can to recreate, in their teaching, the performance teaching they themselves experienced, and who send on to become music educators those students in their ensembles most successful at learning within that model. Round and round goes the wheel.

Change in this well-entrenched system is likely to be hard-won. In some music education institutions the faculty are all devoted to teacher education as a major if not the major mission, and are able to work cooperatively toward shared goals, including that of providing excellent models of teaching performing with understanding. In other institutions, especially those primarily devoted to training professional performers, music education majors are often simply treated as not quite the cream of the crop but to be tolerated nevertheless. After all, the ideal of the professional musicians applies equally to

all, doesn't it? Even in schools, those who elect to perform must rightfully be treated as if they are very young professionals in training, no? So what's the problem with those music education faculty members, who keep pleading for lesson and rehearsal time to be spent on teaching material better confined to theory, history, and literature classes?

Of course there are many performance teachers who, while not music educators in the school-music sense, are nevertheless deeply committed to teaching their students to be understanding performers and who are masters at doing so. Wherever such excellent teachers exist it behooves the fortunate music education faculty there to take full advantage of them, not only in their own programs but by involving them as much as possible in modeling opportunities for the music education community and professional musician communities.

In a perfect world (as music educators are likely to conceive it) all college music teachers, no matter their specialization, would be ready, willing, and able to help prepare music education majors to pursue the values of imbuing their school-age students with deep and broad musical understandings gained through performance experiences, and would provide, in their own teaching, excellent models of how to do so. In a somewhat imperfect world we can only continue to work toward improvement in achieving the values to which we are devoted. In that quest we must enlist all those whose modeling of how to teach performance with understanding provides school music teachers with an internalized image they can then aspire to share with their own students.

The ten guidelines discussed above, along with those that other music educators are likely to want to add, can move the profession firmly and effectively in a direction long sought but too seldom achieved as fully as it deserves to be—the fostering of musical understanding through and in the mode of performing. At this time in history the opportunity to experience music has become easily available to all through listening and is becoming more and more available to all who want to compose by the use of effective computer technologies that allow music to be created and presented without the need for performers. But while performance is no longer the sole or even dominant means for most people in our culture to be involved actively with music, it remains unique and powerful in the opportunities it offers to think, act, create, and understand. The devotion of the music education profession to enable students to fully realize the rich rewards of performing, in both general education settings and a diverse array of elective opportunities, will help ensure that performance remains a vital component of musical culture, and that music education remains a vital component of schooling.

Contributors

BENNETT REIMER is the John W. Beattie Professor of Music Emeritus at Northwestern University, Evanston, Illinois, where he was chair of the Music Education Department, director of the Ph.D. program in music education, and founder and director of the Center for the Study of Education and the Musical Experience. He is the author or editor of fourteen books (with several more on the way) and more than one hundred articles, chapters, and reviews. His writing, teaching, and lecturing have ranged over a diversity of topics including philosophy of music education, curriculum theory, research theory, multicultural issues, musical intelligences, interdisciplinary arts principles, teacher education, international music education issues, and applications of cognitive psychology to music learning.

ROBERT GILLESPIE is a professor of music and is responsible for training string teachers at The Ohio State University. A frequent guest conductor of all-state, regional, and festival orchestras throughout the United States and Europe, he has presented sessions and workshops for string teachers in thirty-nine states. His articles have appeared in all the major music education journals, and he is co-author of the book series *Essential Elements for Strings*.

MARY GOETZE is a professor of music at the Indiana University School of Music, where she chairs the Music in General Studies Department and conducts the International Vocal Ensemble, a School of Music chorus specializing in the recreation of music from outside the European and American art traditions. Recognized for her work with children's choirs, she has served as a clinician and guest conductor.

PATRICIA J. HOY, a professor of music and director of bands at Northern Arizona University, conducts the Northern Arizona University Chamber Winds and Wind Symphony and serves as the major professor in the graduate instrumental conducting program. As a guest conductor, she has appeared with high school, college, semi-professional, and professional organizations in twenty states.

CATHERINE LARSEN directs an educational consulting firm that specializes in development and facilitation of collaborative projects among artists, public agencies, and cultural and educational institutions. She has many years of experience as a music specialist in the public schools and an extensive background in curriculum development, program evaluation, arts administration, and teacher education.

PAUL R. LEHMAN, professor emeritus of music in the School of Music of the University of Michigan, served as president of MENC from 1984 to 1986. He chaired the task force that developed the national voluntary standards for K–12 instruction in music, and since 1992 he has been involved in a wide variety of standards-related publications and activities.

MARVELENE C. MOORE is chair and professor of music education at the University of Tennessee, Knoxville. A specialist in classroom music for students in grades K–8, choral music for students in grades 3–8, and Jaques-Dalcroze Eurhythmics, she has served as clinician and guest conductor for music organizations in forty-four states. Author of the *Jaques-Dalcroze Source Book* and co-editor of MENC's *Making Connections* book and CD, she currently serves as chair of MENC's Society for General Music.

BRUNO NETTL has taught ethnomusicology at the University of Illinois in Urbana since 1964, and he is now professor emeritus. With fieldwork experience in Native American cultures, Iran, and India, he is the author of a number of books, including *The Study of Ethnomusicology* and, most recently, *Heartland Excursions* and *In the Course of Performance*.

LARRY RACHLEFF is professor of conducting and music director of orchestras at Rice University's School of Music in Houston, Texas. A guest conductor of orchestras such as the Los Angeles Philharmonic and the Houston Symphony, he is also music director of The Rhode Island Philharmonic and of Chicago's Symphony II. Rachleff has conducted All-State festivals and orchestras across North America and Europe and has led conducting workshops for the American Symphony Orchestra League and the Conductors Guild.

WILL SCHMID, president of MENC from 1994 to 1996, is a professor at the University of Wisconsin–Milwaukee. The author of more than seventy-five books, CDs, and videos on guitar, choral music, world drumming, and American music, he has given workshops throughout the United States and in Australia, Canada, Japan, and Europe. He chairs the Get America Singing . . . Again! campaign and the MENC/GAMA/NAMM Teaching Guitar workshops.

SUZANNE M. SHULL, retired from thirty years of teaching choral and general music in metro-area Atlanta public schools, works with the Atlanta Symphony's educational outreach program and is an adjunct professor in the Music Education Department at Georgia State University. She serves on the MENC/GAMA/NAMM Guitar Education Task Force.

DOROTHY A. STRAUB is the K–12 music coordinator for the Fairfield (CT) Public Schools. She served as president of MENC from 1992 to 1994. A violist in the Greenwich Symphony and the Greater Bridgeport Symphony, she has presented numerous workshops on music education and string and orchestra education.

MENC Resources on Music and Arts Education Standards

Aiming for Excellence: The Impact of the Standards Movement on Music Education. 1996. #1012.

Implementing the Arts Education Standards. Set of five brochures: "What School Boards Can Do," "What School Administrators Can Do," "What State Education Agencies Can Do," "What Parents Can Do," "What the Arts Community Can Do." 1994. #4022. Each brochure is also available in packs of 20.

Making Connections: Multicultural Music and the National Standards, edited by William B. Anderson and Marvelene C. Moore. 1997. #3020. Book and CD.

Meeting National Standards with Handbells and Handchimes, by Michael B. McBride and Marva Baldwin. 2000. #1712. A publication of Schulmerich Bells, Scarecrow Press, and MENC.

National Standards for Arts Education: What Every Young American Should Know and Be Able to Do in the Arts. 1994. #1605.

Opportunity-to-Learn Standards for Music Instruction: Grades PreK–12. 1994. #1619.

Opportunity-to-Learn Standards for Arts Education. 1995. #1643.

"Opportunity-to-Learn Standards for Music Technology." 1999. #4030.

Performance Standards for Music: Strategies and Benchmarks for Assessing Progress Toward the National Standards, Grades PreK–12. 1996. #1633.

Perspectives on Implementation: Arts Education Standards for America's Students. 1994. #1622.

"Prekindergarten Music Education Standards" (brochure). 1995. #4015 (set of 10).

The School Music Program—A New Vision: The K–12 National Standards, PreK Standards, and What They Mean to Music Educators. 1994. #1618.

Teaching Examples: Ideas for Music Educators. 1994. #1620.

The Vision for Arts Education in the 21st Century. 1994. #1617.

Strategies for Teaching Series

Strategies for Teaching Prekindergarten Music, compiled and edited by Wendy L. Sims. #1644.

Strategies for Teaching K–4 General Music, compiled and edited by Sandra L. Stauffer and Jennifer Davidson. #1645.

Strategies for Teaching Middle-Level General Music, compiled and edited by June M. Hinckley and Suzanne M. Shull. #1646.

Strategies for Teaching High School General Music, compiled and edited by Keith P. Thompson and Gloria J. Kiester. #1647.

Strategies for Teaching Elementary and Middle-Level Chorus, compiled and edited by Ann Roberts Small and Judy K. Bowers. #1648.

Strategies for Teaching High School Chorus, compiled and edited by Randal Swiggum. #1649.

Strategies for Teaching Strings and Orchestra, compiled and edited by Dorothy A. Straub, Louis S. Bergonzi, and Anne C. Witt. #1652.

Strategies for Teaching Middle-Level and High School Keyboard, compiled and edited by Martha F. Hilley and Tommie Pardue. #1655.

Strategies for Teaching Beginning and Intermediate Band, compiled and edited by Edward J. Kvet and Janet M. Tweed. #1650.

Strategies for Teaching High School Band, compiled and edited by Edward J. Kvet and John E. Williamson. #1651.

Strategies for Teaching Specialized Ensembles, compiled and edited by Robert A. Cutietta. #1653.

Strategies for Teaching Middle-Level and High School Guitar, compiled and edited by William E. Purse, James L. Jordan, and Nancy Marsters. #1654.

Strategies for Teaching: Guide for Music Methods Classes, compiled and edited by Louis O. Hall with Nancy R. Boone, John Grashel, and Rosemary C. Watkins. #1656.

Series editor, Carolynn A. Lindeman

For more information on these and other MENC publications, write to or call MENC Publications Sales, 1806 Robert Fulton Drive, Reston, VA 20191-4348; 800-828-0229.